DUEL

OF THE

IRONCLADS

DUEL

OF THE

IRONCLADS

USS *MONITOR* & CSS *VIRGINIA* AT HAMPTON ROADS 1862

Angus Konstam

OSPREY
PUBLISHING

First published in Great Britain in 2003 by Osprey Publishing,
Elms Court, Chapel Way, Botley, Oxford OX2 9LP, United Kingdom.
Email: info@ospreypublishing.com

Previously published as New Vanguard 41: *Confederate Ironclad
1861–65*, New Vanguard 45: *Union Monitor 1861–65*, Campaign 103:
Hampton Roads 1862 – Clash of the Ironclads

ISBN 1 84176 721 2

Editor: Sally Rawlings
Index by Alan Rutter
Design by Melissa Swan, Ken Vail Graphic Design and The Black Spot
Maps by The Map Studio
3D bird's-eye views by The Black Spot
Origination by Magnet Harlequin, Colourpath and the Electronic
Page Company
Printed in China through World Print Ltd.

03 04 05 06 07   10 9 8 7 6 5 4 3 2 1

FOR A CATALOG OF ALL BOOKS PUBLISHED
BY OSPREY MILITARY AND AVIATION PLEASE CONTACT:

Osprey Direct USA, c/o MBI Publishing, P.O. Box 1,
729 Prospect Ave, Osceola, WI 54020, USA
E-mail: info@ospreydirectusa.com

Osprey Direct UK, P.O. Box 140, Wellingborough,
Northants, NN8 2FA, UK
E-mail: info@ospreydirect.co.uk

www.ospreypublishing.com

COVER IMAGE: Battle of 9 March 1862.
(© Copyright from the Collections of The Mariners' Museum)

BACK COVER IMAGE: CSS *Virginia* ramming the CSS *Cumberland*.
(Author's collection)

CONTENTS

INTRODUCTION

The bombardment of Fort Sumter in April 1861 acted as the starting gun for a unique naval arms race. Everyone knew it would be an incredibly one-sided contest. While the Union retained almost all of the old US Navy, the south was starved of ships, guns and above all, resources. Strategically, the Confederacy was on the defensive. Its forces had to defend a long and vulnerable coastline, and although they acquired some guns and a string of virtually obsolete stone-built fortifications, they had no navy with which to contest the Union's control of the seas. Even worse, while the north could draw upon the resources of a vibrant and growing industrial infrastructure, the southern economy was agrarian, and it lacked all but the most rudimentary industrial capacity. Despite these drawbacks or even because of them, it was imperative that the Confederate government found some way of protecting their coastline. This meant they had to build a Navy.

Confederate Secretary of the Navy Stephen Mallory was no ordinary naval administrator. He was something of a visionary, and realised that the Confederacy's only chance to protect its seaboard was to concentrate its meagre resources on the development of an ironclad fleet. The notion of building warships protected by iron was not a new idea. During the Crimean War (1853–56) the French built floating batteries protected by iron plate and used them during the siege of Sevastopol (1855–56). In October 1855, during the bombardment of Kinburn on the Black Sea, three of these steam-powered floating batteries proved invaluable, as their guns demolished the stone-built Russian fortifications while their iron cladding made them proof against even the heaviest Russian shot. After the war, French naval designers developed the concept even further, and on 24 November 1859, the *Gloire* was launched. The world's first true ironclad warship, the *Gloire* entered service in August 1860. She was armed with a broadside battery of 18 rifled guns per side, and her 4-inch wrought-iron hull protected her from the fire of any other warship afloat. The appearance of this formidable warship caused a panic in Britain, and the Royal Navy immediately commissioned an ironclad warship of their own. HMS *Warrior* entered service in October 1861, and the balance of naval power was restored. Both France and Britain then set about producing more ironclads, and by the time the first shells were fired at Fort Sumter, 18 British and French ironclads were on the stocks.

Another technological innovation emerged during the Crimean War. In November 1853, a Russian steam-powered fleet destroyed a Turkish squadron at Sinope, on the Turkish coast of the Black Sea. The smashing victory was achieved in part by a new type of ordnance carried on Russian ships. Shell guns, designed to fire hollow projectiles filled with explosives, were a new development in naval warfare, and the battle demonstrated their effectiveness against wooden-hulled warships. For centuries, naval projectiles tended to be solid shot, such as the roundshot fired by HMS *Victory* or the USS *Constitution*. Overnight, wooden warships were rendered vulnerable to this new type of projectile, which could penetrate their hulls, then explode, causing devastation in the crowded gun-decks of conventional warships. Another ordnance innovation just making its appearance as the Civil War began was the rifled gun. By firing a projectile whose rifled sides locked in grooves in the bore of the gun, the shot could be forced to spin, which greatly improved accuracy. Their range was better than conventional smoothbore guns, and their ability to penetrate wood was also greater. All these innovations were being introduced at exactly the same time as the storm clouds were gathering in the United States. The US Navy was a somewhat hidebound institution in 1861, and its senior officers were resistant to change. While steam-powered marine propulsion systems had become an essential feature in the warships of the main battlefleet, many warships were still powered by sail alone. Shell-firing guns were introduced into service, but the development of rifled ordnance was still at the experimental stage.

During the months before the outbreak of war, many of the scattered units of the fleet were recalled to home waters, and when the war began, President Lincoln was able to order a blockade of the Confederate coastline. In the first year of the war only the major Southern ports could be blockaded, as there were too few ships to create a strong maritime cordon around the coast. What the blockade did achieve from the outset was that it established the boundaries of the naval war between the States. Union strategy would centre around the imposition of the blockade, the conquest of the Mississippi River, and the gradual erosion of the South's coastal defences. For its part, the Confederate Navy needed to keep its ports open, and to try break the blockade in order to import much-needed war material. Mallory believed that this could only be achieved through the use of ironclads. Unlike the ocean-going vessels in the fleets of Britain and France, his ironclad warships would be crude, ungainly vessels, with a limited offensive power and under-powered propulsion systems. These limitations were minor, considering the strategic impact their deployment had on Union naval strategy. Mallory made the best decision he could on how to best use his extremely limited industrial resources. The creation of a small ironclad fleet led to the commitment of Union naval resources to counter this threat. A near hysteria in the North encouraged the development of a Union ironclad shipbuilding program of its own, and eventually this would lead to the creation of a fleet which not only countered the Confederate threat, but it assisted the imposition of a naval stranglehold on the South. Within weeks of the first shots being fired, both Confederate and Union designers were developing their plans for ironclads. Just over a year later, the first of these armored warships would lock horns in combat in a sea battle which would change the face of naval warfare.

The battle of Hampton Roads on 9 March 1862 saw the first ever clash between two ironclad warships. The day before, the USS *Virginia* (sometimes referred to incorrectly as the *Merrimac*) had demonstrated the effectiveness of ironclad warships against wooden vessels. In a singularly one-sided engagement, her guns destroyed two wooden warships, lying at anchor off Newport News, *Virginia*. Although these warships fought back with vigour, their shot proved singularly ineffective against the armour-plated casemate of the *Virginia*. Shot bounced off, and the only real damage was the denting of her plating and the peppering of her smokestack. By contrast her explosive shells tore through the wooden sides of the *Cumberland*, and caused incredible slaughter amongst her gun crews. The *Virginia* was a revolutionary warship in one other aspect. During her attack on the USS *Cumberland*, she rammed the wooden sloop using a purpose-built heavy cast-iron ram fitted to her bow. The collision ripped a hole in the side of the Union warship "wide enough to let in a horse and cart". Although the ramming attempt was a success, it also damaged the *Virginia*, and the ironclad was almost pulled under by the *Cumberland* before it shook itself free. She continued to pour shot into the hull of the stricken Union warship as she backed off, then turned away in search of a new victim. The USS *Congress* was virtually destroyed when the *Virginia* steamed past her at point-blank range, her guns blazing. The cumbersome ironclad then headed upriver to turn around, then returned to finish the job. By the end of the action both Union warships were shattered and sinking, and the rest of the wooden-hulled blockading fleet off Hampton Roads lay at the mercy of the Confederate leviathan. If any naval officer still doubted the effectiveness of shell-guns against wooden warships, or the defensive capabilities of ironclads, these doubts had been dispelled in a single day.

The catastrophe would have been complete if it were not for the Union Navy's own ironclad, which spent the day of the battle steaming south from New York to Hampton Roads. This frail-looking little craft (described by observers as a "cheesebox on a raft") would not only stop any further depredations by the Confederate warship, but it would alter the strategic balance. Many historians regarded the Battle of Hampton Roads as inconclusive. After all, neither the USS *Monitor* nor the CSS *Virginia* who fought their duel on 9 March 1862 inflicted more than minor damage on their opponent. Neither ship was able to gain a significant tactical advantage over the other, and the hard-fought battle petered out when the constraints of ammunition supply and tidal conditions forced an end to the fighting. No fatalities were caused on either side. To take this view is to ignore the incredibly far-reaching impact of the battle.

When it steamed into Hampton Roads on the morning of 9 March, the CSS *Virginia* was prepared to finish the destruction of the Union blockading fleet, a task she had only partially accomplished the day before. Her first victim was going to be the wooden steam frigate USS *Minnesota*, which had run aground during the previous day. Like a sacrificial lamb tied to the altar, she could do nothing to avert her fate. The warship and her crew were saved by the intervention of the *Monitor*, initiating one of the strangest naval encounters in history. The battle between the *Monitor* and the *Virginia* was witnessed by thousands of soldiers, sailors and civilians who lined both sides of Hampton Roads. Few of these spectators were in any doubt that what they were watching was history in the making; the first clash between two revolutionary new warships. The two ironclads appeared as different from each other as it was possible to be. The *Virginia* had been built using the lower hull of the USS *Merrimac*, and her profile underwater was the same as the former steam frigate. On top of this long, narrow hull, the designers constructed an armored box, a wooden framework covered in two layers of iron plating. Looking like a large upturned bath, this "casemate" was pierced with gunports, allowing the deployment of the *Virginia's* main armament of newly-built rifled guns. These were arranged to fire out of fixed positions to each side, while 7-inch rifled pieces in the bow and stern gave the ironclad some degree of all-round firepower.

In complete contrast, the USS *Monitor* was 90 feet shorter than her opponent, and the freeboard of her flat iron deck was so low that the vessel's decks were practically awash. This had almost led to the foundering of the ironclad during her long voyage south, and would play a contributory part in her sinking off Cape Hatteras just ten months later. Her profile was dominated by her iron turret; inside which were two large smoothbore guns. Unlike the *Virginia*, whose guns were aimed by turning the hull, the *Monitor's* turret design was truly revolutionary, permitting the guns to fire in virtually any direction, regardless of which way the ship was heading at the time. What followed would be as much a test of the two doctrines of ironclad construction as a battle between the vessels themselves.

The battle of Hampton Roads was a dramatic demonstration in the defensive strengths of both ironclad designs. For various reasons, shot from the guns of the *Virginia* and the *Monitor* were unable to penetrate the armor of their opponent's ship. While these faults were later rectified, the overall impression of the battle was that ironclads were proof against anything an enemy ship could throw at it. In a single day, wooden warships had been rendered obsolete, and the age of armored fighting ships had begun. As the editor of the *Norfolk Day Book* wrote the evening after the battle; "this successful and terrible work will create a revolution in naval warfare, and henceforth iron will be king of the seas". The first tentative steps of this great naval revolution had been made.

CONFEDERATE IRONCLAD 1861–65

The battle between the *Monitor* and the *Merrimac* (or *Merrimack*), or more properly the CSS *Virginia* is one of the best-known naval conflicts in history. While it is widely regarded as marking a turning point in naval warfare, the battle also tested the prototype of an innovative new ship type. The Confederate ironclad was a technical marvel, given the limited industrial capacity of the Southern states. Although the warship type was initially envisaged as a tool that could break the Union blockade of the Confederacy, experience in action led to a reevaluation. After 1862, Confederate ironclads formed the backbone of the coastal and river defenses of the South, protecting vital cities such as Charleston and Savannah, denying the Union access to the Confederate capital of Richmond, and blocking the rivers of the Atlantic seaboard that pierced the heart of the Carolinas.

The Confederate floating battery at Charleston Harbor, during the bombardment of Fort Sumter, April 12–13, 1861. Its production helped local shipbuilders understand the technical intricacies of the casemate design on ironclads. (SMH)

Superficially these ironclads looked similar, but their form developed through experience gained in combat. Although underpowered, difficult to maneuver, and hellish to serve in, the 22 ironclads that were eventually commissioned provided the backbone of the Confederate Navy. They were also the best possible solution to the strategic defensive problems facing the South. The creation of the Confederate ironclad fleet remains one of the most fascinating, yet under-studied, achievements of the period. This work examines the construction, design, armament, and internal layout of these revolutionary warships, and offers an insight into what it was like to serve on board them in action against the Union Navy.

CREATION OF A FLEET

When the Confederate States of America was formed in February 1861, war with the Union was considered inevitable. Following the firing on Fort Sumter in Charleston Harbor on April 12, the Confederacy was plunged into a conflict for which she was ill prepared. The strategic situation was bleak, as the Confederacy had a long, exposed coastline with inadequate coastal defenses, and numerous inlets and rivers that pierced the interior of the new nation. She also had no navy to undertake its defense. In February, 1861, President Jefferson Davis established a Navy Department, naming Senator Stephen R. Mallory of Key West as its head. The Department was divided into four sections: Ordnance and Hydrography, Orders and Details, Medicine and Surgery, and Provisions and Clothing. The Ordnance Department was responsible for warship construction until September, 1862, when Mallory made John L. Porter his Chief Naval Constructor responsible for all new

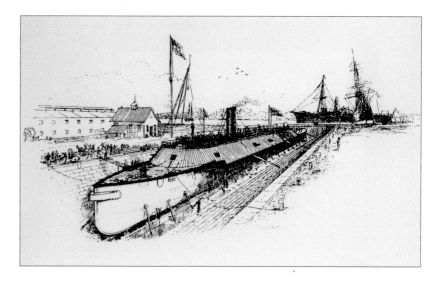

projects. Mallory's vision was to counter the Union's numerical advantage by technology. While his limited staff tried to gather together a scratch force of improvised conventional warships, Mallory tackled the challenge of creating an ironclad fleet. With hindsight, his decision to develop ironclad warships as rapidly as possible was inspired, as all other forms of coastal and riverine defenses proved inadequate.

The final stages of the conversion of the wooden frigate *Merrimac* into the Confederate ironclad *Virginia*. When the US Navy abandoned the Gosport Navy Yard in Norfolk, Virginia, they failed to destroy this dry dock. (SMH)

Alongside Mallory, the author of the Confederate ironclad was his Chief Naval Constructor, John L. Porter. Working with the innovative ordnance expert John M. Brooke and naval engineer William P. Williamson, he spearheaded the design team that produced the first ironclad prototype, the CSS *Virginia*. Although less than perfect, the design provided a test bed for ironclad construction. The lessons learned would be adopted in later ironclad designs. When the war began, Mallory was bombarded by proposals from shipbuilders to build ironclads to their own specifications, and for the most part these proved a failure. By 1862, Porter and the Navy Department had created designs for a new breed of ironclad, incorporating improvements based on experience. Starting with the CSS *Richmond*, built in Virginia, Porter would maintain a tight grip over ironclad production for the duration of the war. By 1864, he was assisted by an experienced team of designers, engineers, and several assistants (Constructors) who supervised projects on a regional basis. By the end of the war, 22 ironclads had been commissioned into the Confederate Navy, and one additional ironclad had been built in France. Numerous other ironclads were never commissioned, and were either abandoned due to lack of materials or destroyed to prevent capture. Of these, the incomplete *Louisiana* was used as a floating battery in New Orleans without being commissioned, and the *Jackson* and *Columbia* were completed but never brought into service. Apart from the CSS *Stonewall*, which was built in France, all of these ironclads were built on the same principle, with an armored casemate protecting a broadside battery. The only non-casemate ironclad ever designed in the South was laid down in Columbus, Georgia, in early 1865. As planned, the vessel was to carry two 11-inch smoothbore guns in a single turret. The war ended before the Confederacy's only monitor-type vessel was even launched. Under

Mallory's supervision, the Confederate Navy performed a miracle, creating a fleet of ironclads which contested control of Southern ports and cities until the very end of the conflict.

IRONCLAD DESIGNS

The Ships

Stephen Mallory's ironclad policy began with the adaptation of the USS *Merrimac* into a casemate ironclad ram. Given the lack of manufacturing capacity in the South, any attempt to produce a design as technically complex as a monitor was beyond the capability of the Confederacy. Following a series of meetings with John L. Porter, John M. Brooke, and William P. Williamson, he decided that the conversion of the burned-out hull of the warship was the easiest way to produce his revolutionary warship. Although the steam frigate's upper works were gone, her lower hull and engines were relatively intact. His directive to start work on the ironclad was issued on June 11, 1861, and she was commissioned into service eight months later (February 17, 1862).

The basic design centered around a wooden casemate (shield) with rounded ends, resembling an upturned bathtub. The wood was approximately two feet thick and sloped at a 35° angle. Original plans called for this wooden frame to be covered by a laminate of three layers of one-inch-thick rolled iron plate, but after experiments into the power of existing naval ordnance, it was decided to use two layers of two-inch plate instead. The armor would extend from the top of the casemate (although the top ("spar") deck was unarmored), down to below the waterline. This decision to extend the armor below the point where the casemate joined the hull (known as the "knuckle") added weight to the vessel, and deliberately sacrificed maneuverability for protection. While contemporary European ironclads had near-vertical casemate sides, the 35° angle on the Confederate prototype gave the vessel an improved resistance to penetrating shot.

Her armament consisted of six Dahlgren smoothbore guns (part of the *Merrimac's* original armament), plus two new 6.4-inch Brooke rifled guns, mounted as broadside weapons on conventional carriages, and two 7-inch Brooke rifles on pivot mounts at the bow and stern. In addition, a 1,500-pound cast-iron ram was fitted to the bow, three feet below the waterline. The hull was all but submerged, offering virtually no target to the enemy. Christened the CSS *Virginia*, the ironclad suffered from a lack of speed, poor maneuverability and a deep draft (23 feet), but her

This engraving by a Confederate artist depicts the CSS *Virginia* the day before the Battle of Hampton Roads. Although slightly inaccurate, it gives an impression of the power and size of the warship. (HCA)

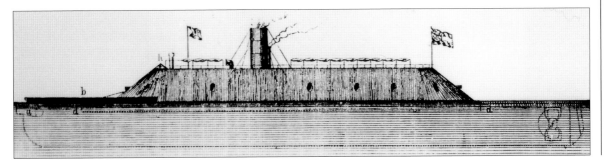

performance at the Battle of Hampton Roads (March 8–9, 1862) proved the basic worthiness of the design. Almost all subsequent Confederate ironclads would follow her basic configuration, although efforts were also made to rectify the numerous inadequacies of her construction.

The CSS *Virginia* was one of six Confederate ironclads that were converted from existing vessels. The CSS *Manassas* (originally built as a privateer), *Baltic* and *Eastport* were all converted during 1861/62, and all of these vessels had significant design flaws. The *Manassas* was converted from a Mississippi tugboat by adding an unusual "turtleback" casemate over her deck. The *Baltic* was originally a cotton transport from Mobile, and the *Eastport* a Tennessee River steamer. In 1862, the Confederate ironclads CSS *Atlanta* and CSS *Mobile* were also converted from existing vessels, the *Atlanta* from the British blockade runner *Fingal*, and the *Mobile* from an existing wooden gunboat.

The USS *Monitor* and the CSS *Virginia*, during their famous engagement on the second day of the Battle of Hampton Roads (March 9, 1862). The engraving also emphasizes the differences in design between the two types of ironclads. (SMH)

In late 1862, work began on five new ironclads, designed from the keel up as armored warships. Of these, four were designed to operate in coastal waters (i.e. offshore), capable of engaging the Union blockading squadrons. The exception was the CSS *Georgia*, which was built to augment the river defenses near Savannah, Georgia. Designed by a Savannah industrialist, she proved a complete failure, and was used as a floating battery for the duration of the war.

The other four vessels (*Louisiana*, *Mississippi*, *Tennessee I*, and *Arkansas*) were all built to assist in the defense of the Mississippi River, particularly its egress into the Gulf of Mexico. Although their designs differed, they were all large and well-armed vessels. The *Louisiana* was built in New Orleans under the direction of a shipbuilder who specialized in constructing Mississippi paddle steamers. This influence was reflected in its unorthodox design, incorporating the twin paddle-wheels and box-like hull of a paddleboat with screw propulsion. Her engines were insufficiently powerful to maneuver the vessel in the waters of the lower Mississippi, and she was still being fitted out when the Union Navy entered the Mississippi Delta in April, 1862. During the Battle of New Orleans (April 24, 1862) she was used as a floating battery, and was destroyed by her own crew following the fall of the city. The *Mississippi* was designed by the entrepreneurial Tift brothers (Old Key West acquaintances of Stephen Mallory), neither of whom had shipbuilding experience. It was a massive vessel, but it was only partially finished when Union forces entered New Orleans, and the vessel was destroyed on the stocks to prevent capture. The *Arkansas* and *Tennessee I* were sister ships, designed by John L. Porter and built in Memphis, Tennessee, at the John

T. Shirley Yard. They were only 165 feet long, designed for use in the upper Mississippi and its tributaries as well as in coastal waters. The *Tennessee* was destroyed to prevent its capture by advancing Union forces, but the *Arkansas* escaped up the Yazoo River and was completed at Yazoo City, Mississippi. Unlike other ironclads, its casemate sides were near-vertical rather than sloped, although the bow and stern sections followed the standard 35° incline of other Confederate ironclads. The CSS *Arkansas* subsequently fought a series of running battles with the Union fleet on the Yazoo and the Mississippi near Vicksburg before its final destruction near Baton Rouge in August, 1862.

By the start of 1863, of the ten Confederate ironclads mentioned above, only the CSS *Atlanta* at Savannah and the CSS *Baltic* at Mobile remained. The latter was considered a "white elephant" and was subsequently decommissioned, its armor used to protect the CSS *Nashville*.

By early 1862, it had became clear that any attempt to break the Union blockade was overoptimistic, and Confederate strategy became centered on the defense of her remaining harbors, rivers, and inlets. Consequently, the new breed of Confederate ironclads reflected this "scaling down" of their role. Two basic designs, based on plans drawn up by Porter, were adopted by the Navy Department. The first of these became known as the "Richmond Class," after the first ironclad of the group, laid down in Norfolk, Virginia, in early 1862. The class comprised the CSS *Richmond, Chicora, Palmetto State, North Carolina, Raleigh, Savannah*, and several others that were never completed, and apart from the *Raleigh*, all were laid down during the first months of 1862. Their length varied from 150 to 174 feet, with a draft of 12–14 feet, and they were powered by a single screw. The most vulnerable part of the *Virginia* was the "knuckle," where the casemate met the hull at the waterline. In the "Richmond class" (and most subsequent ironclads), the knuckle was protected by a two-inch plate of spaced armor, which extended five feet beyond the inner hull all round, and six inches below the waterline.

Later variations of the standard "Richmond class" design were longer, designed to carry a more powerful armament and better armor. These 180-foot vessels (sometimes known as "modified Richmond class") included the CSS *Charleston, Virginia II*, and several others that were never completed. The capture of the CSS *Atlanta* in June, 1863, prompted this alteration of the Richmond design to encompass the lessons learned from the engagement, where Union 15-inch smoothbore guns penetrated the four-inch armor of the Confederate ironclad. The *Virginia II* carried three and in places four layers of two-inch armor, making her one of the best-protected of all the Confederate ironclads. These "Charleston class" ironclads were designed by naval constructor William A. Graves.

Another variation of the "Richmond class" was produced towards the end

The CSS *Manassas* at the Battle of New Orleans, April 23, 1862. The side paddlewheel warship USS *Mississippi* is depicted bearing down on the Confederate ironclad in an attempt to ram her. (HCA)

of the war, with a smaller casemate and a shallower draft. The *Milledgeville* (built at Savannah, Georgia) and the *Wilmington* (of Wilmington, North Carolina) were still not completed when the war ended. The latter was a particularly strange "Richmond class" adaptation, having two small casemates rather than one, each designed to house a single pivot-mounted gun.

A later development of the "Richmond class" designed by Porter incorporated elements of the Graves' "Charleston class", and served as a series of prototypes for the "diamond-hull" ironclads that followed. Although called the "Tennessee class," these vessels were each unique in almost every feature. The *Tennessee II*, *Columbia*, and *Texas* were all approximately 189 feet long, with a draft of 14–16 feet. While the latter two were never commissioned, the CSS *Tennessee* proved her worth in the Battle of Mobile Bay (August 5, 1864) before surrendering to a superior number of Union warships.

A second group of ironclads was designed for use exclusively on rivers rather than in deeper waters. They were therefore flat-bottomed, with an average draft of eight feet. Their design was also simplified, so that plans could be followed by inland builders who lacked the experience of the shipwrights of the Southern coastal cities. Experience had also led to a dramatic reduction in the size of the casemate, a trend which resulted from the critical observation of earlier designs being tested in battle. The trend towards a smaller casemate had already begun with the *Virginia II* where, in order to maintain a workable ratio between displacement and power, thicker armor had been added at the expense of casemate size and consequently of size of armament. Late-war ironclads were therefore better protected, but carried fewer guns in a smaller casemate. Although the size, appearance, and configuration of these vessels varied, they have all been grouped under the category of "diamond-hull" ironclads. The name was a reflection of the shape of the casemate, seen from above, which often resembled an octagonal diamond in form.

The first vessels of this type were the sister ships CSS *Tuscaloosa* and *Huntsville*, built on the Alabama River in Selma, Alabama, during 1862/63. Three similar vessels were also laid down on the Tombigbee River at Oven Bluff, Alabama, and two more at Selma, but they were never completed. Each of the two completed Selma ironclads carried four guns. Neither of the two ironclads saw active service. A second "diamond-hull" duo were the two "Albermarle class" ironclads, CSS *Albermarle* and CSS *Neuse*, both built in North Carolina and designed by

The unfinished ironclad *Louisiana* was towed into place and used as a floating battery during the Battle of New Orleans (April 23, 1862). This engraving is one of the few accurate representations of this super-ironclad. (MM)

Porter. A third vessel of this class was destroyed at Tarboro, North Carolina, before its completion. Although builder's drafts exist, we know the two vessels differed from Porter's plan and from each other in size and configuration. The CSS *Neuse* ran aground on the Neuse River in early 1864 on its maiden voyage and was scuttled. The *Albermarle* had a brief and distinguished career, engaging Union vessels in Albermarle Sound near Plymouth, North Carolina, before she was destroyed by an enemy torpedo attack on October 27, 1864. An improved and lengthened version of the "Albermarle class" was the CSS *Fredericksburg*, built in Richmond and commissioned in March, 1863. It served on the James River until the fall of the Confederate capital in April, 1865. While the original "Albermarle class" specified a 139-foot-long vessel, the *Fredericksburg* was 170 feet in length. The *Jackson* was still being fitted out on the Chattahoochee River at Columbus, Georgia, when the war ended. A "diamond-hull" ironclad, she had twin screws, a six-gun casemate and was 225 feet long. Her construction was also plagued by problems and, although launched in late 1863, she never left the shipyard.

During the mid-war years, two other extremely unusual ironclads were produced, defying the logic employed in the design of other Confederate armored vessels. The CSS *Missouri* was designed by Porter to utilize existing paddlewheel engines available, and consequently the ironclad was powered by a stern-mounted wheel protected by the casemate. She was 190 feet long, but drew a draft of over eight feet. Built at Shreveport, Louisiana, on the Red River she spent the war protecting the river between Alexandria and Shreveport. Apart from the adaptation of the standard "Richmond class" casemate to accommodate the paddlewheel, her armor was similar to that of other Confederate ironclads. Two similar vessels were planned at Shreveport but were never laid down. The CSS *Nashville* was a side-wheel ironclad, designed by Porter to take advantage of available riverboat engines. She was 250 feet long, with a draft of 13 feet, making her larger than most contemporary ironclads. She was built at Montgomery, Alabama, during late 1862 and 1863, and completed at Mobile. Described by one observer as "a tremendous monster," her faults outweighed her strengths. Inadequate protection around her sidewheels and her lack of motive power meant that she was less formidable than her fellow Mobile ironclad the CSS *Tennessee*. Delays in the supply of armor meant that she was still being completed in August, 1864, and was unable to join the *Tennessee* in the defense of Mobile Bay. Although she saw action around Mobile, she proved to be another expensive failure. As with the *Missouri*, other similar vessels were planned but never built.

The gundeck of the *Virginia*, during the Battle of Hampton Roads, as depicted by a French artist. It provides a reasonably accurate portrayal of conditions inside the casemate. (MM)

In conclusion, the design of Confederate ironclads improved as the war progressed, although a few vessels bucked the trend. The basic design conceived by Mallory, Brooke, and Porter remained the best available form of ironclad, given the limitations of the Confederacy in terms of skills, materials and facilities.

Material

Stephen Mallory's ironclad building program was ambitious, even for an industrial power. For the Confederacy, which lacked

The CSS *Arkansas* running through the Union fleet above Vicksburg in July, 1862. Although she passed between the enemy ships at close range, their fire was unable to disable or even damage the Confederate ironclad. (HCA)

sufficient engineering plants, skilled workers, and raw materials, it was incredible. That any ironclads at all were produced was a logistical miracle, and shows the ingenuity and skill at improvisation with which Mallory and his subordinates approached the problems facing them. Apart from ordnance, the main items required for the construction of the Confederate ironclads were wood, rolled iron sheet for armor plating, and propulsion systems. Wood was in plentiful supply, although the ramshackle rail infrastructure often made the transport of shipbuilding lumber more of a problem than it should have been. The remaining two materials were harder to produce in the quality and quantity required by the navy.

Armor

When Stephen Mallory made the decision to convert the burned-out hull of the USS *Merrimac* into a Confederate ironclad, he had to rely on the limited foundry facilities available, the closest being the Tredegar Iron Works in Richmond, Virginia. The initial contract specified that the foundry roll one-inch-thick iron plates, but tests conducted by Lieutenant (later Commander) John M. Brooke at nearby Jamestown proved that a series of one-inch layers would be inadequate protection for the ironclad. The CSS *Virginia* was finally protected with two layers of two-inch iron plate. The Tredegar Iron Works had to halt production to alter their machinery for the new thickness, which was the maximum sheet thickness their machinery would allow. Although Mallory constantly asked for three-inch plate, there is no evidence that any was ever produced in Southern ironworks during the war. Two-inch rolled metal sheets laminated together to form a thicker iron plating became the standard armor for Confederate ironclads during the war, applied using an inner horizontal belt and an outer vertical one. Following the CSS *Atlanta* debacle, where her armor was penetrated by the latest Union guns, three layers of two-inch plate were used on all subsequent ironclads. Small foundries from Virginia to Alabama provided various steel plates for ironclads throughout the war.

In more remote areas, or if rolled iron plate was unavailable, other solutions had to be found. The armor used for the CSS *Arkansas* was railroad "T-rail" iron, drilled and fitted into place over the wooden casemate frame. Railroad iron was also used to protect the CSS *Louisiana, Missouri*, and *Georgia*. Although effective, it was considered inferior to rolled plate armor.

Supplying armor for Confederate ironclads on the eastern seaboard was relatively straightforward, although delays were caused due to lack of raw materials and skilled machinists, strikes, and above all, by a lack of reliable rail transportation. As the war progressed, iron became increasingly scarce, and several half-completed ironclads were abandoned due to a lack of armor plating. Upper decks were never armored, and the top of the casemate (known as the "hurricane deck," "shield deck," or "spar deck") was fitted with metal or even wooden gratings to provide ventilation. Designers did not consider plunging fire a threat. The pilot house (bridge) was always armored in a manner similar to the casemate below it.

Propulsion

The weakest link in the Confederacy's ironclad shipbuilding program was its inability to provide suitable propulsion systems for their vessels. The limited shipyards and industrial facilities were largely incapable of producing the quantity of reliable steam engines and propulsion machinery that the navy required. Even if propulsion systems could be found for the ironclads, the engines were often underpowered and unreliable. Early in the war, a lack of suitable marine engineering plants led to the need to cannibalize steam engines, boilers and propulsion from existing vessels, or from those that had been destroyed or abandoned. The first five ironclads produced by the Confederacy were forced to utilize marine propulsion systems taken from existing vessels, and on the whole these proved unsatisfactory. Most of the handful of heavy engineering works that the South possessed were adapted to produce weapons and munitions for the Confederate Army. Of the few works that specialized in marine engineering, almost all proved incapable of building the powerful engines required.

The impetus for change came from Mallory's plan to build a series of ironclads that could be used to defend the Mississippi River. In late 1861, the Navy Department ordered the production of purpose-built engines and propulsion system from engineering works scattered throughout the South. These contractors supplied the systems installed in the ironclads *Louisiana, Mississippi*, and *Arkansas*, although some components were still taken from

The building of the Confederate ironclad *Arkansas* was achieved in primitive conditions on the Yazoo River in Mississippi. Here, the cranes of a riverboat are being used to install the ironclad's armament. (HCA)

existing vessels. By mid-1862, the Navy Department established its own engineering works, leasing the Columbus Iron Works in Georgia and Richmond's Schockoe Foundry. While Columbus produced the complete propulsion systems used in the ironclads *Tennessee, Columbia, Milledgeville,* and *Jackson,* the Richmond plant (renamed the Confederate Naval Works) provided similar components for the *Fredericksburg, Virginia II, Raleigh, Albermarle,* and *Neuse.* The navy's Engineer-in-Chief, William P. Williamson, designed all the purpose-built machinery and propulsion systems produced in these plants. Other ironclads still relied on engines and propulsion parts salvaged from other vessels, but Williamson and his Engineering Department oversaw their installation. By the end of the war, engines supplied for use in Confederate ironclads were efficient, although they still lacked power.

Marine propulsion was going through something of a transition at the start of the Civil War. On Southern rivers, riverboats were usually propelled by high-pressure steam engines, which powered paddlewheels. Elsewhere, more conventional low-pressure single-cylinder engines were used to power screw propellers. Ironclad engines were usually reciprocating, single-expansion machines, the exact nature of which varied due to the location of the cylinders. The boilers were usually horizontal fire-tube boilers with a return (double) flue. Some vessels, such as the CSS *Tennessee,* also had a fan to ensure a constant draft in the firebox. This helped maintain steam pressure. The CSS *Albermarle* had two parallel-mounted boilers, which was a common configuration, but more were sometimes fitted. The massive CSS *Mississippi* was exceptional, being designed to carry 16 boilers.

Throughout most of the war, the engines in Confederate ironclads were inadequate for the tasks they had to perform, and were also prone to mechanical failure. A lack of trained machinists and engineers exacerbated this problem, as did the lack of spare parts, and a reliable transport system to move parts and labor where it was required. The lack of speed of almost all Confederate ironclads was largely the result of inadequate propulsion systems, which lacked the power to propel the heavy vessels. This lack of speed also made them notoriously difficult to maneuver.

THE EUROPEAN OPTION

While efforts to produce ironclads within the South proved remarkably successful given the lack of industrial resources and capacity, the Confederacy was singularly unsuccessful in buying suitable ironclads overseas. Using funds raised by the "Cotton Loan" (a scheme arranged between the Confederate Treasury and the German banking house of Erlangers) and other sources, Confederate agents tried to buy or build suitable vessels. Although money was no problem, government policy was. Both the French and British governments had proclaimed their neutral status in the conflict, and the British also had a statute called the Foreign Enlistment Act, whereby it was illegal to supply or equip vessels for a foreign power currently at war without a special dispensation from the government. The Confederates had to employ every legal ploy and deception to try to circumvent the law, while Union diplomats lobbied to have it enforced.

Soon after the outbreak of the war, the Navy Department sent Lieutenant James H. North to Europe, where he failed to buy the ironclad battery ship *Gloire* from the French government. In May, 1862, he signed a contract with the Clydeside shipbuilding firm J & G Thomson to produce a large seagoing ironclad ram. As she was to be built in Glasgow, she was nicknamed the "Glasgow," or the "Scottish Sea Monster," although her official shipyard designation was simply ship "No. 61." Designed to carry a broadside armament of 20 guns, she was completely unsuited to the needs of the Confederacy. The inexperienced Lt. North was probably influenced by the vessels being produced for the British and French navies, rather than considering the special needs of the South. She was clearly a warship, and quickly came under the scrutiny of US spies and British officials, forcing Lt. North to cancel the contract in December, 1863, before the vessel was completed. If work had continued, she would have been confiscated by the British authorities under the terms of the Foreign Enlistment Act.

The Confederate agent James D. Bulloch was far more successful. In June, 1862, he signed a contract with the British shipbuilders Laird's, of Birkenhead, for the production of two armored rams. The "Laird Rams" differed from other European ironclads in that they each had two revolving turrets rather than a casemate battery. Each turret would carry two 9-inch Armstrong rifled guns (RMLs, or rifled muzzle-loaders). A large iron ram was to be fitted to their bows, and the latest steam plants available provided power for their engines,

The surrender of the CSS *Tennessee* in Mobile Bay in August, 1864. Surrounded by enemy warships, the Confederate Admiral Buchanan surrendered more because of his hopeless position than due to damage to his ironclad. (MM)

although both also carried a suite of masts and sails. Union diplomatic pressure on the British government intensified as work proceeded, despite a legal smokescreen thrown up by Bulloch and his British lawyers. He even arranged a fake sale of the vessels from Laird's to the Egyptian government, and the two rams were renamed *El Toussan* and *El Monassir*, but the scheme was exposed. The British government impounded the two vessels in July, 1863, but Bulloch continued his legal efforts to have them restored to him. It was only after the authorities finished an exhaustive investigation into the vessels' ownership, involving British and French shipowners and the Egyptian court, that the ships were purchased for service in the Royal Navy. They eventually became HMS *Scorpion* and HMS *Wivern*.

The CSS *Tennessee* engaging the wooden steam sloop USS *Monongahela*, during the Battle of Mobile Bay, 1864. The Union ironclad USS *Chickasaw* is shown to the left of the Confederate ironclad. (MM)

In the summer of 1863, Bulloch travelled to France and signed another contract for two seagoing ironclad rams with the Bordeaux yard of Lucian Armand. Bulloch had been introduced to the shipyard owner through the French shipping agents who helped him obscure the origins of the "Laird Rams," and was told Armand was a Southern sympathizer. Initial negotiations between Armand and the Confederate agent Matthew F. Maury had already fallen through, as the Maury vessels were too large for the capacity of the yard. The Bulloch vessels were smaller, and better suited to the needs of the Confederacy and the competence of the shipyard, being designed exclusively for use in the confined coastal waters of the South. There is evidence that Stephen Mallory planned to use them to spearhead an attempt to recapture the Mississippi Delta. Armand had already produced similar small ironclads for the French navy. Unlike the "Laird Rams," the two vessels commissioned by Bulloch were turretless, and carried two pivoting guns in a casemate, and a 9-inch rifled gun on a pivot mount on the forecastle. The vessels were named the *Cheops* and *Sphinx* to disguise the identity of their future owners. Four wooden corvettes were also commissioned at the Bordeaux yard by the Confederate government.

In September, 1863, the US Ambassador to France was informed about the vessels, and he brought diplomatic pressure on the French to follow the British example and impound the two ironclads. By this stage, the Confederates had already lost the Battle of Gettysburg (July, 1863), and were on the defensive. Their political status in Europe was falling as a consequence of Confederate military setbacks, and the French Emperor, Napoleon III, became convinced that the Confederate cause was lost. Unwilling to back the losing side, he notified Armand that the vessels were denied permission to leave France, and could not be placed in Confederate hands. He demanded they were sold to "legitimate" customers, and consequently when it was completed, the *Sphinx* was sold

The ironclad *Albermarle* was built on a riverbank in North Carolina, a logistical feat of immense proportions. Designed by Naval Constructor Porter, the vessel was modified during construction to suit local conditions and available materials. (HCA)

to Denmark and the *Cheops* to Prussia. Bulloch was powerless to prevent the loss.

By exceptional fortune, the *Sphinx* was offered for resale by the Danish government in late 1864. Bulloch arranged an undercover purchasing scheme involving French shipping agents, and in January, 1865, the ironclad was handed over to the Confederate Navy in a transfer in the Bay of Biscay. The vessel was renamed the CSS *Stonewall*, the only active Confederate ironclad to be commissioned in Europe rather than at home. She sailed to El Ferrol in Spain, and narrowly escaped a battle with two Union cruisers before she escaped into the Atlantic. She stopped in Lisbon (again avoiding her Union pursuers) and crossed the Atlantic to Cuba. Finding that General Robert E. Lee had already surrendered, and that the Confederacy was finished, the CSS *Stonewall* was handed over to the Spanish authorities in Cuba. It was subsequently sold to the US government.

Although the European option produced no vessels that influenced the naval campaign, different political circumstances and legal verdicts could have given the Confederacy a suite of extremely powerful ironclads.

SHIPBUILDING

Unlike the North, the Southern states had very few operational shipyards in 1861. Although over 140 shipyards have been identified, most of these were virtually nonexistent: stretches of riverbank where small riverine vessels were built by local craftsmen. The only real shipyards were concentrated in the main coastal cities: Norfolk, Wilmington, Charleston, Savannah, Mobile, and New Orleans. Shipyards for river craft were also located in towns like Baton Rouge, Selma, Columbus, and Memphis. When the war broke out, several of the local shipyard owners submitted bids to build warships, including ironclads. For example, Asa Tift of Key West, a friend of Stephen Mallory, submitted a model for an armored vessel, which could be built by relatively unskilled builders. Mallory eventually commissioned its construction, and the vessel became the ironclad *Mississippi*. The Savannah shipbuilder Henry Willink Jr. won a contract to built two ironclads in his yard, while E. C. Murray won a bid to build a large ironclad called the *Louisiana* at his Jefferson City (New Orleans) yard. The construction of the *Louisiana* and the *Mississippi* strained the resources of Louisiana, and work was constantly delayed by lack of skilled men, vital materials, or available transportation. These yards were lost when New Orleans was captured by Union forces in April, 1862.

When the Union Navy withdrew from the Gosport Navy Yard (at Norfolk, Virginia), it tried unsuccessfully to destroy the naval construction facilities there. Within months, the yard was operational again, and work had begun on the conversion of the former USS *Merrimac* into an ironclad. When Norfolk was abandoned in May, 1862, the CSS *Virginia* was destroyed, and the incomplete ironclad *Richmond* was towed up the James River to Richmond, where a new yard was set up (Rockett's Navy Yard). Much of the equipment, stores, and workforce from Gosport

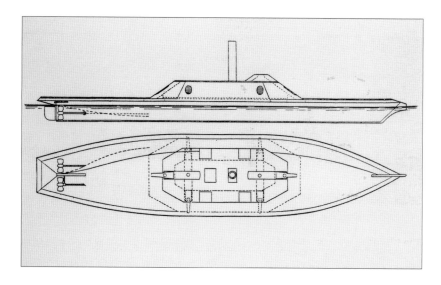

The CSS *Albermarle* and her sister vessel the CSS *Neuse* were both armed with 6.4-inch Brooke rifles. Note the pivot arrangement for the guns, which were employed as the bow and stern weapons in most Confederate ironclads. (MM)

were also transferred to Richmond. During the war, the ironclads *Fredericksburg, Virginia II,* and *Texas* were built there, although the *Texas* was unfinished when she was burned to prevent her capture in April, 1865. The losses of Norfolk and New Orleans were a severe blow to the Confederacy, as they contained the most-developed shipyards in the South. Subsequently, the lack of shipbuilding facilities dictated the size, shape, and construction methods of Confederate ironclads.

With an unbreakable Union blockade around the coast, ironclads could not be transported far from their place of construction. It was evident that shipyards would have to be constructed from nothing, alongside rivers or estuaries where no facilities had previously existed. In the west, the ironclads *Tennessee* and *Arkansas* were being constructed at Memphis, Tennessee, when the city fell to the Union. The *Arkansas* escaped, and a temporary shipyard was established at Yazoo City, Mississippi, so that the ironclad could be completed. Under the supervision of Lieutenant Isaac Brown, local slaves, laborers, and blacksmiths were pressed into service, working 24 hours a day in shifts. This makeshift solution worked, and by July, 1862, the newly commissioned CSS *Arkansas* was ready for action.

Shipbuilder Henry Basset agreed to build two ironclads at his yard in Selma, Alabama, and despite a lack of facilities, the *Huntsville* and *Tuscaloosa* were constructed within a year, together with the *Tennessee II.* Other small, temporary yards on the Red River in Louisiana and the Alabama and Tombigbee rivers in Alabama were also created for the production of ironclads, although they never proved as productive as the facility established at Yazoo City. Work on these western projects was supervised by Captain Ebenezer Farrand of the Navy Department. Naval Constructor John Shirley retained overall control of all western ironclad construction throughout the war.

On the Atlantic seaboard, "Richmond class" ironclads were constructed at existing yards in Richmond, Wilmington, Charleston, and Savannah, and temporary shipyard facilities were established in North Carolina to construct the *Albermarle* and the *Neuse.* Of these, Gilbert Elliot, the builder of the CSS *Albermarle,* created a shipyard at Edwards Ferry in what was once a cornfield! Attempts to create a new Naval Yard

at Columbus, Georgia, were largely unsuccessful, and apart from Richmond and the temporary yards in North Carolina, ironclad building on the Atlantic seaboard of the Confederacy was left in the hands of local shipyards at Wilmington, Charleston, and Savannah.

The CSS *Albermarle* is rammed by the USS *Sassacus* during a skirmish in Albermarle Sound. The Union vessel was unable to cause any significant damage to the ironclad. (HCA)

THE IRONCLAD'S ROLE

When Stephen Mallory lobbied for a Confederate Navy that embraced the latest technical innovations, he was attempting to offset the numerical superiority of the Union Navy. His emphasis on the development of an ironclad fleet was only part of a concerted strategy that also included the use of mines, rifled guns, submarines and commerce raiders, all revolutionary elements in naval warfare. At first, Mallory envisaged ironclads as a strategic tool capable of breaking the Union blockade of Southern ports, and of taking the war to the enemy. As the war progressed, and increasing inroads were made into the Confederacy's coastal defenses, the role of ironclads was scaled back. By the end of the war, they were little more than floating coastal batteries, trying to protect the few surviving Confederate ports from an overwhelming force of Union warships and troops.

To traditional naval officers, the ironclads designed by the Confederates were "monsters," "iron elephants," or "gunboxes," lacking the aesthetic beauty of traditional, masted warships. However, these officers also recognized their naval potential. As 22 ironclads were commissioned by the Confederacy, any description of their basic characteristics has to be general, although the development of their design has already been discussed. The majority had a uniformity of appearance, with an iron casemate whose sloping sides were pitched at a 35° angle. The basic design was not a new one; the central armored casemate set upon a low-freeboard hull was first employed in the design of floating batteries built by the French during the Crimean War (1854/56), although the Confederates improved upon this design to produce a fully operational type of warship.

The first true ironclad warship was the *Gloire*, commissioned into the French Navy in 1859. The following year, the British commissioned the even more powerful HMS *Warrior*. Both navies followed these with a succession of improved versions of these original designs. With a few exceptions, most European armored warships produced between 1859 and 1865 were broadside casemate vessels, designed for use on the open sea. By contrast, Confederate ironclads (and for that matter the Union monitors) were coastal vessels at best, lacking the seaworthiness of their European counterparts. This reflected a difference in strategic role. The navies of Britain and France existed to support the global aspirations of their governments. The role of the Union Navy was to enforce a blockade of Southern ports, and to wrest control of coastal waters and rivers away from the Confederacy. For the South, the defense of her ports, rivers, and inland waterways was of paramount importance. The role assigned each nation's ironclad warships reflected these strategic objectives.

The casemate ironclad suited the defensive strategy of the Confederacy, and reflected the realities of her shipbuilding capabilities. Although the *Virginia* had several significant flaws, it was a successful experimental prototype, and it allowed the Navy Department to develop a series of improved casemate designs throughout the war. Near the end of the war, Mallory wrote: "For river, harbor and coastal defense, the sloping shield and general plan of the armored vessels adopted by us … are the best that could be adopted in our situation … In ventilation, light, fighting space and quarters it is believed that the sloping shield presents greater advantages than the Monitor turret …" In other words, the design was ideally suited to the industrial capacity and requirements of the Confederacy.

Early ironclads were designed to operate in coastal waters, reflecting an attempt to contest the Union blockade. The failure of the Confederacy to break the Union stranglehold led to a shift in policy around the summer of 1862. From that point on, ironclads were designed for local coastal defense only, marking a significant change in role. They became defensive rather than offensive vessels. This reflected a realization that the Confederate ironclad was incapable of undertaking a more demanding role, due to the constraints of its design. In 1862, work began on the ironclad CSS *Richmond*, designed as a harbor or river defense vessel. The design was better suited to this new defensive role than the *Virginia* and other early ironclads. Although designs changed, subsequent Confederate ironclads were built from the keel up for local defense.

A second reassessment of the role of the ironclad took place in mid-1863, following the capture of the CSS *Atlanta*. Later ironclads were better armored, and even limited independent forays against Union vessels were discouraged. This meant that from late 1863, the role of the Confederate ironclads was to form part of an integrated coastal defense system. The provision of mobile support to static defenses (minefields and fortifications) became the new role of the ironclad, marking an even greater surrender of strategic initiative to the Union. Given the numerical, logistical,

A hydraulic press such as this was used to press the iron sheets into the armored plate produced by Southern foundries. The standard thickness used on ironclads was 2 inches, and two or even three layers were laminated together to create the casemate armor. (Collection of Chris Henry, Southsea, Hampshire)

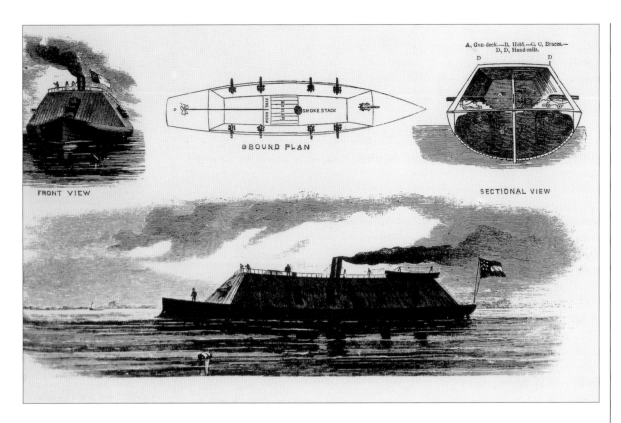

A, Gun-deck.—B, Hold.—C, C, Braces.—
D, D, Hand-rails.

GROUND PLAN

FRONT VIEW

SECTIONAL VIEW

The CSS *Richmond* was the first of the "Richmond class" Confederate ironclads designed by John Porter. Their limited motive power and seagoing abilities reflected their role as harbor or river defense vessels. (MM)

and strategic disadvantages of the Confederate Navy, this represented the best possible role for the warships.

OFFICERS & MEN

The officers who served in the Confederate Navy were all former US Navy officers who resigned their commissions and "went south." Of the 1,550 naval officers in the US Navy at the start of the war, about a quarter of them resigned their commissions and sought service in the Confederacy. The decision these men faced was an unenviable one, torn between loyalty to the service, the nation, their home state or even to a particular ideology. Not all Southern officers "went south," but most resigned when their home state seceded from the Union. Those who remained were often viewed with suspicion, although the vast wartime increase in the Union Navy meant that every available officer was almost certain of promotion and financial reward. After Lincoln took office, resigning officers were deemed as "deserters," and faced arrest unless they fled south of the Mason-Dixon line. The prospects for those who allied themselves with the Confederacy were bleak, as at first the Confederate Navy only had a handful of ships at its disposal. Compared to their counterparts in the army, promotion prospects remained poor throughout the war, and commanders of major warships in the US Navy found themselves commanding converted river steamers in the South. These men had all made a huge sacrifice for the cause, and their treatment by the Confederate government never reflected the personal traumas they went through.

In April, 1862, the Confederate Congress established posts for four admirals, ten captains, 31 commanders, 125 lieutenants (first and second), plus a corresponding number of non-line posts, such as paymasters and surgeons. Promotion to most of the senior slots was by merit, to encourage the younger officers, a system that ran contrary to that of the old navy. Until ships were produced, many of these men found themselves commanding coastal fortifications or overseeing construction programs. The Confederacy even introduced an officer training program, to reinforce the skilled commissioned officers available to them. The training ship CSS *Patrick Henry* served as a midshipman's training ship, and operated in that capacity on the James River near Richmond from August, 1863.

The "Richmond class" ironclad CSS *Palmetto State* is depicted ramming the wooden screw sloop USS *Mercedita* in a detail of an inaccurate contemporary engraving by a British artist. (Charleston Museum, Charleston, SC)

The Confederate Navy operated through a regional command system, where a senior officer would command the naval defenses of a stretch of coastline, say from Savannah to Georgetown. He often held command of a warship in his district, usually the most powerful ironclad, although he could devolve control of these vessels to a subordinate senior officer. A lack of clarification of duties and spheres of responsibility by the Navy Department in Richmond plagued the navy throughout the war, and some regional commanders exerted almost no real authority beyond their immediate squadron. Often, the area or local station commander had responsibility for land batteries in the area.

Within the ironclads, command followed the procedures set up for the US Navy, and the captain or senior officer present commanded the vessel in action from his command post in the pilot house, which replaced the quarterdeck on a conventional warship for this purpose. His executive officer was responsible for maneuvering the vessel in action, and coordinating damage control. He was assisted by the master, responsible for seamanship and navigation, and a number of midshipmen who relayed orders from the pilot house (effectively the bridge) to the rest of the ship. In some cases vessels were controlled by the army, but naval officers still commanded them, a command problem that hindered the effective defense of areas such as Charleston, Mobile Bay, and New Orleans. Wherever they served, the officer corps of the Confederate Navy distinguished itself by an almost unblemished record of devotion to duty, courage under fire, and improvisation. Faced with overwhelming odds, they did more than was expected of them.

As for the crew, they proved more of a problem. With no navy to speak of, the Confederacy had to recruit one from scratch, and the defection of seamen to the South in no way matched the substantial movement of officers. Most of the navy's manpower came from the army, drafted by order of local military commanders partly to fulfil the requests for men made by the Navy Department. Naturally, there was a tendency to send the men who these commanders wished to be rid of, so the navy was effectively given the "dregs of the barrel," or as one commander put it: "misfits sent by lesser army officers." One problem was that the South did not have a substantial pool of seamen to draw from. Although naval recruiting stations were set up in most major Southern ports, and bounties of $50 were offered, recruitment levels were poor. Many real seamen preferred the army, which offered higher pay, or service on blockade runners, where the potential financial rewards were even greater. Ages ranged from 14 upwards, with the teenagers being classed as "boys." Surprisingly, colored recruits were sometimes employed as coal heavers, stewards, or local pilots, although their numbers and duties were restricted.

Ranks ranged from petty officer, though promotion to this rank was by meritorious service, down to seaman, ordinary seaman, landsman, coal heaver, fireman, and boy. Development from landsman to ordinary seaman and seaman was based on maritime experience and length of service. If recruits had any technical skills (such as carpentry, metalworking, or engineering), they were usually placed where their skills would do the most good. As most army recruits were landsmen, training was of the utmost importance. Receiving ships were set up at most major naval stations, and the landsmen were given a basic naval training before they were sent on active service. Ironclads were unpopular assignments because of their uncomfortable living conditions, since only the engineers, firemen, and coal heavers had to endure the stifling heat of the engine rooms on other ships. On ironclads, the whole ship was usually uncomfortably hot. Despite their lack of training and seamanlike qualities, most of these recruits performed their duties well. An ironclad in action against a superior enemy would have been a terrible assignment for anyone. It is to the credit of these Southern landsmen turned sailors that they fought to the best of their abilities.

The CSS *Atlanta* during her duel with the Union ironclad USS *Weehawken*, in June, 1863. Note the torpedo on a spar fitted to the bow of the Confederate vessel. It could be lowered into position when required. (MM)

ORDNANCE

The Confederate Navy was fairly successful in providing its ironclads with the weapons they needed. From 1863 on, except in the more remote corners of the Confederacy, ordnance was in relatively good supply. The capture of the Norfolk (Gosport) Navy Yard in April, 1861, meant that 1,198 heavy guns were available to the Confederacy, meeting almost all of the nation's initial requirements for coastal fortifications and for the navy. Most of these pieces were muzzle-loading smoothbores, including just under 1,000 32-pounders, although it also included over 50 9-inch Dahlgren pieces, among the most modern pieces of ordnance then available. Of the smoothbore guns, most were of the Columbiad pattern, a design introduced in 1811, but improved and enlarged during the intervening half century. The ordnance designer Thomas J. Rodman developed an improved version during the 1840s that became a standard form of naval weapon, capable of greater range and penetration. The ordnance developed by John A. Dahlgren between 1847 and 1855 was cast from the solid, then bored out, creating an even more powerful barrel. What the US Navy lacked when the war broke out was rifled weapons, although the conflict would serve as an impetus for designers on both sides.

The Confederate Navy Department's policy of emphasizing the use of rifled weapons meant that the navy pushed for the production of additional rifled guns. Their superior range and penetration were demonstrated by the Union when they reduced Fort Pulaski (guarding Savannah, Georgia) to rubble on April 10–11, 1862. As an interim measure, many of the 32-pounders captured at Norfolk were reinforced at the breech and rifled. By the end of 1861, the navy began to produce its own rifled guns under the supervision of Commander John M. Brooke.

The large Dahlgren and Columbiad smoothbore guns captured at Norfolk were designed so that the barrel thickened considerably towards the breech, allowing the gun to withstand the explosion of the main charge. The new guns designed by Robert Parrott in New York mirrored those produced in Britain by Armstrong and Blakely in that the barrels had parallel sides, but wrought-iron reinforcing bands were coiled around the breech end of the guns. The Parrott rifle was just being patented in late 1861, and details of the weapon were released to the US Navy before Brooke "went south." Evidently, he had access to these designs. Brooke designed his guns to copy this feature, as it made the weapons easier to produce. In his weapons, a series of iron bands were heat-shrunk around the barrel. Initially, a single two-inch-thick reinforcing band surrounded the breech end of the tube. In later and larger Brooke

The "Laird Rams" *El Tousson* (left) and *El Mounassir* (right) following their confiscation by the British government. HMS *Majestic*, shown between the two ironclads, acts as a guard ship. Built in Merseyside for the Confederacy, they were never completed. (SHM)

This depiction of the interior of the CSS *Albermarle*, during her action with the USS *Sassacus*, takes place just after the ironclad was rammed by the gunboat. It is probably the best depiction availalbe of the inside of a casemate ironclad in action. (HCA)

pieces, additional bands were added, up to the three-banded reinforcement on his 10-inch rifled guns. His guns were first mounted in the CSS *Virginia* (ex-USS *Merrimac*), and in testing the first of the two 7-inch rifles he designed for the ironclad, he fired a 100-pound projectile 4.5 miles. When the *Virginia* fought its duel with the USS *Monitor* in March, 1862, the efficiency of his design was proven, and consequently orders for more guns were placed.

Throughout the war, Brooke rifles and smoothbores were noted for their accuracy, reliability, range, and penetration. They became the standard armament for Confederate ironclads for the remainder of the war. The majority were of 6.4-inch or 7-inch calibers, and these were carried on ironclads such as the vessels of the "Richmond class." After the loss of the CSS *Atlanta* (June, 1863), larger calibers were developed, and some of the earlier guns had their reinforcing increased, so they could handle larger powder charges (thereby increasing penetration). Typically, 7-inch guns were used as bow and stern pivot-mounted weapons, while the 6.4-inch rifles were mounted on traditional carriages and used as broadside weapons.

Not all the guns carried on Confederate ironclads were rifles, as it was considered that shells fired from smoothbore guns had a greater destructive power against wooden warships. Consequently, some ironclads carried a mixture of rifled and smoothbore guns. For example, among the vessels of the James River Squadron, the ironclad CSS *Richmond* carried a matched armament of 7-inch Brooke rifles, but the CSS *Fredericksburg* and CSS *Virginia II* both carried a stern-mounted 10-inch Brooke smoothbore gun (both were rearmed with Brooke 11-inch pieces in 1864). Brooke 10-inch (double-banded) and 11-inch (triple-banded) smoothbore guns continued to be produced from 1862 until the end of the war, to satisfy the demand for a mixed armament. Most ironclads also carried one or two small 12-pounder howitzers, mounted on modified field carriages for use against boarding parties. These were almost never employed in action, as nobody tried to board the ironclads.

Vessels built or purchased overseas often carried European guns. The French-built CSS *Stonewall* was armed with Armstrong (Blakely) rifled guns (11-inch and 6.4-inch RMLs), while the "Laird Rams" were earmarked to carry 7-inch Armstrong rifled guns. The huge 300-pound, 11-inch Armstrong mounted in the bow of the CSS *Stonewall* was never fired in anger. The CSS *Huntsville* and CSS *Tuscaloosa*, built in Selma, were reputedly armed with a single 7-inch Armstrong (Blakely) rifled gun which was installed alongside domestic pieces. Presumably, the two pieces were brought into the Confederacy by a blockade runner.

In late 1862, the Confederate government secured an industrial site in Selma, Alabama, and converted it into an ordnance foundry. In May, 1863, the former executive officer of the CSS *Virginia*, Commander Catesby ap Jones, took control of the plant on behalf of the Navy Department. He saw the production of Brooke rifles and smoothbores as its primary function, and adapted the formerly joint-service facility to suit the needs of the Confederate Navy. The Naval Gun Foundry at Selma also provided guns for the army, supplying ordnance for batteries along the Mississippi River, but otherwise the guns produced at the foundry were almost exclusively used to arm the Confederate ironclads. By early 1864, the first gun was completed at the plant, a 7-inch Brooke rifle which was used on the CSS *Tennessee*. By the spring, Jones was producing 6.4- and 7-inch rifles, and 8-, 10-, and 11-inch smoothbores, fulfilling all the ordnance needs of the navy. Further guns were sent to improve coastal defenses, and the foundry even produced smaller Parrott rifles for the navy's gunboats. On April 2, 1865, Union troops entered Selma, the day before the Confederate capital at Richmond fell. The yard was destroyed, together with the Army Ordnance Foundry located nearby. During its operation, the plant supplied 102 Brooke pieces for the navy, and almost all of the later ironclads were armed using pieces produced in Selma.

The CSS *Albermarle*, photographed after the Confederate ironclad was raised by Union engineers. The figure on the stern gives an impression of the vessel's size. (USN)

To sum up, from about 1863 onwards, the Confederate Navy had all the guns it needed, and the weapons were of the highest quality. It could even be argued that Brooke guns were better than anything in the Union naval arsenal.

NAVAL GUNNERY

Each gun division consisted of a heavy gun, or a battery of two or three broadside pieces. Each was commanded by a lieutenant, with a midshipman to assist him. They provided fire control, ordering a change of target, the substitution of a different kind of ammunition, or supervised the safety of the crew. A gun captain, usually a petty officer, oversaw each gun, and his crew varied in number depending on gun size and crew availability. A large piece on a pivot mount such as a 10-inch Brooke rifle, required a crew of 27 men, an 8-inch broadside gun needed 19 men, and small pieces such as the 32-pounder in the bow of the CSS *Manassas* had a crew of 11 men.

When the ironclad went into action, the crew gritted the deck with sand, and gun tools were brought out and stationed beside each weapon. The guns were unlashed from the sides of the casemate, and powder and shot was brought up from the magazine. The officers commanding each gun division ordered the type of shot to be loaded, and then each gun crew prepared its individual piece. The master gunner stationed himself in the magazine and supervised the flow of ammunition and the safety of the gun crews. Each gun crew consisted of a number of men who in regular ships were called on to serve as

CSS *Arkansas*

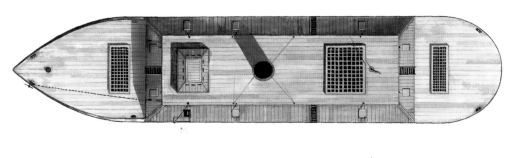

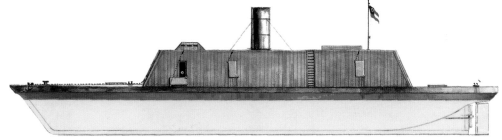

CSS *Fredericksburg*

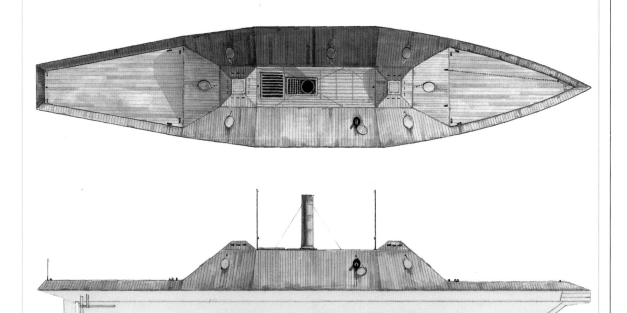

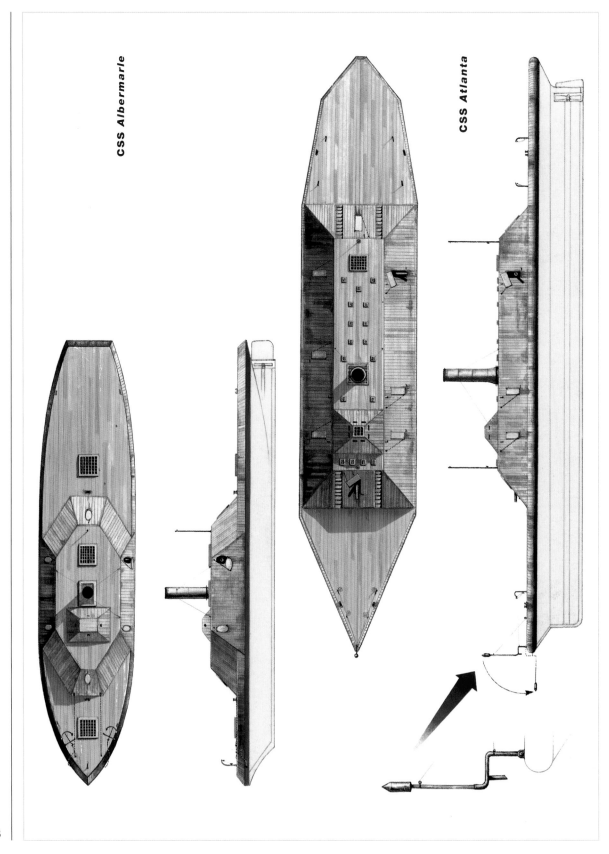

CSS *Albermarle*

CSS *Atlanta*

B

The Battle of New Orleans, 1862

C

CSS *VIRGINIA*
(Merrimac inset)

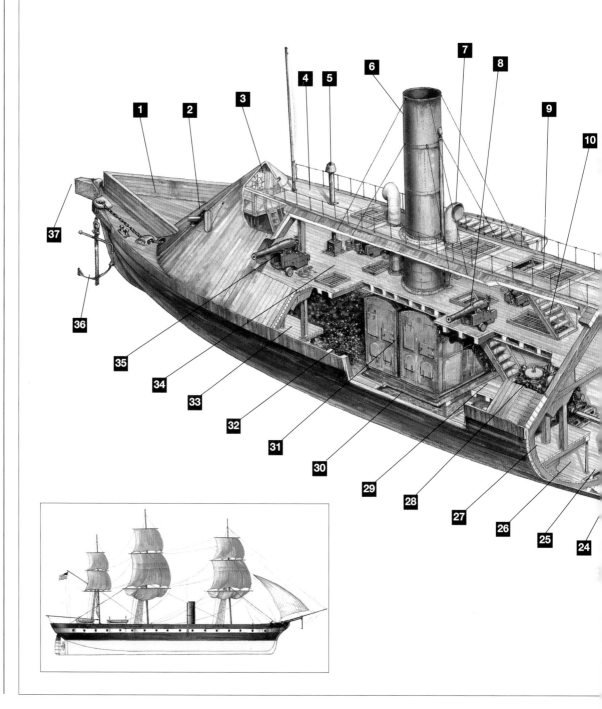

1
2
3
4
5
6
7
8
9
10
24
25
26
27
28
29
30
31
32
33
34
35
36
37

1. "False" bow
2. Gunport shutter and chain pulley
3. Pilot house
4. Spar deck
5. Stove and chimney
6. Funnel
7. Ventilator
8. 6.4-inch Brooke rifled gun on Marsilly carriage
9. Ventilation grating
10. Main companion-way
11. Powder magazine
12. Ship's galley
13. Shell magazine
14. Dry provisions store
15. Main ensign staff and Confederate ensign
16. 7-inch Brooke rifled gun on pivoting wooden casemate structure
17. Iron chain cover
18. Steering chain mechanism
19. Rudder
20. Twin-bladed Griffiths pattern propellor
21. Copper-sheathed lower hull
22. Outer layer of 6-inch wide 2-inch rolled iron plate (vertical)
23. Inner layer of 6-inch wide 2-inch rolled iron plate (horizontal)
24. Propellor shaft
25. Bilge
26. Orlop deck
27. Berth deck
28. Horizontal Back-acting engine
29. Location of temporary sick bay
30. Brick foundation to boilers
31. Twin tubular boilers
32. Coal bunker
33. Temporary cabins (partitions removed in action)
34. Gun deck
35. 9-inch Dahlgren smoothbore gun on Marsilly gun carriage
36. Main anchor
37. Bolt-on ram (1,500 lb)

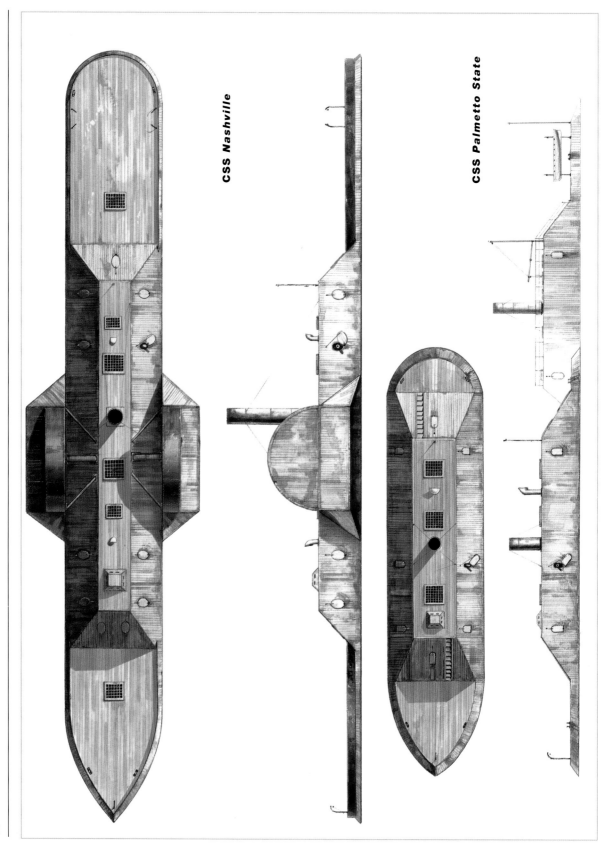

CSS Nashville

CSS Palmetto State

E

CSS *Huntsville*

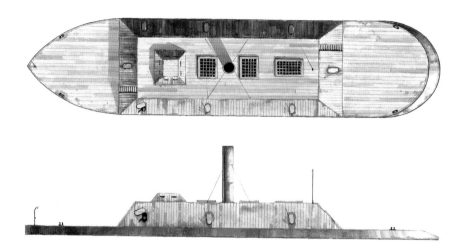

CSS *Stonewall*

boarders. On ironclads, their main function was to assist firefighting parties or repair teams when required.

The loading and firing sequence was identical to that practiced in the US Navy. After unlashing the gun and rolling it back, the first order given by the gun captain was to "Serve vent and sponge." His assistant (the second gun captain) sealed the vent with his gloved thumb while the sponger and loader swabbed out the barrel with a dampened sponge. Following the next order of "Charge with cartridge," the powder man passed the loader a pre-measured, color-coded cartridge that was set into the barrel and gently rammed home. When it was in place, the loader yelled "Home." Next, the gun captain ordered "Charge with shot." Two shot men brought the shot or shell forward to the muzzle and inserted the projectile into the barrel mouth, followed by a cloth wad, which acted as a sealant. The rammer and loader then rammed it home against the cartridge. The gun was then almost ready to be fired. Ammunition varied from solid shot, spherical shell, grape or canister for smoothbore weapons to grooved conical shells or solid shot for rifled guns. Smoothbore guns firing spherical shot could also be double-shotted, for extra effect at close range. (A variation to the standard drill could be used when a faster rate of fire was desired, although this was achieved at the expense of safety. On the order "Quick fire," the charge and projectile could be loaded at the same time.) At the order "Run out," the gunport shutter was opened by two port tackle men, one on each side of the muzzle. Two side tackle men pulled on their heaving ropes to run the gun forward on its wheels or slide carriage until the muzzle projected from the gunport. At the next command of "Point," two handspike men shifted the carriage to left or right until it pointed at the target. On pivot carriages, these men turned cranks to train the piece. This was done under the supervision of the gun captain, who also determined the amount of elevation. He then ordered "Prime," and the second gun captain pricked the cartridge bag by ramming a wire pricker through the touch-hole, then the gun captain inserted a priming tube into the vent, and attached a lanyard to it. The gun was then ready to fire. The gun captain held up a clenched fist and yelled "Ready" to signal to the officer commanding the gun division that the weapon was ready to fire. All the gun crew stood well back from the gun, and waited for the order to fire. Following approval from the division officer, the gun captain yelled "Fire," and pulled the lanyard. The gun recoiled as far as its breeching ropes if mounted on a regular carriage, or back against its rear chocks on a sliding pivot carriage. The process

The Confederate ironclad CSS *Stonewall*, photographed after the end of the war. The French-built vessel was finally sold to the Japanese, who named her the *Adzuma*. (National Archives, Washington, DC)

would then be repeated. A well-trained crew could reload a 6.4- or 7-inch Brooke rifle in five minutes, although heavier smooth-bore guns had a slower rate of fire (approximately one round every eight or ten minutes). When the engagement was over, the crew were given the order "Secure," and they cleaned the gun, secured it in its normal position and then returned the gun tools to their proper storage racks.

The CSS *Chicora* was a "Richmond class" ironclad that formed part of the Charleston Squadron. She differed from her sister, *Palmetto State*, by having a shorter casemate, and fewer guns. (LOC)

As for range and penetration, the maximum range of a typical Brooke rifle was around four miles, with an effective range against non-armored targets of less than two miles. Against armored opponents, the guns were fired at ranges of less than 600 yards in order to have any effect, and even then, penetration was rare at ranges beyond 100 yards. As the war progressed and gun sizes increased, penetration became easier, necessitating an increase in armored protection.

LIFE ON BOARD

Confederate ironclads were functioning warships, and lacked the relative comfort of other contemporary wooden vessels. They were effectively a floating gundeck, powered by steam engines. The interior layout of almost every casemate ironclad was similar. The "gun deck" was the portion of the main deck located inside the protective casemate. As on a steam- or sail-powered wooden warship, most of the crew ate and slept between the guns. Hammocks and mess tables were stowed away when not in use. Below the gun deck was the "berthing deck," which contained additional crew quarters forward as well as the galley, and berths for the officers (in the wardroom), the midshipmen's berth, the captain's cabin, the paymaster's office, and the sick bay. As the CSS *Virginia* was taken into action before she was completed, only temporary dividing partitions were installed using canvas screens, and all but the sickbay were taken down before the ironclad went into battle. Later ironclads had wooden partitions between the main stores, cabins, and office spaces. This berth deck was usually only a partial or mezzanine deck, fitted around the engine and boiler that rose from the orlop deck to the gun deck. Below this second deck, a third "orlop deck" contained storerooms forward and aft, as well as the spirit room, shell room(s), and magazine(s). The magazine was usually located forward of midships, dry provision stores nearer the bow and wardroom stores sited at the stern. All these spaces were below the waterline, so dampness was a major problem. To the stern of this deck, or sometimes on a lower deck, were fresh water tanks, the boiler room, and the engine room, with all their attendant machinery. Although exact configurations varied (often between vessels of the same class), this basic internal layout was adopted for virtually all Confederate ironclads.

Living conditions on these ironclads were virtually intolerable, particularly during the summer. Where ventilation existed, it was primitive, with temporary canvas wind-shutes installed rather than mechanical fans or blowers. Light and fresh air was provided through the gratings on the upper ("spar") deck, and through the open gunports. When the ironclad was under way, heat generated from the engine turned the whole vessel into a large furnace. Dampness from rain, spray or (even more commonly) leaks in the hull created an unhealthy, humid atmosphere. Consequently, the crew of the ironclads was prone to sickness brought on by the dank, dark, hot conditions in which they served. There was little opportunity for exercise, leading to even further medical problems. Historians have claimed that on average about 20 percent of the crew of an ironclad would be sick at any one time. In action, it was common for sailors to collapse from heat exhaustion, and "intense thirst usually prevailed."

The conditions encouraged discontent and desertion. It was therefore important to provide alternative accommodation for the crew when the ironclad was not operating overnight. On the CSS *Tennessee*, the crew slept on board a barge anchored in Mobile Bay, and the same arrangement was used for the CSS *Arkansas*. The crews of the CSS *Albermarle*, *Tuscaloosa*, and *Hunstville* slept in warehouses ashore, while the vessels of the Charleston Squadron were allocated barracks. This was fine when the ships were in port or at anchor, but many went on operational patrols during the night, so the crew still suffered.

On the CSS *Tennessee*, the appallingly humid condition after weeks of nearly continual rain created "that opressiveness which precedes a tornado." It was impossible to eat or sleep below decks because of the heat and humidity, and the decks were always wet . "Then men took their hardtack and coffee standing … creeping out of the ports on the after deck to get a little fresh air." In winter, ice would cover the decks, and the iron hull retained the icy cold of the air and water that surrounded it. Perhaps the worst of all the ironclads was the CSS *Atlanta*, where one officer wrote: "I would defy anyone in the world to tell me when it is day or night if he is confined below without any way of marking time … I would venture to say that if a person were blindfolded and carried below, then turned loose, he would imagine himself in a swamp. For the water is trickling in all the time, and everything is damp."

Overall, naval service was no soft alternative to life in the Confederate army. The living conditions in ironclads were the worst of any group of

The former Confederate ironclad *Atlanta*, photographed while serving as a Union warship off Savannah, Georgia. This view from off the starboard bow gives a good impression of the slope of her casemate, sloping inwards at a 35° angle. (LOC)

ships in the fleet. Battle at least brought the promise of a temporary end to the suffering. As the surgeon of the CSS *Tennessee* reported: "everyone looked forward to the impending action which, regardless of the outcome, would provide a positive feeling of relief." If men preferred to risk their lives rather than continue to endure life at anchor in port, then conditions must have been truly appalling.

TACTICS

This rare view of the *Atlanta* in dry dock shows the shape of her lower hull, and the relatively deep draft of a typical early- or mid-war ironclad. The lack of cladding on the underside of the hull led to irreparable rotting in both the *North Carolina* and the *Baltic*. (National Archives, Washington).

For the Confederate officers who commanded or served in ironclads, no tactical manual existed. They were at the forefront of a naval revolution, and had to devise their own modus operandi. Much was dictated by the characteristics of the casemate ironclad. Most Confederate vessels were underpowered, and lacked maneuverability. By contrast, Union monitors had little problem bringing their guns to bear on their Confederate opponents. Apart from bow and stern guns (most of which could also train to face port or starboard), the Confederate ironclads engaged the enemy by presenting their main broadside battery to the target and firing. In consequence, they presented a larger target to enemy guns than the vessels of the monitor design. The CSS *Virginia* demonstrated the effectiveness of the ironclad against unarmored opponents on March 8, 1862, when she sank the wooden steam frigates USS *Cumberland* and *Congress* with ease. Against an armored opponent, things were very different. During the engagement between the *Virginia* and the *Monitor,* a divisional gunnery officer, Lieutenant Eggleston, ordered his men to cease firing, as "it would be a waste of precious powder and ammunition. I can do her just about as much damage by snapping my thumb at her every two minutes and a half." The CSS *Virginia's* guns were unable to penetrate the armor of the USS *Monitor.* Although the armor plates on the Confederate vessel were damaged, towards the end of the action some plates were knocked away, exposing unarmored timbers in the casemate. Although the design flaws were rectified in later ironclads, the casemate design continued to provide a target to the enemy that was almost impossible to miss. The increasing power of Confederate rifled guns as the war progressed was a response to the ineffectiveness in gunnery against ironclads, while increasingly strong armor and the reduction in size of the casemate helped counteract the inherent vulnerability of the Confederate design. Experiments with armor-piercing ammunition were unsuccessful, although the use of steel bolts as projectiles was considered but never implemented.

A contemporary artist's view of the CSS *Arkansas*. There is still discussion about the slope of her casemate but, unlike other vessels, her sides were vertical or nearly so. She is depicted steaming down the Yazoo River after her completion. (MM)

The Confederate ironclad *Tennessee*, photographed after her capture by the Union in August, 1864. Typically, deck awnings and even huts were erected when the ironclads were at anchor for long periods. (LOC)

Early in the war, the crew organization of ironclads called for a boarding party to be ready to attack enemy vessels. During the battle with the *Monitor*, some officers from the *Virginia* suggested boarding the Union vessel, to immobilize the turret and seal the hatches. It was never undertaken and, apart from the occasional use of sharpshooters, Confederate ironclads abandoned these traditional tactics and developed their own. One innovative weapon was the ram, first introduced on the *Virginia* and used in her attack on the *Cumberland*. Rams were subsequently fitted to over half of the ironclads that were commissioned into the Confederate Navy. Ramming saved powder and shot, and against vulnerable vessels such as monitors or wooden gunboats, the tactic was a sound one. The greatest drawback was the lack of speed and maneuverability of the Confederate vessels, meaning that the blow might damage the enemy, but would probably not sink it. There was also a significant risk of damage being inflicted on the ramming vessel.

Ironically, the lack of maneuverability of Confederate rams made them vulnerable to attack by ramming, and ramming attacks were conducted on both the CSS *Tennessee* and the CSS *Albermarle* by wooden Union steam warships. A development of the ram tactic was the addition of a spar torpedo to the armament of the CSS *Atlanta*, mounted on the end of a pole which could be lowered into position on the ironclad's bow, extending ahead of it like a bowsprit. Similar fittings might have been contemplated for other vessels, but were probably never installed.

Conditions in action were almost indescribable, with the crew working its guns in the darkness of the casemate, illuminated only by light from lanterns. Although penetration of the hull by enemy shot was unlikely, in the last battle of the CSS *Atlanta*, wooden splinters from the backing caused by the impact of Union shot wounded about

50 crewmen. Damage to the engines could also fill the hull with scalding steam, as happened on Union river ironclads, and gun crews were exposed when they raised their gunport lids to fire. During the Battle of Mobile Bay in 1864, the CSS *Tennessee* was only penetrated once, when a 15-inch (440 pound) shot from the monitor USS *Manhattan* pierced the casemate armor. Like the *Atlanta* action, far worse was the effect of concussion:

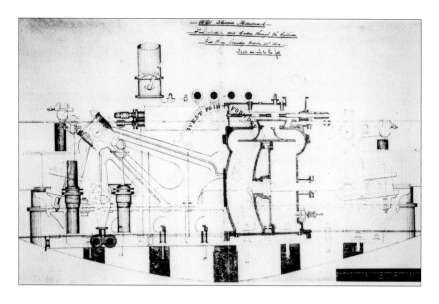

The engines of the USS *Merrimac* were reused for the ironclad *Virginia*. Chief Engineer William P. Williamson performed miracles, but the old frigate's engines were still underpowered, given the extra weight of the *Virginia*'s iron casemate. (USN)

"For an hour and a half the monitors pounded us with solid shot, fired with a charge of sixty pounds of powder from their eleven-inch guns, determined to crush in the shield of the *Tennessee*, as thirty pounds of powder was the regulation amount. In the midst of this continuous pounding, the port-shutter of one of our guns was jammed by shot, so that it could neither open or shut, making it impossible to work the piece.

"The admiral then sent for some of the firemen from below, to drive the bolt outward. Four men came up, and two of them holding the bolt back, the others struck it with sledgehammers. While they were thus standing there, suddenly there was a dull-sounding impact, and at the same instant the men whose backs were against the shield (casemate) were split to pieces. I saw their limbs and chests, severed and mangled, scattered about the deck, their hearts lying near their bodies. All of the gun's crew and the admiral were covered from head to foot with blood, flesh and viscera … The fragments and members of the dead men were shovelled up, and struck below."

Although protected by a thick iron casemate, the crews of Confederate ironclads were still vulnerable. The *Atlanta* and the *Tennessee* both surrendered when the casualties and psychological pressure created by enemy fire became too intense to bear, not because their armored protection was ineffective. In 1865, the British naval officer Philip Colomb wrote *Modern Fleet Tactics*, incorporating many of the lessons learned from ironclad actions of the American Civil War. For the officers and men who manned the Confederate ironclads, these lessons were learned the hard way.

Stephen Mallory was Secretary of the Navy in the Confederate Government. This unassuming Floridian was widely criticized for the navy's lack of success during the war, but his vision of an ironclad fleet greatly improved the protection offered to Southern ports and harbors. (HEC)

THE CONFEDERATE IRONCLADS

Although over 50 ironclads were laid down in the Confederacy, only 22 were commissioned; the rest were never completed. Of the others, only the *Louisiana* saw action before she was destroyed. Of the ironclads built in Europe, only the CSS *Stonewall* entered Confederate service.

CSS *ALBERMARLE*, CSS *NEUSE*

(Note: order of data is *Albermarle/Neuse*)

Dimensions:	152'/140' length, 34' beam, 9' draft
Displacement:	375 tons
Armor:	6" iron, with wood backing
Armament:	2 x 6.4" Brooke rifles
Engines:	twin-screw
Speed:	4 knots
Built:	Edwards Ferry, North Carolina / White Hall (now Seven Springs), North Carolina
Laid down:	April, 1863
Commissioned:	April, 1864
Crew:	50

On April 19,1864, the CSS *Albermarle* attacked a Union squadron in the Albermarle Sound off Plymouth, North Carolina, sinking the USS *Southfield*. On May 5, she was damaged in another engagement with Union warships in the river, and withdrawn up the Roanoke River for repairs. On October 28, she was sunk at her moorings by a Union torpedo boat. The CSS *Neuse* ran aground at Kinston on her voyage down the Neuse River to attack New Bern. She was repaired, but destroyed, to prevent her capture on March 9, 1865.

CSS *ARKANSAS*

Dimensions:	65' length, 35' beam, 11' 6" draft
Displacement:	unknown
Armor:	2" iron, with wood backing
Armament:	2 x 8" Brooke rifles,
	2 x 9" smoothbores,
	2 x 32-pdr. smoothbores
Engines:	twin-screw
Speed:	8 knots
Built:	Memphis, Tennessee
Laid down:	October, 1861
Commissioned:	May 26, 1862
Crew:	200

The *Arkansas* was completed on the Yazoo River, and on July 15, she engaged Union ironclads on the river, then ran past the Union fleet on the Mississippi to reach Vicksburg. On July 22, she fought off the Union ram, USS *Queen of the West*, at Vicksburg, and on August 6 she battled with the USS *Essex* above Baton Rouge. Badly crippled, she was destroyed by her own crew.

CSS *ATLANTA*

Dimensions:	165' length, 35' beam, 11' 6" draft
Displacement:	1,000 tons
Armor:	4" iron, with wood backing.
Armament:	2 x 7" Brooke rifles,
	2 x 6.4" Brooke rifles, spar torpedo
Engines:	triple-screw
Speed:	8 knots
Built:	Savannah, Georgia
Laid down:	spring, 1861
Commissioned:	September, 1862
Crew:	145

The *Atlanta* was converted from the blockade runner *Fingal*. The ironclad was based in Savannah, guarding the approaches to the city. In June, 1863, she engaged two Union monitors in Wassaw Sound, 12 miles south-east of Savannah. The monitors inflicted severe damage to her, driving the ironclad aground, and forced her surrender.

CSS *BALTIC*

Dimensions:	186' length, 38' beam, 6' draft
Displacement:	unknown
Armor:	4" iron, with wood backing
Armament:	4 rifled guns (caliber unknown)
Engines:	twin side paddlewheels
Speed:	6 knots
Built:	Selma, Alabama
Laid down:	summer, 1861
Commissioned:	August, 1862
Crew:	approx. 150

CSS *CHARLESTON*

Dimensions:	189' length, 34' beam, 14' draft
Displacement:	unknown
Armor:	4" iron, with wood backing
Armament:	2 x 9" smoothbores,
	4 x 6.4" Brooke rifles
Engines:	twin screw
Speed:	6 knots
Built:	Charleston, South Carolina
Laid down:	December, 1862
Commissioned:	July, 1864
Crew:	150

Known as the "Ladies Gunboat," as female subscriptions helped pay for her, the CSS *Charleston* served in the Charleston defense squadron until she was burned to prevent her capture when Charleston fell on February 15, 1865.

She formed part of the James River Squadron in defense of Richmond, and participated in the Battle of Trent's Reach (January 24, 1865). She was destroyed to prevent capture when Richmond fell in April, 1865.

CSS FREDERICKSBURG

Dimensions:	188' length, 40' beam, 9' draft
Displacement:	unknown
Armor:	6" iron, with wood backing
Armament:	3 x 7" Brooke rifles, 1 x 11" Brooke smoothbore
Engines:	twin-screw
Speed :	4 knots
Built:	Richmond, Virginia
Laid down:	autumn, 1862
Commissioned:	May 12, 1863
Crew:	125

An unsuccessful vessel due to her lack of power, she served out the war as a floating battery guarding Savannah. She was destroyed when the city fell in December, 1864.

CSS GEORGIA

Dimensions:	250' length, 60' beam, 13' draft
Displacement:	unknown
Armor:	4" iron, with wood backing
Armament:	4 x 6.4" Brooke rifles, 2 x 10" Brooke smoothbores
Engines:	single-screw
Speed:	3 knots
Built:	Savannah, Georgia
Laid down:	March, 1862
Commissioned:	July, 1863
Crew:	200

Initially built as floating batteries, these river ironclads were used to defend Mobile Bay from early 1864 onwards, but they were very slow and virtually unseaworthy. Following the Battle of Mobile Bay in August, 1864, they helped defend Mobile's forts in March, 1865. They were both scuttled off the city on April 12, 1865.

CSS HUSVILLE, CSS TUSCALOOSA

Dimensions:	(between) 150-175' length, 30' beam, 7' draft
Displacement:	unknown
Armor:	4" iron, with wood backing
Armament:	2 x 7" Brooke rifles, 2 x 42-pdr., 2 x 32-pdr. smoothbores
Engines:	single-screw
Speed:	3 knots
Built:	Selma, Alabama
Laid down:	summer, 1862
Commissioned:	summer, 1863
Crew:	140

Converted from the river steamer *Enoch Train* into an ironclad privateer, she was commandeered by the navy and added to the fleet guarding the mouth of the Mississippi River. She participated in the Battle of New Orleans on April 24,1862, where she was deliberately ran aground and destroyed.

CSS MANASSAS

Dimensions:	143' length, 33' beam, 17' draft
Displacement:	387 tons
Armor:	1" of iron, with wood backing
Armament:	1 x 64-pdr. smoothbore
Engines:	single screw
Speed:	4 knots
Built:	Algiers (New Orleans), Louisiana
Converted:	summer, 1861
Commissioned:	September 12, 1861
Crew:	104

CSS MISSOURI

Dimensions:	183' length, 54' beam, 9' 6"draft
Displacement:	unknown
Armor:	2" iron, with wood backing
Armament:	1 x 11", 1 x 9" smoothbores,
	1 x 32-pdr. smoothbore
Engines:	single stern paddlewheel
Speed:	4 knots
Built:	Shreveport, Louisiana
Laid down:	December, 1862
Commissioned:	September 12, 1863
Crew:	145

The CSS *Missouri* was considered worthless as a warship, and was used to ferry troops and supplies on the Red River. Unable to participate in the Red River campaign of early 1864, she remained on the upper reaches of the river until the end of the war. She never fired a shot in anger.

CSS NASHVILLE

Dimensions:	270' length, 62' beam, 13' draft
Displacement:	unknown
Armor:	6" iron, with wood backing
	(2" over paddlewheels)
Armament:	3 x 7" Brooke rifles
Engines:	twin side paddlewheels
Speed:	5 knots
Built:	Montgomery, Alabama
Laid down:	February, 1863
Commissioned:	March 18, 1864
Crew:	130

Although an impressive-looking warship, she suffered from poor armored protection over her paddlewheels, and a lack of power. The *Nashville* participated in the defense of Mobile in March, 1865, then escaped up the Tombigbee River, where she remained until the Mobile Squadron surrendered on May 8.

CSS RICHMOND, CSS CHICORA, CSS PALMETTO STATE, CSS NORTH CAROLINA, CSS RALEIGH, CSS SAVANNAH

Dimensions:	172' 6" length, 32' beam, 12' draft
Displacement:	unknown
Armor:	4" iron, with wood backing
Armament:	varied (see table)
Engines:	single screw
Speed:	6 Knots
Crew:	180

All these ironclads were built according to the design produced by John Porter, but they all differed in minor details, particularly in the placement of gunports and in armament. The *Richmond* was completed in Richmond, serving on the James River in defense of the Confederate capital, and participated in several small engagements before her destruction on April 3, 1865. *Chicora* and *Palmetto State* helped to defend Charleston, and both participated in an attack on the Union fleet in January, 1863. They were scuttled on February 18, 1865. The *Raleigh* and *North Carolina* helped protect Wilmington, but the latter vessel suffered from severe structural problems due to poor construction. The *Raleigh* was wrecked on Wilmington bar during an engagement with Union forces on May 7, while her sister ship sank at her moorings on September 27, 1864. The *Savannah* helped to defend her home port until its city capture. She was burned by her crew on December 21, 1864.

	BUILT	LAID DOWN	COMMISSIONED	ARMAMENT
CSS *Richmond*	Norfolk and Richmond,Virginia	1862	July, 1862	4 x 7" Brooke rifles
CSS *Chicora*	Charleston, South Carolina	April 25, 1862	November, 1862	2 x 9" smoothbores, 4 x 6.4" Brooke rifles
CSS *Palmetto State*	Charleston, South Carolina	January, 1862	September, 1862	10 x 7" Brooke rifles
CSS *North Carolina*	Wilmington, Georgia	1862	December, 1863	4 guns (prob. rifles, size unrecorded)
CSS *Raleigh*	Wilmington, North Carolina	early 1863	April 30, 1864	4 x 6.4" Brooke rifles
CSS *Savannah*	Savannah, North Carolina	April 1862	June 30, 1863	2 x 7" Brooke rifles, 1 x 10" smoothbores, 2 x 6.4" Brooke rifles

The largest ironclad in the Mobile Bay Squadron, she served as the flagship of Admiral Buchanan. Together with two wooden escorts, she engaged the Union fleet that entered Mobile Bay on April 5, 1864. She surrendered following a one-sided engagement against a superior number of enemy warships.

CSS *TENNESSEE II*

Dimensions:	209' length, 48' beam, 14' draft
Displacement:	1,275 tons
Armor:	6" iron, with wood backing
Armament:	2 x 7" Brooke rifles,
	4 x 6.4" Brooke rifles
Engines:	single-screw
Speed:	5 knots
Built:	Selma, Alabama
Laid down:	October, 1862
Commissioned:	February 16, 1864
Crew:	133

The CSS *Virginia* was converted from the remains of the wooden screw frigate USS *Merrimac*. Consequently, she was often referred to by this name. The first Confederate ironclad to see action, her battle against the USS *Monitor* on March 8, 1862, was considered a turning point in naval history. When Norfolk was abandoned, she had too deep a draft to steam up the James River, so she was burned to avoid capture on May 11, 1862.

CSS *VIRGINIA*

Dimensions:	263' length, 51 beam, 22' draft
Displacement:	3,200 tons
Armor:	4" iron, with wood backing
Armament:	2 x 7" Brooke rifles, 2 x 6.4"
	Brooke rifles, 6 x 9" smoothbores
Engines:	single screw
Speed:	5 knots
Built:	Norfolk, Virginia
Converted:	June, 1861
Commissioned:	March, 1862
Crew:	320

Part of the James River Squadron, she participated in the Battle of Trent's Reach in January, 1865, and was destroyed by her crew when Richmond was captured on April 3, 1865.

CSS *VIRGINIA II*

Dimensions:	201' length, 47' beam, 14' draft
Displacement:	unknown
Armor:	4" iron, with wood backing
Armament:	3 x 7" Brooke Rifles,
	1 x 10" Brooke smoothbore
Engines:	single-screw
Speed:	10 knots
Built:	Richmond, Virginia
Laid down:	spring, 1863
Commissioned:	May 18, 1864
Crew:	160

While under construction, the CSS *Stonewall* (codenamed the *Sphinx*) was seized by the French government, and sold to the Danish Navy. She was subsequently sold in secret to the Confederate government. She eluded Union cruisers and reached Havana on May 11, 1865; when her crew discovered the war was over she was surrendered to the Spanish authorities. She was the only ocean-going ironclad to serve in the Confederate Navy.

CSS *STONEWALL*

Dimensions:	186' 9" length, 32' 6" beam,
	14' 3" draft
Displacement:	1,390 tons
Armor:	4", with wood backing
Armament:	1 x 11" (100-pdr.),
	2 x 6.4" (70-pdr.) Armstrong rifles
Engines:	twin-screw
Speed:	10 knots
Built:	Bordeaux, France
Laid down:	1863
Commissioned:	January, 1864
Crew:	unknown

The Tredegar Iron Works, Richmond, on the banks of Virginia's James River. Iron plating produced at this yard was used to protect most of the Confederate ironclads built in the Confederate Atlantic states. (LOC)

RIGHT **Naval Constructor John L. Porter was charged with designing the prototype Confederate ironclad *Virginia*, and he continued to develop improvements to the basic ironclad design throughout the war. (LOC)**

FAR RIGHT **John Mercer Brooke was the Confederacy's leading ordnance expert, and his rifled guns were fitted in virtually every ironclad built in the South. He was also a leading member of the team who designed the *Virginia*. (HEC)**

THE PLATES

A: CSS *Arkansas*, CSS *Fredericksburg* (profiles)
CSS *Arkansas*

The CSS *Arkansas* was laid down in Memphis, Tennessee, but when Union forces threatened, the half-finished ironclad was towed to safety up the Yazoo River. She lay at Greenwood for a month until Lieutenant Brown arrived to take charge. Local workers were pressed into service, and work continued round the clock until she was commissioned. On July 14, 1862, she steamed down river, and the following morning she fought a skirmish with the ironclad USS *Carondolet* before reaching the Mississippi. She forced her way through the Union fleet before reaching the relative safety of Vicksburg. A week later she fought off a determined attack before continuing on to Baton Rouge to help the Confederate defenders there. On August 6, she was attacked by the USS *Essex* when her engines failed. Brown ran her aground and the *Arkansas* was then destroyed by her own crew.

CSS *Fredericksburg*

Built in Richmond, the *Fredericksburg* was completed in May, 1863. Together with the ironclads CSS *Richmond* and *Virginia II* she formed part of the James River Squadron, defending Richmond from riverine attack. During General Butler's attack across the James, the squadron protected the Confederate defenses, and helped contain the Union attack. While General Grant's army invested Petersburg, the *Fredericksburg* kept Butler's army isolated, and for the rest of the year the squadron harried the cross-river supply lines between Grant's and Butler's forces. The ironclad played a minor role in the Battle of Trent's Reach (January 24, 1865), and saw no further action until the fall of Petersburg forced the destruction of the squadron off Drewry's Bluff on April 2.

B: CSS *Albermarle*, CSS *Atlanta* (profiles)
CSS *Albermarle*

During 1863, the Confederates laid down two ironclads to contest the waters of the Carolina sounds. The CSS *Neuse* was built on the river after which she was named, but took no active part in the war. Her sister vessel, the CSS *Albermarle*, was built in a cornfield on the Roanoke River above Plymouth. On April 17, 1864, the *Albermarle* broke

ABOVE **A Confederate ordinary seaman, portrayed on shore duty at Manassas Junction in 1861. The engraving was first published in *Harper's Weekly*, 1861. (SMH)**

LEFT **Gilbert Elliot, the builder of the CSS *Albermarle*, who created a shipyard in a cornfield at Edwards Ferry on North Carolina's Roanoke River. In doing so he altered the strategic naval balance in the Carolina sounds. (Private Collection)**

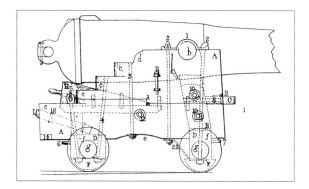

This Dahlgren carriage was a common gun mount used in the broadside armament of Confederate ironclads. The reinforced carriage was secured to the sides of the ironclad by breeching ropes. This example is shown carrying a 64-pounder smoothbore gun. (HEC)

The Marylander Franklin Buchanan (1800–1874) became an admiral in the Confederate Navy in February, 1862, and commanded the ironclads *Virginia* and *Tennessee* in action. (HC)

through Union river defenses and attacked two wooden sidewheel steamers that were chained together. The ironclad rammed and sank the USS *Southfield*, and chased the USS *Miami* into Albermarle Sound. A simultaneous attack by land forces recaptured Plymouth for the Confederacy. On May 5, the Albermarle attacked a Union gunboat flotilla in the Sound. The resulting skirmish was inconclusive, and although the USS *Sassacus* rammed her, the ironclad was hardly damaged. She withdrew to Plymouth, where she was trapped by a powerful Union blockade. On the night of October 27, she was attacked by a steam launch fitted with a spar torpedo. The ironclad was sunk at her moorings.

CSS *Atlanta*
In the spring of 1862, work began to convert the British blockade runner *Fingal* into an ironclad to defend the port of Savannah. In September, 1862, she was commissioned into service. Unlike other Confederate ironclads, she had an iron hull, a legacy from the *Fingal*. Operations against the Union blockaders were avoided as there were doubts about the *Atlanta*'s operational capabilities, but her presence deterred any direct Union attack on Savannah. At dawn on June 17, 1863, Captain Webb led the *Atlanta* out into Wassaw Sound to fight the blockaders. She met two powerful Union ironclads, the USS *Weehawkeen* and the *Nahant*, both armed with 15-inch guns. The *Atlanta* ran aground at the start of the engagement and, unable to defend herself against the enemy, she surrendered within 20 minutes.

C: CSS *Manassas*, CSS *Louisiana*
The Battle of New Orleans, 1862
In the spring of 1862, the only operational defenses of New Orleans and the Mississippi Delta were the two forts of Fort St. Philip and Fort Jackson, plus a motley collection of hastily armed riverboats. The only operational ironclad available was the CSS *Manassas*, a privately built privateer which had been commandeered by the Confederate Navy. Her unusual "cigar-shaped" hull was only lightly protected, and her armament was limited to a single 32-pounder gun and a ram. Two other ironclads, the *Mississippi* and the *Louisiana*, were still being completed in the city's shipyards.

On the night of April 23, Admiral Farragut led his fleet of 23 wooden Union warships up the Mississippi and broke

through the line of obstructions that crossed the river below the forts. The *Louisiana* had been towed into position near Fort St. Philip, where she acted as an immobile floating battery. Five fire-rafts were unleashed on the Union fleet, then both sides closed for a melee fought at short range. The *Manassas* rammed two Union warships before being forced aground, her crew escaping ashore.

The plate depicts the *Manassas* heading towards Farragut's flagship the USS *Hartford*, as the Union vessel is busy fending off a fire-raft. In the background, the *Louisiana* and Fort St. Philip direct a heavy fire against the Union screw sloop. Farragut recorded that it seemed "as if all the artillery of heaven were playing on the earth." A ramming attack by the USS *Mississippi* forced the *Manassas* to veer away, then she became embroiled in her own private battle against four enemy gunboats. The *Hartford* escaped to fight another day.

D: CSS *Virginia* (ex-USS *Merrimac*)
(cutaway view)
Secretary of the Navy Stephen Mallory decided to convert the burned-out hull of the wooden steam frigate *Merrimac* (or *Merrimack*) into the first Confederate ironclad. A committee headed by John L. Porter designed this prototype, which used the lower hull and machinery of the frigate, but from the waterline up, the design was completely revolutionary. A wooden casemate was covered with two layers of two-inch-thick iron plating. Her armament consisted of six 9-inch smoothbore Dahlgrens, two 6.4-inch Brooke rifles, with 7-inch Brooke rifles at the bow and stern. Although well armed and protected, her greatest drawbacks were her propulsion and steering systems. At best, she was capable of making five knots, and her turning circle was twice that of the original Merrimac. Her steering chains also ran across the exposed deck, and were therefore extremely vulnerable.

On March 8, 1862, she sortied out of Norfolk into Hampton Roads. Impervious to Union shot, she rammed and sank the USS *Cumberland*, then set the USS *Congress* on fire, and returned to Norfolk. The following day she tried to

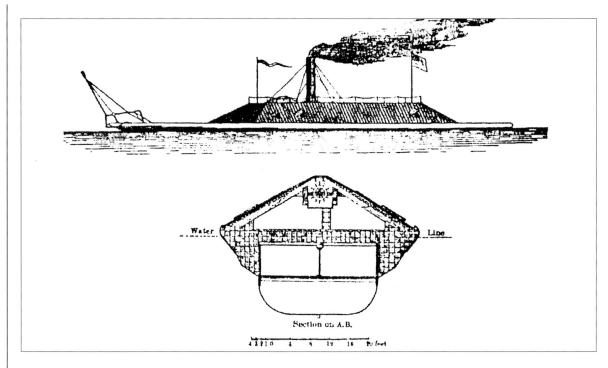

Plan and cross-section of the CSS *Atlanta*, drawn after her capture by two Union monitors at Wassaw Sound, south of Savannah on June 17, 1863. Note the spar torpedo carried on her bow. (USN)

complete her one-sided engagement, but instead she met the USS *Monitor*. The clash between the two ironclads was inconclusive, but proved to be a revolutionary moment in naval warfare. The Virginia failed to break the blockade, but every subsequent time she sortied, the Union ships fled. Any victory was fleeting, as on May 11, the Confederates abandoned Norfolk. Unable to steam up the James River to safety in Richmond, the ironclad was destroyed by her own crew. Although destroyed, her legacy lived on, and the lessons learned from her construction and performance were applied to subsequent generations of Confederate ironclads.

E: CSS *Nashville*, CSS *Palmetto State*
CSS *Nashville*

The *Nashville* was an unusual warship; together with the CSS *Baltic* and *Missouri*, she used a paddlewheel mechanism for propulsion. She was built in Montgomery, Alabama, and then taken for completion to Mobile, although the supply of materials delayed her commissioning. Armor plating was taken from the condemned *Baltic*, as armor plating was unavailable elsewhere. Although commissioned in March, 1864, she was only ready for active service in September. Her broadside armament consisted of 7-inch rifles, weapons that were usually reserved for bow and stern guns on Confederate ironclads. The light armor plating over her side paddlewheel boxes made her vulnerable, and her slow speed made her virtually useless in tidal waters. She participated in the defense of Mobile in March, 1865, then escaped up the Tombigbee River. She remained there until the end of the war.

CSS *Palmetto State*

The *Palmetto State* and her sister ship the *Chicora* were built with great speed during 1862, as the inhabitants of Charleston considered that a Union attack was imminent. By November, both ironclads were in service, and together they formed the backbone of the Charleston Squadron. Commodore Ingraham used them as part of a coordinated defense, which included Fort Sumter and other coastal defenses. Both were "Richmond class" ironclads, although they varied from the original vessel of the class. On January 31, 1863, the ironclads attacked the blockading squadron, the *Palmetto State* ramming the wooden USS *Mercedita*, forcing it to surrender, while the *Chicora* attacked the USS *Keystone State*. The ironclads continued to defend the harbor until the city fell to General Sherman. The two vessels were blown up on February 18, 1865, together with the ironclads CSS *Charleston* and the unfinished *Columbia*.

F: CSS *Tennessee*
The Battle of Mobile Bay, 1864

A Union attack on Mobile Bay had been expected throughout the war, but in August, 1864, the only Confederate ironclad capable of operating in the Bay was the CSS *Tennessee II*. She was the flagship of Admiral Buchanan, who last saw action in the CSS *Virginia*'s fight against the USS *Monitor* two years earlier, and she was assisted by two wooden paddlewheel gunboats. A string of fortifications, centered around the brick Fort Morgan and Fort Gaines, protected the entrances to the bay, while underwater obstructions and torpedoes (mines) were strung across the main ship channel.

At dawn on August 5, 1864, Admiral Farragut led his fleet past Fort Morgan, with the ships lashed together in pairs. The USS *Brooklyn* led the column, followed by the USS *Hartford*. Four monitors formed a separate column. One, the monitor USS *Tecumseh*, struck a mine and sank. After the two

A 6.4" Brooke rifle pictured outside the old Richmond National Battlefield Park Headquarters (Chimborazo site). This was the standard broadside weapon fitted in most Confederate ironclads. (author)

Confederate gunboats were driven off, the majority of the Union fleet attacked the ironclad, the *Tennessee*. She was rammed by the wooden warships, USS *Monongahela* and the *Lackawanna*, without damage, her fire crippling the Union ships. At one point, the *Hartford* and the *Tennessee* lay alongside each other, exchanging broadsides at point-blank range. The three surviving Union monitors entered the fray, their guns repeatedly slamming projectiles into the *Tennessee*'s armored casemate. Her steering gear was shot away, and her gunport shutters jammed. Helpless, the *Tennessee*'s crew surrendered to the inevitable. The plate depicts the *Tennessee* in the foreground, attacked by (from the left), the USS *Chicasaw*, *Monongahela*, *Kennebec*, and the *Hartford*. Another six Union warships were equally busy attacking the ironclad off her bow and starboard side.

G: CSS *Huntsville*, CSS *Stonewall*
CSS *Huntsville*
The CSS *Huntsville* and her sister ship the CSS *Tuscaloosa* were built in the summer of 1862 at Selma, Alabama, and were originally designed as floating batteries. Other sister ships were never completed. Although the city contained an ironworks and a gun foundry, construction was dogged by problems, and in the spring of 1863 the two vessels were still

not complete. They were taken downriver to Mobile for fitting out, and both were commissioned by mid-summer. Both were used in the defense of Mobile, as their slow speed and poor seaworthiness made them unsuitable for use in Mobile Bay. Following the Battle of Mobile Bay (August 5, 1864), the ironclads provided the only effective naval defense of the city until Mobile's fall in April, 1865. The vessels retreated up the Tombigbee River, only to be scuttled on April 12.

CSS *Stonewall*
The only Confederate ironclad commissioned outside the Confederacy, the *Stonewall* was built in Bordeaux, at the Armand shipyard. Before her completion, she was impounded by the French government, and then sold to Denmark. By luck, the Danes reneged, and Armand's agents secretly resold the vessel to the Confederacy. In January, 1865, she was transferred at sea to Confederate command, and later put into the Spanish port of El Ferrol for repairs. Trapped by two Union cruisers (the USS *Niagara* and *Sacramento*), she sailed out to fight her way past them, but they declined to fight. At Lisbon, the *Stonewall* escaped her blockaders due to the observation of neutrality laws. On May 11, she reached Havana, where her crew discovered that the war was over. She was duly surrendered to the Spanish.

A pivot carriage of this kind was frequently used to mount bow and stern guns on Confederate ironclads. The gun could be traversed through 90° to each side, and the rear portion of the carriage absorbed the recoil. Brooke rifles were commonly mounted on these carriages. (HEC)

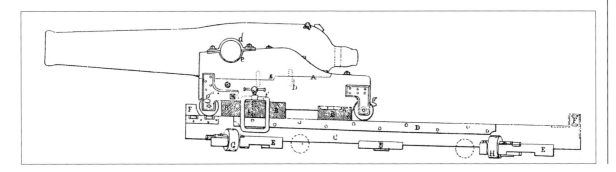

The Officers of the USS *Monitor*, photographed in July 1862 while the ironclad lay at anchor off Norfolk, Virginia. Rumours that a new Condederate ironclad was being built at Richmond helped fuel "monitor fever", and meant that the crew of the Union ironclad had to remain vigilant. (U.S. Army Military History Institute, Carlisle, PA)

UNION MONITOR 1861–65

The popularity of the Civil War as a period of historic interest is reflected in the thousands of books on the subject, but of these, very few cover any aspect of the naval war. Even more noticeably, the ships of the Union Navy have been dealt with in a cursory fashion, as the focus of naval historical research has concentrated on the engagements themselves. It is hoped that this book will go some way towards making information on these vessels more accessible.

Even more so than her adversary the *Merrimac* (renamed the CSS *Virginia*), the USS *Monitor* represented a revolution in warship design. Not only was the vessel fully armored, but she mounted her guns in a revolving turret, which in theory was capable of firing in any direction. Following the first fight between two ironclads at the Battle of Hampton Roads (March 9, 1862) the North was swept by "monitor fever," as everyone from President Lincoln down became convinced that victory in the naval war would be achieved through the creation of a fleet of "monitor" ironclads. The original USS *Monitor* therefore spawned a host of successors, and gave her name to a new type of warship.

The USS *Monitor* as depicted in a Northern newspaper in 1862. Her diminutive and unusual appearance led the Confederates to underestimate her potential as a warship. (HCA)

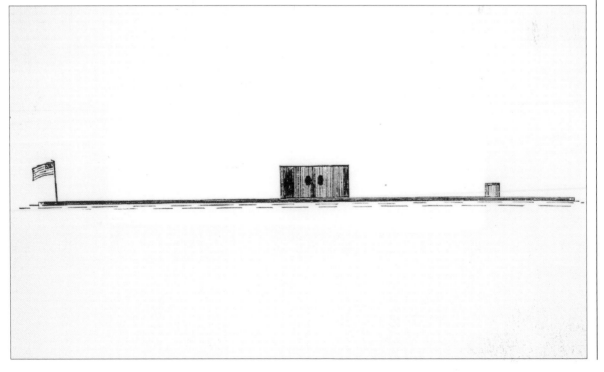

MONITOR DESIGN

Gideon Welles and the Navy Department

On March 4, 1861, Gideon Welles became President Lincoln's Secretary of the Navy. A month later the country was irrevocably plunged into war. When Lincoln approved the "Anaconda Plan," devised by General Winfield Scott, he committed his navy to a course for which it was ill-prepared. The strategy envisaged the encirclement of the Confederacy by both a naval blockade of Southern ports and a drive down the Mississippi River. Scott's Anaconda would constrict his victim, squeezing the life out the Confederacy by applying pressure to its borders. When the war was declared in April 1861 the US Navy had just over 90 warships at its disposal, but 48 were either in refit or were unfit for service, and another 28 vessels were deployed overseas. The remaining vessels were clearly insufficient to put into effect any blockade of the Confederate coast, so Welles instituted a huge expansion of the fleet. This included the acquisition and conversion of merchant ships until new purpose-built vessels could be constructed. He also considered the construction of armored warships. Both Welles and his Confederate counterpart were aware of the introduction of ironclad warships into the French and British fleets. During 1861 Welles became increasingly convinced that his naval plans would necessarily involve the adoption of a new breed of ironclad warships.

Welles had a limited knowledge of naval matters, but he was able to fill the Navy Department with highly competent subordinates. In August 1861 he made Gustavus V. Fox his Assistant Secretary, charging him with running the daily affairs of the department. His small department was gradually expanded to encompass the growing needs of the service. Originally it was divided into five Bureaus, overseeing construction, provisioning, medicine, dockyards and ordnance. A sixth Bureau of Steam Engineering was added later. For guidance on strategic matters, Welles formed a body referred to as the Blockade Strategic Board, while

This engraving was based on the photograph taken of the USS *Monitor* after her battle with the CSS *Virginia*, but depicts her without the subsequent modifications to her smokestacks, turret or pilothouse. (HCA)

another group advised him on scientific issues. An administrative section headed by a Chief Clerk covered more mundane matters and oversaw the navy's finances. Both the Senate and House of Representatives maintained standing Naval Affairs Committees, who occasionally met to investigate naval matters when required, and had the power to curb department spending.

Welles appointed businessman George D. Morgan to help the navy purchase and convert civilian ships, while another office in New York supervised dealings between the department and civilian contractors. This office, headed by Admiral Francis Gregory, inevitably became dubbed "The Monitor Board." The board operated independently of the department's own Bureau of Construction, headed by John Lenthall, a division of responsibilities that would cause problems in the future.

An even more influential advisory committee was formed in August 1861 after the Union authorities heard of Confederate plans to convert the former steam frigate *Merrimac* into an ironclad. This time Welles formed a three-man "Ironclad Board," whose members were to advise him on the development of ironclads, although none of them was expert in naval construction or ordnance. For all their lack of experience, it was this board which would recommend the construction of both the *Monitor* and the *New Ironsides*.

The naval yards were not equipped to build ironclad warships, so it was inevitable that almost all ironclads would be built under contract by private shipyards. Government policy also dictated that contracts were awarded to the lowest tender. A handful of private firms had the equipment and expertise necessary, and the majority of these were in New York or on the New Jersey shore. In many instances, contracts were awarded for the ship, while another more specialized firm was contracted to produce the engines. In other instances, the private contractor sub-contracted much of the work to improve profits.

The monitor USS *Chickasaw* and the former ironclad USS *Galena* depicted during the Battle of Mobile Bay (August 1864). This Milwaukee class warship commanded by Lieutenant-Commander George H. Perkins was one of four monitors to participate in the battle. (HCA)

The high cost of converting the necessary machinery and the rigorous government regulations surrounding contracts meant that only a handful of companies were willing to work on the construction of monitors, so a handful of yards specialized in the production of that type of vessel. One bizarre example of government regulations was the "Performance Bond," where the designer was liable for all costs until the vessel proved itself in naval service. This meant that when the USS *Monitor* fought the CSS *Virginia*, she was still legally owned by designer John Ericsson.

Somehow, despite such obstacles, the navy overcame the resistance of serving officers and the inertia of government bureaucracy to develop a fleet of ironclad warships. In the end Welles and his subordinates managed to find the right advisers, designers and private contractors to push forward the construction of an ironclad fleet. While the Confederate ironclad fleet was built as a result of a series of decrees by the government, the Union monitor fleet came about as a result of committees and entrepreneurial initiative. These naval and civilian advisers, these public servants and these designers, engineers and investors would combine to change the course of history.

The first ironclad contracts

Prior to the Civil War, the US Navy had made one unsuccessful attempt at producing its own ironclad. In 1842 the designer Robert L. Stevens was authorized to construct a large ironclad, although work was delayed until 1854. Stevens died two years later, and "Stevens' Battery" languished in his family's yard at Hoboken, New Jersey, until the outbreak of the war. Although the designer's brother offered to complete the work at his own expense in 1861, the navy viewed the vessel as a white elephant and rejected the offer. No more work was carried out on the battery until after the war.

When reports reached Washington that the Con-federates were converting the former screw frigate *Merrimac* into an ironclad, Congress was duly alarmed, as the Union had no vessel with which to counter the Confederate warship. In response Welles asked Connecticut financier Cornelius S. Bushnell to use his influence with Congress to allocate funds to produce a Union ironclad squadron. Bushnell pushed a bill through both houses, and Welles formed his

Captain John Ericsson, the Swedish-born inventor of the USS *Monitor*. Under his direction dozens of monitors were built for the Union Navy during the war. (HCA)

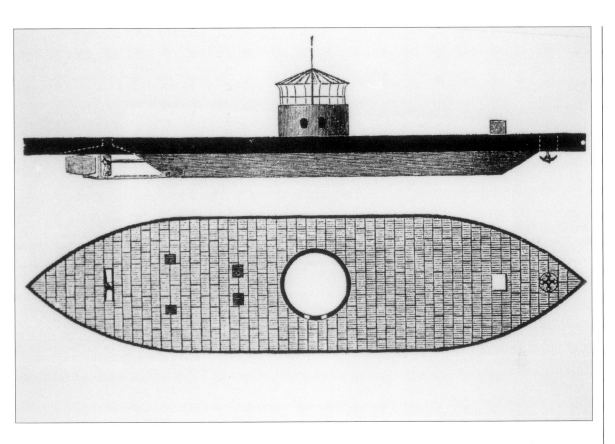

Ironclad Board on August 3, 1861, the day Congress allocated $1.5 million to be spent on new ironclad projects.

Welles's first step was to advertise for bids for ships "either of iron, or wood and iron combined, for sea or river service." He also specified the required draft, armor and coal capacity. Seventeen proposals were laid before the board, and on September 16, it presented its selection of three prototype vessels. The broadside ironclad (*New Ironsides*) proposed by Merrick and Sons of Philadelphia was almost a direct copy of the French *Gloire*, and the conventional design must have appealed to the board's more conservative members. A second successful bid was the ironclad gunboat (*Galena*), designed by Samuel Pook of Connecticut, who planned to have the vessel built at Mystic River, Connecticut. Both these vessels were named shortly before they were completed.

Bushnell influenced the award of the Connecticut contract, but in the process of lobbying he met Cornelius Delamater, the owner of a New York ironworks. The industrialist introduced Bushnell to his friend John Ericsson, and together they examined the plans for the ironclad gunboat. Ericsson showed the financier his own plans for an ironclad, and Bushnell was impressed with the design. He became a convert, and convinced both Welles and his business partners (John Winslow and John Griswold) that Ericsson's ironclad was the ideal vessel to counter the threat of the *Merrimac*. Despite the adamant opposition of board member Commander Charles Davis, Welles and Bushnell forced the board to accept the Ericsson plan. A determining factor was speed of construction, as the other vessels would take longer to build. Ericsson was awarded the third contract, and the *Monitor* legend began.

The *Monitor* and "monitor fever"

The hesitation of the Ironclad Board to approve Ericsson's design was understandable, as it was a completely revolutionary one. One board member even tried to force Ericsson to add masts and sails to the design, but the inventor refused. The design centered around a revolving gun turret containing two smoothbore guns. The guns were protected by eight layers of 1 inch iron plate, bent into gentle curves to create the 20 foot diameter turret. The hull was constructed in two parts, the upper portion sitting on top of the conventionally shaped lower hull like a raft. This upper portion was protected by two $\frac{1}{2}$ inch plates laid over the deck beams, and 5 inches of side armor in five 1 inch strips, backed by 25 inches of oak. When the guns were fitted the freeboard was less than 18 inches, meaning her hull was almost impossible to hit if fired at by another warship. The thin deck armor did mean the warship was vulnerable to plunging fire from fortifications.

The hull was flat-bottomed, with a 35 degree slope atop the bilge. The screw was protected by a recess in the upper deck section, which meant the vessel had a draft of just 10 ft 6 in. The screw was powered by two "vibrating-lever" engines designed by Ericsson himself, which propelled the vessel at a top speed of 6 knots. Smaller engines powered a ventilation system and the turret rotation mechanism, which took 24 seconds to turn the turret through a complete circle. The mechanism was controlled by a clutch inside the gun turret itself. Ericsson's 120 ton turret was designed to house two 15 inch Dahlgren smoothbores, but when the time came to mount the guns, only 11 inch pieces were available, so these were fitted instead. The turret was designed to turn on a thick central spindle, but first the turret itself had to be raised up off the deck from its "stowed position." When not in use it rested on a brass ring set in the deck. Iron shutters could be lowered over the gunports when the guns were not in use.

When she was completed, the *Monitor* was 179 feet long, with a beam of 41.5 feet, and looked like no warship which had ever been seen before. She was constructed at the Continental Iron Works at Greenpoint, Brooklyn, and newspapermen who watched her construction dubbed the vessel "Ericsson's Folly." The designer built the vessel with the financial support of Bushnell and his partners, who also benefited from the sub-contracting of parts of the project to their own yards, or those of their friends. As the date of the launch approached, Gustavus Fox wrote to Ericsson asking him what he planned to call the ironclad. He replied that his ironclad: "will thus prove a severe monitor to those [Confederate] leaders. Downing Street will hardly view with indifference this last Yankee notion, this monitor … On these and many similar grounds I propose to name the new battery *Monitor.*"

The arrival of the USS *Monitor* in Hampton Roads, during the evening of March 8, 1862, came too late to prevent the destruction of two Union warships at the hands of the CSS *Virginia*. In this engraving the monitor is dwarfed by the wooden steam warship USS *Minnesota*. (HCA)

The *Monitor* was launched on January 30, 1862, and commissioned into service less than a month later. Lieutenant John L. Worden was placed in command of her 48 man crew, and on March 4, he steamed south towards Hampton Roads and his historic engagement with the *Monitor*'s Confederate opponent. Arriving in Hampton Roads on March 8, Worden was too late to prevent the first sortie of the *Virginia* that day, which resulted in the loss of two Union warships and the grounding of two more. When the *Virginia* renewed her attack the following morning, the *Monitor* sailed to meet her. For almost four hours the two ironclads battered each other, but with little visible effect. Soon after noon the *Virginia* retired to Norfolk as her deep draft made her a liability in the falling tidal waters of the Roads. The *Monitor* had proved her effectiveness, and held the larger Confederate ironclad at bay.

Worden was wounded in the engagement, and as he was taken to Washington for treatment, Gustavus Fox came on board to congratulate the crew and dine with the officers. By the time Worden reached the capital, the action was being hailed as a victory, and both Welles and Lincoln basked in the reflected glory. Both men were also keenly aware that as Ericsson's *Monitor* had countered the threat posed by the *Virginia*, the possibility of further Confederate ironclads breaking the Union blockade was unlikely. The industrial North could easily out-produce the South. A whole fleet of monitors would effectively seal off the Confederacy from the rest of the world. Lincoln also realized that the Battle of Hampton Roads was the last genuine opportunity for the Confederates to encourage the political and naval intervention of Britain and France to break the blockade. The failure of the *Virginia* to defeat the *Monitor* sealed the long-term fate of the Confederacy.

After the Battle of Hampton Roads, as the two days of fighting became known, "monitor fever" swept the country. While the crewmen of the USS *Monitor* were lauded as heroes, Ericsson and his ironclad design were also placed on a pedestal. The only group who maintained some reservations about the monitor design were the officers of the ship and their Navy seniors. Although Ericsson later claimed his design was created exclusively to counter Confederate ironclads, this was after the debacle at Fort Sumter in 1863. In early 1862 he had written that: "this structure [the *Monitor*] will admonish the leaders of the Southern rebellion that the batteries on the banks of their rivers will no longer present barriers to the entrance of the Union forces." The views of the navy's leaders were swept aside in the general excitement, which even extended to include President Lincoln and Welles. Other ironclad designs were abandoned in favor of monitors, and Ericsson could do no wrong.

This longitudinal interior view of the USS *Monitor*'s rudder, engine and propeller shaft assembly shows the overhanging upper deck structure which protected the rudder and screw from damage. (HCA)

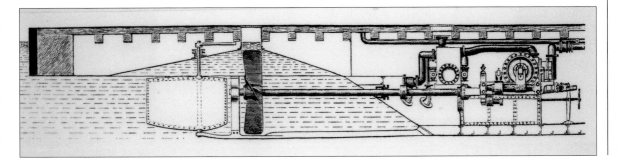

Casemate ironclads

The success of the *Monitor* effectively ensured that three other ironclad prototypes would not lead to further vessels of their type. The USS *New Ironsides*, the USS *Galena* and the USS *Keokuk* therefore represented a dead end in warship design. Of these, the *New Ironsides* was by far the most powerful. Displacing over 4,000 tons, she carried an armament of 16 guns, mounted in broadside batteries. Although fitted with a ram bow, she was too under-powered to use it in anger. The central casemate was protected by up to 4.5 inches of iron backed by 15 inches of wood, which made her impervious to most Confederate shot. During her attack on Fort Sumter in April 1863, sandbags were added to provide more protection to her deck. She served as Admiral Du Pont's flagship in this battle, and although an under-powered and awkward vessel, her formidable firepower and adequate protection ensured her position as one of the most valuable vessels in the fleet. She also had the distinction of being in action more times than any other Union warship in the blockading squadrons.

The USS *Galena* was built in Mystic, Connecticut, while her engines came from New York. She carried six guns, capable of firing from fixed broadside gunports on either side of her hull, but her 3.25 inch armor lacked extensive wooden backing, and her deck was unarmored. Her iron plating was fitted in the form of rows of interlocking iron planks, and although her tumblehome was designed to encourage shot to glance off, it also left her more vulnerable to plunging fire. It was unfortunate that her first action was against the Confederate fortifications at Drewry's Bluff on the James River (May 15, 1862), and the ironclad was badly damaged in the engagement. She was subsequently stripped of her armor and recommissioned as a wooden gunboat.

The former ironclad USS *Galena* was sketched after the Battle of Mobile Bay, following her conversion from an ironclad gunboat to a wooden one. She fell victim to monitor fever, and was relegated from the ranks of the ironclad fleet even though she could still have played a useful role. (HCA)

The USS *Keokuk* was an "armored gunboat" designed by Charles W. Whitney, a financial partner of John Ericsson, and her plans were first submitted to the Navy Department as early as April 1861. She had high, sloping sides and a cambered deck, topped by two small casemates which resembled gun turrets, but were immobile. Each was designed to house a single 11 inch Dahlgren on a 360 degree pivot mounting, capable of firing through one of three fixed gunports. An armored pilothouse was sited between the two casemates. Although Whitney's plans were dismissed, he re-submitted them in the wake of Hampton Roads, and was given a contract. The *Keokuk* was duly built at the Underhill Yard in New York, and she was commissioned in March 1863, in time to participate in the attack on Fort Sumter. She proved a costly disaster, as her thin armor proved incapable of preventing the penetration of Confederate shot. After being hit over 90 times (including 14 hits below the waterline), her crew were unable to prevent her from taking in water, and she sank the following morning.

The casemate ironclad USS *New Ironsides* photographed soon after she was commissioned in August 1862. The shutters of her gunports have been opened to provide extra ventilation. Her bark-type sailing rig was later removed. (Smithsonian)

The USS *Galena* in the summer of 1862, viewed from forward of the funnel on the port side, looking astern. Her pronounced tumble-home and her steel hull cladding are clearly visible. (Naval Institute)

Passaic class

Within a week of Hampton Roads, Congress approved the allocation of funds for a new class of ten improved versions of the *Monitor*, following plans drawn up by Ericsson while the original *Monitor* was still under construction. These vessels were described as "monitors," the first use of the term as a type of vessel rather than an individual ship. These vessels became known as the Passaic class. Ericsson's design was almost rejected in favor of plans drawn up by John Lenthall, the Chief of the Bureau of Construction and Repair. Lenthall's ironclads relied on the superior British-designed Coles turret, and might well have become more effective warships, but extensive lobbying by Ericsson and his financial partners ensured he rather than Lenthall was awarded the contract, provoking a feud between the two men that would outlast the war.

The reports of the *Monitor*'s officers were examined by Ericsson and the Navy Department, and their suggestions were incorporated into the new design. All the monitors were 200 feet long, with a 46 foot beam, making them larger and more stable than the original *Monitor*, but they retained their prototype's shallow draft. Compared to the *Monitor* the hull was more streamlined, with a slight sheer towards the bow and stern, and a cambered upper deck to allow breaking waves to run off the hull more easily. The most significant post-Hampton modification was to mount the pilothouse on top of the turret, which allowed better communications between the conning position and the gun turret. The turret was designed to carry two 15 inch Dahlgren smoothbores, but a shortage of suitable ordnance forced the compromise of fitting one 15 inch piece alongside an 11 inch Dahlgren smoothbore. All these considered, the Passaic class monitors were a great improvement over their prototype.

The failings of the Passaic class reflected the inadequacies of the original *Monitor*. When they were conceived, these vessels were designed to fight enemy ironclads, not fortifications, so the deck armor remained thin. Similarly, Ericsson's engines were inadequate, and the Passaic class ships were barely able to steam at 6 knots. The vessels should have been equipped with improved engines, but Ericsson's vibrating-lever engines were fitted with only minor modifications. As the vessels were larger than the *Monitor*, it was inevitable that they would be under-powered.

The Passaic class monitor USS *Weehawken* in an engraving based on a photograph taken of the ironclad within days of the disastrous attack on Fort Sumter in April 1863. The monitor was hit 53 times during the battle. (HCA)

The USS *Montauk* commanded by John Worden (the former commander of the *Monitor*) attacked and destroyed the Confederate paddlewheel raider *Nashville* on the Ogeechee River in Georgia on February 28, 1863. Note how the monitor is shown towing her boats astern to reduce the risk of damage to them. (HCA)

Contracts for these vessels were placed in six different yards from Boston, Massachusetts, to Wilmington, Delaware, and the first of them, the USS *Passaic,* was commissioned in December 1862. By the time Admiral Du Pont launched his monitors against Fort Sumter in April 1863, eight more Passaic class monitors were available, and seven in all

This cross-section of a Passaic class monitor emphasizes the improvements of the design over the USS *Monitor*. The location of the pilothouse over the gun turret ensured better communication between the captain and the gunnery officer. The turret rotation mechanism was also far more efficient, allowing a faster rotation speed. (HCA)

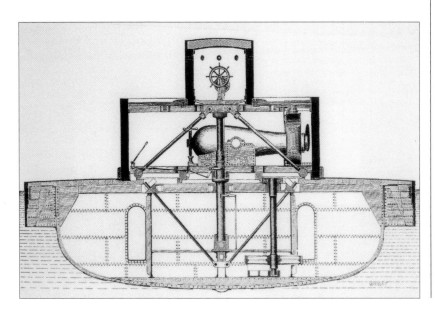

A Passaic class monitor, possibly the USS *Lehigh*, photographed on the Stono River south of Charleston in late 1864. Her turret and pilothouse are screened by canvas awnings, and a small howitzer can be seen on her forecastle. (Naval Institute)

took part in the attack. A tenth Passaic class, the USS *Camanche,* was built in San Francisco, and commissioned in May 1865.

The attack on Fort Sumter in April 1863 was a failure, and most of the participating monitors were damaged by non-penetrating hits. The action also highlighted the vulnerability of the joint between the turret and the hull, as several monitors had their turrets jammed by shot damaging the brass turret ring. That summer a protective ring was added around the base of the turret, and extra plate was added to the exterior of the pilothouse. As the engagement between the USS *Weehawken* and the ironclad CSS *Atlanta* showed, these monitors were highly effective in combat against other ironclads, the task they were designed to perform. They were less well suited to attacking powerful fortifications.

Canonicus class

As Ericsson's star stood high in the firmament in 1862, the designer was virtually assured of further contracts, and in July he was awarded a contract to build nine more ironclads. The result was the Canonicus class, a further development of Ericsson's original *Monitor* design. Five of these were commissioned before the war ended. Ericsson had been working on improvements to his *Passaic* design as early as the summer of 1862, primarily to increase their speed and performance. Improved versions of his own engines were installed, and sharper bows and longer hulls improved their passage through the water. The ordnance supply problems which plagued the navy in 1862 had been overcome, so the turrets carried two 15 inch Dahlgren smooth-bores, with improved carriages to allow the muzzles to protrude further through the gun ports. The ships were laid down in the fall of 1862, five in yards on the Atlantic coast, and four more in yards in Pittsburg and Cincinnatti. Although the monitors built in the

The bombardment of Fort Fisher, North Carolina (January 13–15, 1865), lasted over 60 hours. In this lithograph three Canonicus class monitors (USS *Mahopac*, USS *Canonicus* and USS *Saugus*) accompanied by the USS *Monadnock* are shown in the background, bombarding the Confederate fort at close range. (HCA)

Atlantic yards were all commissioned in 1864, none of the vessels produced in western yards was ever commissioned.

These monitors were all still on the stocks when the reports of the performance of the Passaic class monitors at Charleston were read by Welles and the Navy Department. Consequently recommendations were made to incorporate modifications to the Canonicus design. The turret was to be protected by a thick glacis ring, and the pilothouse was to be heavily armored.

Three monitors of this class were commissioned in April 1864, and two more were added to the list by the fall. A further two vessels (*Catawba* and *Oneota*) were built in Cincinnati, Ohio, but were never commissioned. Instead, they were sold to the Peruvian government, which renamed them *Atahualpa* and *Manco Capa*. Two more vessels were laid up at New Orleans, and were never commissioned until the 1870s. The five Canonicus class monitors which saw service during the war proved effective warships, although the USS *Tecumseh* was sunk by a torpedo (mine) as she entered Mobile Bay. The modifications incorporated during construction also ensured they were better suited to engagements with fortifications than previous Ericsson designs.

The USS *Canonicus* photographed long after the war, at a naval review held in Hampton Roads in 1907. Although decommissioned in 1877, she remained in mothballs until the review, and was sold the following year. Remarkably, apart from her smokestack, her appearance had remained unchanged since the end of the war. (USN)

USS *Roanoke*

Described as the unfortunate victim of "monitor fever," the steam frigate USS *Roanoke* was commissioned in 1857, and she was present at the Battle of Hampton Roads in March 1862. As a result of the engagement, she was sacrificed on the altar of naval experimentation, and less than three weeks later she was decommissioned, and sent to the aptly named Novelty Iron Works in New York city. The conversion of the steam frigate was the brainchild of John Lenthall (Chief of Naval Construction) and Benjamin F. Isherwood (Chief of Steam Engineering). Her upperworks were cut down to her main gundeck, and it was planned to install four Coles turrets on her upper deck. As these were unavailable, Lenthall reluctantly agreed to substitute three Ericsson turrets instead. Each turret carried one smoothbore and one rifled gun. The hull was protected by 4.5 inches of iron in one-piece slabs rather than in the usual series of 1 inch laminated plates. *Roanoke* was recommissioned in

The ironclad ram USS *Roanoke* was converted from a steam frigate by cutting down her upper hull and removing her masts. Her four smoothbores and two rifled guns were mounted in three turrets, which made the vessel top-heavy, and strained the existing wooden frames of the hull. She was never used in action. (USN)

late June 1863, but on her voyage back to Hampton Roads it was discovered she was too top-heavy to operate safely in open waters. The wooden deck was also strained by the weight of the turrets. The design was considered a costly failure, and she remained as a harbor defense ship in Hampton Roads for the remainder of the war.

A similar wrong turning was the *Dundenberg*, a casemate ironclad which loosely resembled the CSS *Virginia*. Designed by James Lenthall, she was a 7,000 ton ironclad ram whose technical requirements and attendant problems strained the Brooklyn Navy Yard. Lenthall's original design incorporating two turrets was altered following the failure of the *Roanoke*, and the casemate was the alternative solution. The use of unseasoned timber caused delays in construction and, although she was launched in July 1865, she was never completed. The following year she was sold to France.

Milwaukee class

Although the study of Mississippi River ironclads is beyond the scope of this book, 24 ironclads were built, converted or captured and used on the Mississippi River and its tributaries during the war. Of these, nine were monitors. Unlike the rest, the four monitors of the Milwaukee class were not just pure riverine vessels, but were capable of operating in the coastal waters of the Gulf of Mexico.

In May 1862 the Navy Department awarded a contract to James Eads, a shipbuilder and designer who owned the Union Iron Works at Carondolet, Missouri, a few miles south of St Louis on the banks of the Mississippi. Eads had already successfully built ironclads to designs supplied by Samuel Pook. His new design was for a twin-turreted monitor, combining the shallow draft of most riverboats with a cambered armored deck with a low freeboard. His vessels were driven by four horizontally laid engines, which powered four screws, giving the monitors a top speed of 9 knots. The turret configuration was also unusual, as he designed the vessels to carry an Ericsson after turret and

a turret of his own design further forward. These Eads turrets were a significant improvement over the Ericsson design as they not only used steam engines to rotate the turret, but steam power was also used to run the guns in and out, elevate them and operate the gunport stoppers. Unlike the Ericsson turret which turned on a central spindle, the Eads turret extended below the upper deck and rotated on bearings running in a circular track. These ironclads were commissioned in the spring and summer of 1864, and served in the Western Gulf Blockading Squadron. Both the USS *Chickasaw* and the USS *Winnebago* participated in the Battle of Mobile Bay in 1864, where they proved their effectiveness in action against the ironclad CSS *Tennessee*. It has been argued that of all the monitors produced during the war, the Eads vessels were the most successful.

Twin-turreted monitors

The Navy Department had considered the creation of twin-turreted monitors since the spring of 1862, and in the frenzy of "monitor fever," four were ordered in 1862, while a further vessel was ordered the following year. Of these, only two were commissioned before the end of the war.

Shipbuilder and designer George W. Quintard was given a contract to produce a twin-turreted monitor on May 26, 1862, less than three

The Milwaukee class monitor USS *Chickasaw* shown engaging the ironclad CSS *Tennessee* during the closing stages of the Battle of Mobile Bay (August 1864). Although they were designed for use on the Mississippi River and its tributaries, two Milwaukee class monitors participated in the battle.

The powerful twin-turret monitors USS *Miantonomoh* (left) and the USS *Terror* (formerly the *Agamenticus*) photographed at anchor off Portland, Maine, in 1870. Although laid down in 1862, both were commissioned after the end of the conflict. (Peabody Museum, Salem, Massachusetts)

weeks after the Battle of Hampton Roads. His vessel was to be constructed entirely from iron, giving the hull a far greater strength and longevity. The *Onondaga* was built at the Continental Ironworks in Brooklyn (the same yard that built the original *Monitor*), while the engines were built at the neighboring Morgan Iron Works, which was owned by Quintard. Her armament was varied, with a 150-pdr Parrot rifle and a 15 inch Dahlgren smoothbore in each turret (the rifled guns were mounted on the left of each pair). The USS *Onondaga* was 226 ft long and almost 50 ft wide, making her shorter but more beamy than previous monitors. She entered service in March 1864, and served on the James River throughout the war. During the Battle of Trent's Reach (January 24, 1865) her 15 inch shot penetrated and seriously damaged the ironclad CSS *Virginia (II)*, and prompted a Confederate retreat. Although she had her faults (namely her poor coal capacity and engines), she was regarded as a highly successful design.

By contrast the Monadnock class of two twin-turreted monitors (*Monadnock* and *Agamenticus*) were criticized for their poor hulls. The subsequent *Miantonomoh* and *Tonawanda* were both slight variations of the same design. All four vessels were designed by John Lenthall, and were seen from the outset as Navy Department vessels. Lenthall decided to use wood for their construction (as had Ericsson in his single-turreted monitors) because it permitted the vessels to be constructed in naval yards. Consequently, the *Monadnock* was built in the Boston Navy Yard, the *Agamenticus* in Portsmouth, the *Miantonomoh* in Brooklyn and the *Tonawanda* in the Philadelphia Yard. Lenthall replaced Ericsson's raft hull with a more streamlined design, and raised the freeboard, which increased the vessels' seakeeping qualities at the expense of protection. As the hulls carried 4.5 inches of iron backed by oak, this was not seen as a significant problem. The engines (designed by Benjamin Isherwood) were powerful, generating speeds of up to 9 knots. Lenthall's mistake was to rely on wooden frames to support the twin turrets. Like his *Roanoke* conversion, the weight of the turrets weakened the structural integrity of the vessels, and the hulls were prone to rotting and cracking. Only the USS *Monadnock* was in service before the end of the war. She participated in the attack on Fort Fisher in January 1865, and successfully sailed to San Francisco via Cape Horn soon after the end of the war.

Four additional twin-turreted ironclads (referred to as the Kalamazoo class) were commissioned in late 1863 and early 1864, based on a design submitted by Benjamin F. Delano. Like the Lenthall ironclads, these vessels were designed to be constructed in the same four naval yards, which lacked the facilities to construct metal-ribbed vessels. These were true white elephants, and their planned displacement of 5,660 tons was almost six times that of the original *Monitor*. Designed as ocean-going monitors, they were never completed, and rotted on the stocks.

The powerful twin-turret ironclad USS *Onondaga*, photographed on the James River during the summer of 1864. She participated in several actions on the river, including the Battle of Trent's Reach on January 24, 1865. (Naval Institute)

Ericsson's ocean-going monitors

The USS *Dictator* was another Ericsson design, a monitor which was almost twice the size of his original *Monitor*. This was Ericsson's vision of a "sea-going monitor." His original name for the vessel was *Protector*, but the Navy Department favored a more aggressive name. She differed from his previous designs in several vital aspects, apart from the sheer scale of the vessel. The overhang of the upper hull was less pronounced than in previous ironclads, and at the bow the upper and lower hull sections were blended together to form a unified bow structure. This meant she had cleaner hull lines than previous monitors, and therefore made it easier for her engines to drive her through the water. She also had twice the draft of a Passaic class monitor, which made her a better seagoing vessel, but reduced her operational value in coastal waters. The wide smokestack and a ventilation shaft were armored, while a light flying bridge (or "hurricane deck") was added behind the turret. Her two 15 inch Dahlgrens were protected by an impressive 15 inches of armor. The *Dictator* was commissioned in November 1864, but engine failure prevented her taking part in the bombardment of Fort Fisher, and she played no further part in the conflict. Nevertheless she remained in service for another two decades after the war, and she was generally regarded as a useful coastal defense vessel.

Her half-sister *Puritan* was laid down in 1863 in the Continental Yard in New York, and was virtually an enlarged version of the *Dictator*.

Ericsson planned to arm her with two of Dahlgren's new 20 inch smoothbores, but production problems prevented their delivery before the end of the war. Although the *Puritan* was launched in July 1864, she was never completed and she languished in New York for another decade before she was scrapped. Although impressive, these large sea-going ironclads went against the trend of concentrating on shallow draft coastal and riverine monitors. They were also extremely costly, and at $1.3 million, they were five times more expensive than the original *Monitor* and double the price of the USS *Canonicus*.

The light-draft monitor fiasco

The Navy Department decided that there was a need for shallow draft monitors which were capable of operating in extremely shallow rivers, such as the smaller tributaries of the Mississippi. Ericsson produced preliminary sketches for a design in two days during the summer of 1862, but went no further than to submit these to Gustavus Fox. Fox then passed the draft plans to Chief Engineer Alban B. Simers for study. Instead, Simers developed fully-fledged plans, then modified these following the attack on Fort Sumter in April 1863. Simers was attached to the Monitor Board in New York, and John Lenthall had little or no communication with it, while Ericsson and Simers fell out, and refused to co-operate on the project. The result was that the plans were approved without serious scrutiny, and Simers ordered the construction of 20 of his light draft monitors, and $14 million was appropriated for their construction. Dubbed the Casco class, the vessels were built in Atlantic yards and also in Pittsburg, Cincinnatti, and St Louis.

Of the 20 Casco class monitors ordered, only three entered service before the end of the war (*Casco*, *Chimo* and *Naubuc*). The design proved a disaster, as although the original design was reasonably sound, a stream of subsequent modifications made by Simers increased the weight of the vessels, but failed to compensate for the extra stress on the hull. The result was a series of vessels whose freeboard was less than 3 inches, and whose wooden frames were unable to support the weight of the reinforced turret structure. Simers was removed from control of the project, and Ericsson was called in to try to remedy the fiasco. The

When the war ended many of the monitors were mothballed. In this photo a turretless Casco class monitor lies in the foreground, while three Canonicus and Passaic class monitors are seen astern of her in the background. The turretless vessel has been tentatively identified as either the USS *Casco* or the USS *Chimo*. (USN)

The Casco class monitor USS *Chimo* (left) and the powerful USS *Tonawanda* (right) pictured at anchor off the Washington Navy Yard after the war. Although the *Chimo* was commissioned in January 1865, the *Tonawanda* was still being completed at the war's end. The captured Confederate raider *Stonewall* is visible in the background. (USN)

only practical solution was to raise the hulls of the monitors by almost two feet, which added to the weight of the vessels. Consequently, just before the first vessels were completed, the turrets were removed, and the first three monitors were converted into torpedo boats, armed with 11 inch Dahlgrens on an open mount, and a spar torpedo, placed on a retractable pole extending from the bows of the vessels. None saw active service, but they were used as guard boats. The remainder of the Casco class were laid up as they were completed, an embarrassing flotilla of white elephants. The entire fiasco was the result of a lack of control within the Navy Department, and Welles and his senior subordinates were duly castigated for the affair.

MONITOR CONSTRUCTION METHODS

At the start of the war, Naval Yards were not equipped to build ironclad warships. While facilities were gradually improved in these dockyards, this took time, and private iron foundries had to fill the gap. In fact, all but a handful of wartime monitors were built under contract with private yards, under the supervision of the Monitor Board in New York.

This cross-section of the USS *Monitor* is based on a series of more detailed plans and shows the forward facing of her two boilers and furnaces. A similar boiler configuration was adopted in Passaic and Canonicus class monitors. (HCA)

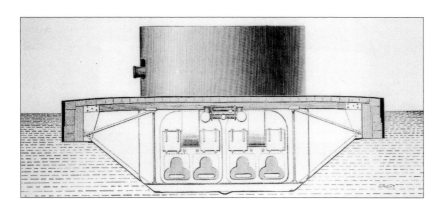

The original *Monitor* was designed to allow its construction using existing facilities in these foundries, and by conventional metal fabrication techniques. Ericsson also provided detailed plans of every aspect of construction, allowing the fabrication of different elements in other sites. This speeded production, and when the elements were

A planing machine like this was used to produce a smooth finished surface to the armored plates used to protect the turrets and hulls of Union monitors. This particular machine was installed at the Continental Ironworks in Greenpoint, New York. Engraving from *Scientific American*, October 25, 1862. (Author's collection)

brought to the Continental Ironworks in Brooklyn, the vessel could be assembled under the supervision of the designer. It was therefore built in a manner which differed from every previous ship construction project. This notion of sub-contracting was repeated in the construction of most subsequent monitors, as foundries specialized in certain aspects, such as engines, turrets or armor plating.

The Continental Ironworks had the ability to forge plate iron into large slabs, but for the construction of most monitors rolled plate was used. It was produced by passing molten iron between two sets of rollers, which formed it into flat sheets. Although the maximum thickness of rolled plate at the time was 2.5 inches, this involved a costly re-configuration of machinery. Consequently, most monitors used a series of 1 inch rolled plates which were laminated together. Flat metal plates could then be shaped by means of a hydraulic ram. Before assembly they were cut and drilled, and each plate was given a reference number, to ensure each piece was fitted exactly where the designer wanted it to go.

Taking the *Monitor* as an example, her keel was laid in a specially constructed assembly shed, and consisted of a series of 7.5 ft long metal plates. The major bottom plates (each 11 ft x 3 ft) were bolted in strakes on each side of the keel, and secured by heated rivets, which tightened the joint as they cooled. The exterior of the lower hull was then surrounded by a 4 ft wide metal plate, secured by angled brackets and set 5 ft below the top of the lower deck structure. In effect it formed an iron shelf, running around the ship. 1 ft square oak beams sat vertically around the shelf, and were bolted to the inner hull. These beams were then covered by horizontally laid pine beams. This wooden backing was finished off by adding five layers of 1 inch thick iron plating, which was bolted in place to complete the lower hull. This ledge of wood and iron formed the side armor of the vessel.

The upper hull was essentially a deck, supported by 10 inch square oak beams and diagonal bracers. This was covered by pine planking, then two layers of $\frac{1}{2}$ inch iron plating, extending over the top of the wood backing until it joined with the layers of hull armor. At the bow and stern, additional "truss frames" supported the deck beams and side armor, as the upper deck extended beyond the lower hull. These also formed protective covers for the propeller assembly and the anchor well.

The turret was constructed by bending a series of 1 inch iron plates, each measuring 9 ft x 3 ft. These were assembled in a workshop around a 20 ft diameter wooden framework, and each layer was drilled to provide holes for rivets. The gunports were also cut out of the appropriate plates. The process was repeated with eight successive layers of plating. The completed structure was then riveted together. The turret construction was then taken to the ship assembly shed and lowered over the hole left in the upper deck. It was secured to a beam that formed the turret base-plate, then reinforced with additional plating. The guns were then lowered into their mountings by crane, and the turret rotation mechanism attached to the baseplate assembly. A ledge around the interior of the turret top was used to support the iron beams that formed the turret roof.

Once the monitor was launched, finishing work took place on interior wooden partitions surrounding the living spaces, and stores, equipment and other small items were added. Once this was finished the vessel was commissioned into service, and a naval crew took over control of the vessel though, in theory, the vessel remained the responsibility of the designer until the captain reported he was happy with the performance of the ship.

Bending 1 in. thick metal plates in a New York foundry, 1862. This particular hydraulic press produced curved plates for gun turrets by applying up to 1,400 tons of pressure to the metal plate. From *Harper's Monthly Magazine*, September 1862. (Author's collection)

BENDING THE PLATES.

MONITORS IN OPERATION

The role of the monitors

The original *Monitor* was designed to fight enemy ironclads but, contrary to his later statements, the designer John Ericsson also claimed the vessel could successfully engage shore batteries. The success of the USS *Monitor* in countering the threat of the CSS *Virginia* led to a gross overestimation of the potential of Ericsson's design. The monitor as a ship type was imbued with qualities that exceeded the limitations of the design. Consequently, when these vessels were sent into action against powerful fortifications such as Fort Sumter and the coastal defenses surrounding Charleston, South Carolina, the result was a near disaster. This debacle led to a re-evaluation of monitor design, but not of the role given to these warships.

As a warship with which to counter the threat of enemy ironclads, the monitor design proved highly successful. The ease with which the Passaic class monitor USS *Weehawken* defeated the casemate ironclad CSS *Atlanta* in June 1863 demonstrated the superiority of these improved versions of the original monitor over Confederate casemate ironclads. This superiority was further demonstrated during the Battle of Mobile Bay in August 1864, when the Milwaukee class monitor USS *Chickasaw* was able to pound the ironclad CSS *Tennessee* into submission. During the Battle of Trent's Reach fought on the James River in January 1865, the twin-turreted monitor USS *Onondaga* clearly outclassed the ironclad CSS *Virginia (II)*.

The weakness of the monitor designs lay in their poor buoyancy and lack of seaworthiness. Given the use of monitors to bolster the blockade of the Confederate coast, it was inevitable that these vessels were placed at risk of loss through rough seas or underwater obstructions. Consequently, of all the operational monitors which were lost during the war, only the USS *Keokuk* sank as a result of enemy fire. The USS *Monitor* and the USS *Weehawken* foundered in rough seas, while the USS *Tecumseh*, the USS *Patapsco* and the USS *Milwaukee* were sunk after hitting enemy torpedoes (mines). No monitor was ever lost or even seriously damaged while in action with an enemy ironclad, while two Confederate ironclads

The USS *Weehawken* depicted in a storm, 1863. The Passaic class monitor played a leading role in the blockade of Charleston but, on the afternoon of December 6, she lay at anchor when a gale sprang up from the north-east. Water flooded in through a forward hatch, and she went down by the bow within five minutes. (Author's collection)

USS Keokuk

USS Weehawken

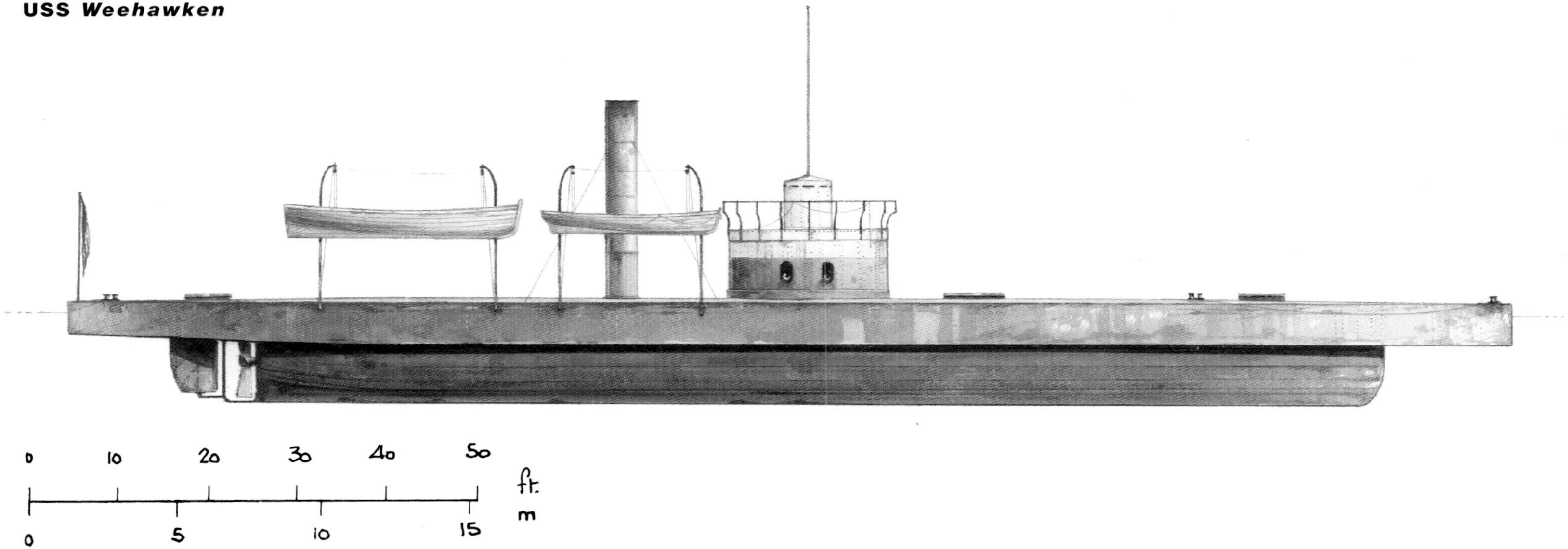

ft.

m

50 40 30 20 10 0

15 10 5 0

A

B

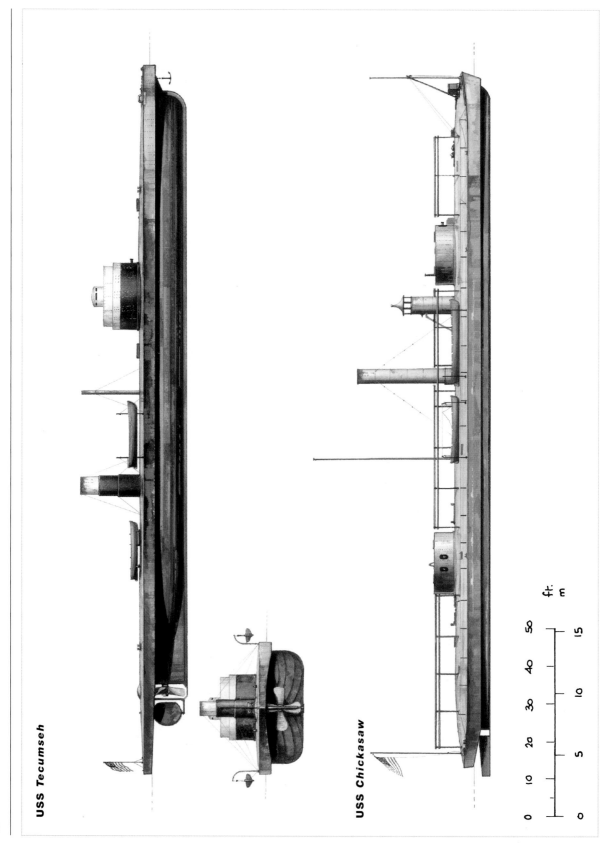

USS *Tecumseh*

USS *Chickasaw*

ft.
m

0   10   2o   3o   4o   5o
0   5   1o   15

The bombardment of Fort Sumter, 1863

C

USS *MONITOR*

D

1. Anchor
2. Anchor Well
3. Boatswain's Locker (both sides)
4. Hand-powered Windlass
5. Chain Locker
6. Tiller Actuating Ropes
7. Timber Deck Beams
8. Deck Beam Supports and Bracings
9. Main Bulkhead
10. Brass Turret Ring
11. Hull Armor
12. Ship's Wheel
13. Observation Slit (0.5 in.)
14. Pilothouse
15. Deck Plating
16. Captain's Cabin (Stateroom on Starboard Side)
17. Officers' State Rooms

18. Store Rooms
19. Crews' Quarters (Berth Deck)
20. Glass Deck Lights (covered in action)
21. Turret Traverse Mechanism
22. Turret Support Beams
23. Gun Carriage Rails
24. Turret Frame Stanchions (2.5 in.)
25. Gunport Stopper (shown open)
26. Turret Hatch (1 of 2)
27. Boiler (1 of 2)
28. Blower Engine (on both sides)
29. Coal Bunker Bulkhead
30. Smokestack (1 of 2)
31. Engine
32. Ventilator
33. Propeller Housing
34. Rudder
35. Propeller Well and Access Hatch
36. Condenser (Starboard side only)
37. Steam Discharge Pipes and Stop Valves
38. Engine Bulkheads
39. Main Turret Beam
40. 11 in. Dahlgren smoothbore

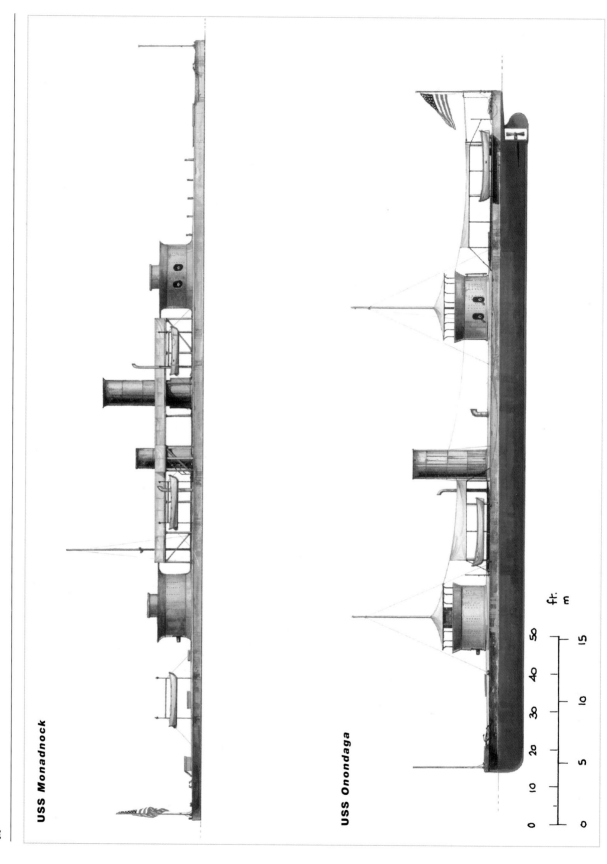

USS Monadnock

USS Onondaga

ft.
m

0   10   20   30   40   50   ft.
0   5   10   15   m

The bombardment of Fort Fisher, 1865

F

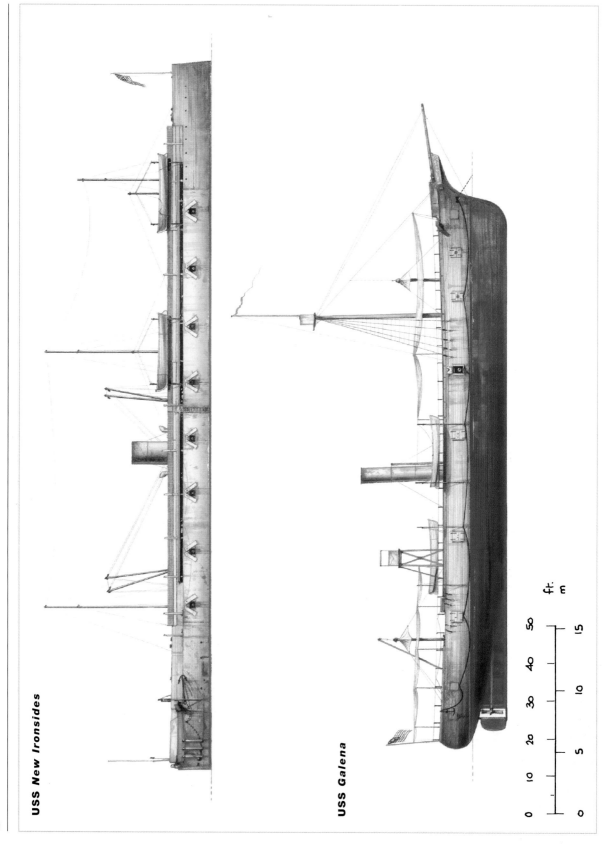

USS *New Ironsides*

USS *Galena*

| 0 | 10 | 20 | 30 | 40 | 50 | ft. |
| 0 | | 5 | | 10 | 15 | m |

were captured following engagements with monitors. This is perhaps the greatest justification for the faith placed by the US Navy in John Ericsson's revolutionary design.

Crewing the monitors

The original *Monitor* had a crew of 58 men. As monitor designs became larger and more complex, the vessels consequently needed increasingly large crews. Passaic and Canonicus class monitors required a crew of 65–88 to operate, while double-turreted monitors such as the USS *Onondaga* required a crew of 130–150, as did the armored gunboat USS *Galena*. The most manpower intensive of the Union ironclads was the USS *New Ironsides*, which had a complement of 460 men. In theory, the USS *Roanoke* had a full complement of 350, but she never received more than a fraction of her full complement because of her limited usefulness.

These crews were divided into two watches in the same manner as the rest of the fleet, and these were further subdivided into divisions, where each was responsible for a particular area of the ship's operation (e.g. turret division or engineering division). Taking the USS *Monitor* as an example, her 58 hands included 13 officers and 45 sailors of various rates. Five of the officers and 17 sailors were engineers, responsible for the operation of the engines and all machinery, including the turret rotation system. A further 5 officers (including the captain) and 21 sailors were "of the line," responsible for gunnery, and all tasks relating to seamanship. The Surgeon and Paymaster were officers without operational duties, while the Ship's Clerk was a petty officer. In addition the crew included seven "waisters," an archaic term applied to the storemen, clerks, cooks and stewards who were not required to keep watches. The quota of officers included 5 ensigns, 3 of whom were engineers. While the crew of the USS *Monitor* were all volunteers, subsequent monitors had their crews drafted to them in the same manner as all other vessels in the fleet.

The crew of the USS *Monitor*, in an engraving based on a photo taken two months after the Battle of Hampton Roads. Although improvements were made to the crew quarters on subsequent monitors, conditions in these ironclads were probably the worst in the entire fleet. (HCA)

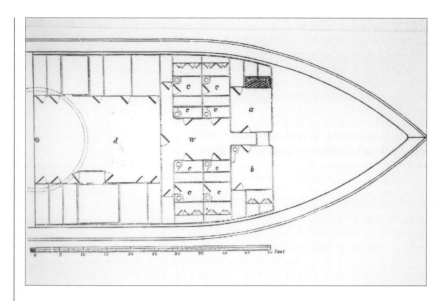

The Line officers were considered superior to the engineers, an elitism which was less pronounced in monitors than in the rest of the fleet because of the inherently technical nature of the vessels themselves. Most officers who served in monitors volunteered to do so, and were therefore more willing to accept the technical aspects of many of their duties which differed from those in conventional warships.

Among the most useful members of the crew were the petty officers, whose ranks included the boatswain, the gunner's mates and the quartermaster, all of whom were set apart in terms of responsibility. In addition these senior rates included skilled machinists and engineers, responsible for the maintenance, operation and repair of the monitor's machinery. For the "black gang" in the engine room, conditions were appalling, with temperatures only partially helped by often inefficient ventilation systems. There was also the near-constant risk of a build-up of poisonous fumes, and during the *Monitor*'s journey to Hampton Roads, fumes forced the abandonment of the engine room for several hours. If conditions were bad for most of the personnel in the engine room, they were worse for the firemen and coal heavers, whose duty was to keep the boiler furnaces trimmed and supplied, two of the dirtiest and most exhausting jobs on board.

When off duty, officers were able to relax in their own private staterooms, while the captain had two such cabins. While the petty officers enjoyed their own communal mess, the rest of the monitor's crew ate, slept and relaxed on the berth deck, which was poorly ventilated and often damp. A common complaint was the heat on board a monitor, particularly during the summer. In winter, the reverse was the case, and only the engine room was comfortably warm. Boredom was also common, particularly when monitors were on blockade. The iron hulls of most monitors "sweated," creating a humid atmosphere below decks. One monitor sailor reported it was like "living in a well." Sailors serving in monitors had to endure these conditions for months on end, but occasionally a monitor would be allowed to put into ports such as New Orleans, Key West or Port Royal for supplies, maintenance, and a "run ashore." For more significant repairs, monitors returned north to

New York, Boston, or some other major port. Although conditions were primitive, service on board a monitor carried with it an element of glamor, as the vessels were almost guaranteed to be in the forefront of any major engagement.

Ordnance and gunnery

By the start of the Civil War, the US Navy was well equipped with ordnance, and throughout the war the service relied exclusively on smoothbore shell guns designed by John Dahlgren and rifled guns designed by Robert Parrott. Apart from a few exceptions, all monitors were fitted with Dahlgren smoothbores.

John A. Dahlgren was a serving naval officer who was assigned to ordnance duty in 1847. He developed a new system of naval ordnance, and produced plans for several new guns. These included his 11 inch and 15 inch smoothbores, but he also developed 12-pounder "boat howitzers" for use against boarders or to arm small launches. In 1861 Commander Dahlgren became commander of the Washington Navy Yard, and in July 1862 he was promoted to captain and named as Chief of the Navy Department's Ordnance Bureau before returning to active service with the fleet in 1863.

Dahlgren's first 9 inch smoothbore shell gun entered service in 1850, and it was easily identifiable through its "soda bottle" shape. The larger guns which Dahlgren installed in Union monitors were simply bigger versions of this weapon. The following year he produced an 11 inch smoothbore, which weighed 15,700 pounds (just over 8 tons) and fired a 135 pound shell. It was also capable of firing a 165 pound solid roundshot. The shot was propelled by a 15 pound charge of powder, but after the guns of the USS *Monitor* failed to penetrate the hull of the CSS *Virginia*, Dahlgren ordered the charge increased to 20–25 pounds, which improved the penetrative power of the shot.

Dahlgren also produced a 10 inch smoothbore for use on a pivot carriage, and the USS *Galena* carried four 9 inch Dahlgrens on similar pivot mounts, designed to fire out of either side of the hull. Conventional warships carried these guns mounted on wooden "Marsilly" carriages, a French design with two front wheels, and these were also used on board the USS *New Ironsides*. Monitors required special treatment, and consequently special sliding carriages were developed by John Ericsson, working in consultation with Dahlgren.

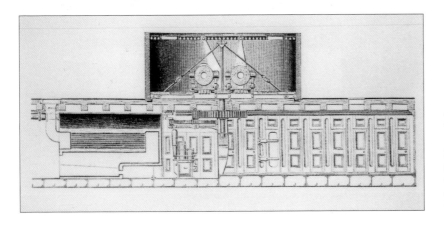

A cross-section of the turret of the USS *Monitor*, showing her 11 in. Dahlgren smoothbore guns run forward into their firing position. Her turret turning mechanism was improved in subsequent monitor designs. (HCA)

Dahlgren was also working on designs for 13 inch, 15 inch and 20 inch smoothbores when the war broke out, and of these, the 15 inch was ready for production, and was rushed into service during 1862. The first became available in September, but technical problems at their foundry prevented them appearing in sufficient quantities until the following year. Consequently, only one of each of these new guns was fitted into the turrets of Passaic class monitors rather than the two which had been planned. These 15 inch guns weighed 42,000 pounds (21 tons), and fired a 330 pound shell or a 440 pound solid shot. The sheer weight of the gun and projectile necessitated the adoption of mechanical loading systems, and again, Ericsson and Dahlgren worked together to produce a viable design, which was introduced into the Passaic class monitors and all subsequent ironclads. While the 11 inch smoothbore could be reloaded in three minutes, the 15 inch piece

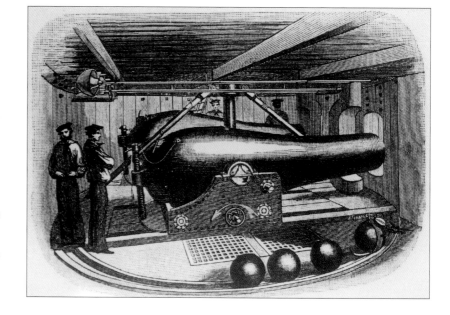

required 5–6 minutes. Also, the 11 inch was designed to be fired by a crew of 16 men, although it could be operated by a crew of eight. The 15 inch smoothbore normally needed a crew of 14 men, which would have led to overcrowding within the turret. By relying on mechanical aids, the gun could be operated by a crew of eight men. The largest Dahlgren to enter production was the 20 inch smoothbore, which weighed 100,000 pounds, and these were available to the navy by late 1864. Although Ericsson planned to fit two of these guns into his ocean-going monitor *Puritan*, the vessel never entered service.

In 1861, Robert P. Parrott had designed a series of small rifled guns for naval use, including a 100 pounder (6.4 inch) rifle. By the end of the year his 150 pounder (8 inch) Parrott rifle entered service. The US Army classified the same weapon as a 200 pounder Parrott rifle. It fired a 152 pound shell over five miles, which was approximately four times the range of an 11 inch Dahlgren. Despite these figures the principle of rifling a gun had never been fully accepted in the pre-war US Navy, as naval tacticians emphasized weight of firepower over range and accuracy. While the Confederate Navy relied on rifled guns to provide the principal armament in their ironclads, the Union Navy tended to avoid these weapons, and instead relied on the immense battering power of Dahlgren's smoothbores.

The only coastal monitor to carry rifled guns was the USS *Roanoke*, and she never saw active service. The USS *Galena* carried two 100 pounder Parrott rifled guns, while the USS *New Ironsides* was armed with two 150 pounder rifles and two 50 pounders in addition to her main battery of 11 inch Dahlgren smoothbores. Unlike Dahlgren's guns which were completely reliable, Parrott rifles were occasionally prone to bursting, and following an incident on the *New Ironsides* during the bombardment of Fort Fisher, the 150 pounder guns were withdrawn from service. Dahlgren also designed 50 pounder rifled guns.

Due to the restricted space inside a gun turret, mechanical aids were used to perform many gunnery functions. Pulleys were used to raise port stoppers, and hand-cranks were used to run the guns out and in. Guns were trained by rotating the turret, and at action stations an engineer was detailed to operate the crank inside the turret which engaged the turret rotation system. It was found it was often difficult to stop the turret turning when the enemy was on target, so the gun was sometimes fired while the turret was still in motion. After firing the turret was normally trained fore and aft to allow powder and shot to be passed up from the magazine, although a small ready-use supply was stored inside the turret itself. An overhead gantry

The interior plan of the turret of a Canonicus class monitor. The turret interior of a Passaic class monitor was similar, except the right-hand gun was an 11 in. piece. The two 15 in. Dahlgren smoothbores are shown run back for reloading. An overhead gantry was used to load the projectiles. Engraving from "US Navy Ordnance Instructions, 1866." (Author's collection)

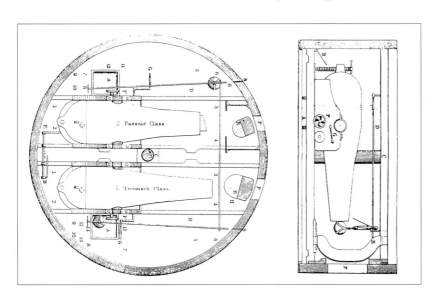

was used to transport the shot of a 15 inch gun across the turret to the muzzle, but 11 inch shot was loaded by hand, using a shot holder, which resembled a small stretcher, carried by two men. In action the smoke, noise and confusion must have been indescribable, and it was easy for the gunnery officer in charge of the turret to become disorientated. On monitors where the pilothouse was fitted over the turret (it remained stationary through its attachment to a central spindle), the control of the gun was far easier, as the helmsman was able to confirm when the guns were facing the target.

Monitors in action

Naval officers were unable to draw on any body of tactical experience when the war began. The only naval tactical manuals available which were relevant in an age of rapid technological change were of little use to the commanders of the Union monitors. All that commanders like Lieutenant John Worden of the USS *Monitor* had to base their tactics on were the claims of designers such as Ericsson and their own common sense.

During the Battle of Hampton Roads, Worden decided to take advantage of his warship's maneuverability, and the ability of his guns to fire regardless of the direction his ship was heading. The only blocked field of fire was directly forward to prevent damage to the pilothouse. Worden chose to circle his opponent, firing his guns at as close a range as possible. In action he found his guns could fire every eight minutes, a significantly slower rate of fire than expected. After the first few shots the gun crew discovered the stratagem of leaving the cumbersome port stoppers open, and turning the turret away from the enemy to reload. As bearing marks inside the turret were quickly obliterated, it became almost impossible to aim the turret with any degree of accuracy. Lieutenant Dana Greene elected to fire "on the fly," rotating the turret until the *Virginia* became visible through an open gunport, then firing one of the guns. This meant that Greene was able to hit the target with almost every shot, but it also made it virtually impossible to concentrate fire on one particular spot on the *Virginia*'s casemate. Although fire from the *Virginia* struck the turret, the shots were unable to penetrate the armor. To ensure communications between the turret and the pilothouse, Lieutenant Keeler and a clerk ran back and forth between the two locations with messages. After almost four hours of fighting, a rifled shell from the *Virginia* struck the *Monitor*'s pilothouse and exploded, wounding Worden and tearing away part of the protective armor. Creene soon took over command of the ship, but by that time the *Virginia* had withdrawn back to Norfolk.

The action was studied by other future monitor commanders, and when the Passaic class vessels entered service, their officers knew what they might expect. The engagement between the USS *Weehawken* (supported by the USS *Nahant*) and the casemate ironclad CSS *Atlanta* was a brief, one-sided battle. The *Atlanta* ran aground while

John L. Worden, the captain of the USS *Monitor*, was the first man to command such a vessel in action, and was wounded during the engagement with the CSS *Virginia*. His after-action report was crucial to the modification of subsequent monitor designs. He went on to command the USS *Montauk* off Charleston, and eventually became an admiral. (HCA)

maneuvering for position, and the *Weehawken* captained by Commander Rodgers closed to within 300 yards, taking up a raking position which prevented the Confederates from returning fire with more than one rifled gun. The seven hits scored by the rifle failed to penetrate the monitor, but the *Weehawken*'s 11 inch and 15 inch guns hit the enemy ironclad four times, twice with each gun. Both of the 15 inch shots caused penetrating damage to the *Atlanta*, and she surrendered within 15 minutes. The effectiveness of Dahlgren's smoothbore guns firing heavy solid shot was clearly demonstrated in the engagement, and consequently roundshot was considered the projectile of choice against enemy ironclads.

During the Battle of Mobile Bay in August 1864, the ironclad CSS *Tennessee* was effectively pinned by wooden warships, allowing the USS *Chickasaw* to take up a raking position 50 yards from the enemy's stern. Fire from her 11 inch guns tore away parts of the *Tennessee*'s armor plating, and sent chunks of backing timber scything through the casemate. The *Tennessee* duly surrendered. During the Battle of Trent's Reach on the James River, the USS *Onondaga* fired solid shot from her 15 inch guns at the CSS *Virginia (II)*, scoring two hits which penetrated the ironclad's armor. The engagement proved without doubt that, ship for ship, the monitor design was superior to the casemate ironclad, especially if the Union vessel carried 15 inch guns.

The performance of monitors against static fortifications was less impressive. During Admiral Du Pont's attack on Fort Sumter in April 1863, only the USS *New Ironsides* proved herself to be virtually invulnerable to enemy fire. The Confederates poured shot into the fleet, and an officer on the USS *Passaic* reported that 15 shots passed his ship in the opening seconds of the battle. She was struck 36 times during the engagement, while the USS *Weehawken* suffered 53 hits, two more than the USS *Nantucket*. All these shots dented the armor of the various turrets, but none of them penetrated, although several injuries were caused by concussion. If a crewman happened to be leaning against the turret side when it was hit, he could be seriously injured or even killed by the concussion. Despite this, Ericsson's armored plate functioned well under what was probably its most severe test of the war. Two turrets were jammed by enemy shot striking the join between the turret and the deck, effectively putting the ships out of action. Two other monitors suffered hits to their guns, which damaged them and put them out of action.

The lessons learned that day bore fruit when the monitor fleet was given the task of bombarding Fort Fisher. This time each vessel was assigned specific targets, such as individual embrasures. Although on the first day the USS *Canonicus* was hit 36 times, no serious damage was inflicted, largely due to the protective glacis that had been fitted around the turret. By contrast, almost every gun in the fort was dismounted and damaged during the bombardment. To cause maximum damage, monitors first fired one of their guns at a target, which inevitably drove the defenders behind cover. The gunners would then wait until the Confederates re-emerged before firing again. Although monitors were ill-designed for fighting powerful shore fortifications, and fire from Confederate positions regularly struck the ships, no monitor was ever seriously damaged in a bombardment, although the casemate ironclad *Keokuk* sank as a result of enemy fire. After modifications to the turret protection of the Passaic class, monitors were virtually invulnerable to enemy fire, and could inflict far more damage to enemy fortifications than they received.

The USS *Monitor* sank in a gale off Cape Hatteras in late December 1862. In this engraving the USS *Rhode Island* is shown coming to the aid of the sinking vessel. All but 16 of her crew were rescued before the *Monitor* foundered. (HCA)

CATALOG OF OCEAN-GOING UNION MONITORS

Although the Milwaukee class ships were not designed as ocean-going monitors, they have been included in this list because two of the class joined the ocean-going Gulf Blockading Squadron, and participated in the Battle of Mobile Bay in 1864. Also, although the USS *New Ironsides* and USS *Galena* were not monitors, they have been included as they were ocean-going ironclads, and fought alongside monitors in action. Similarly the spar torpedo boat USS *Spuyten Duyvil* has been included as it was of ironclad construction, and supported the monitor USS *Onondaga* during the Battle of Trent's Reach in 1865.

All other Union monitors and casemate ironclads were not ocean-going vessels, and will form part of a later Osprey study.

MONITOR	
Built:	New York, NY
Displacement:	987 tons
Dimensions:	179 ft × 41 ft 6 in. × 10 ft 6 in.
Speed:	9 knots
Armament:	2 × 11 in. smoothbores in a single turret
Armor:	9 in. pilothouse, 8 in. turret, 4.5 in. hull, 2 in. deck
Crew:	49
Service:	Commissioned February 1862; foundered December 31, 1862

GALENA	
Built:	Mystic, CT
Displacement:	950 tons
Dimensions:	210 ft × 36 ft × 12 ft 8 in.
Speed:	8 knots
Armament:	2 × 100 pdr rifles + 4 × 9 in. smoothbores, broadside mounted, capable of firing to either side
Armor:	3.5 in. hull, unarmored deck
Crew:	150
Service:	Commissioned April 1862

NEW IRONSIDES

Built: Philadelphia, PA
Displacement: 4,120 tons
Dimensions: 232 ft × 57 ft 6 in. × 15 ft 8 in.
Speed: 6 knots
Armament: 2 × 150 pdr rifles + 14 × 11 in. smoothbores, broadside mounted, capable of firing to one side only
Armor: 10 in. pilothouse, 3–4.5 in. hull, 1 in. deck
Crew: 460
Service: Commissioned August 1862

ROANOKE

Built: New York, NY (Converted from steam frigate)
Displacement: 6,300 tons
Dimensions: 278 ft × 52 ft 6 in × 24 ft 3 in.
Speed: 6 knots
Armament: 1 × 15 in. smoothbore + 1 × 150 pdr rifle (forward turret)
1 × 15 in. smoothbore + 1 × 11 in. smoothbore (middle turret)
1 × 11 in. smoothbore + 1 × 150 pdr rifle (after turret)
Armor: 9 in. pilothouse, 11 in. turrets, 4.5 in. casemate, 3 in. hull, 2.5 in. deck
Crew: 350
Service: Commissioned June 1863; re-designated a harbor-defense vessel Hampton Roads July 1863

KEOKUK

Built: New York, NY
Displacement: 677 tons
Dimensions: 159 ft 6 in. × 36 ft × 8 ft 6 in.
Speed: 9 knots
Armament: 2 × 11 in. smoothbores on pivot mounts in two casemates
Armor: 4 in. hull and deck, 4.5 in. turrets and pilothouse
Crew: 92
Service: Commissioned March 1863; foundered April 8, 1863

PASSAIC CLASS

10 in class
Built: Jersey City, NJ (2), New York, NY (3), Philadelphia, PA (2), Boston, MA (2), Wilmington, DE (1)
Displacement: 1,335 tons
Dimensions: 200 ft × 46 ft × 11 ft 6 in.
Speed: 7 knots
Armament: 1 × 15 in. smoothbore + 1 × 11 in. smoothbore in a single turret (except Camanche 2 × 15 in. smoothbores)
Armor: 8 in. pilothouse, 11 in. turret, 5 in. hull, 1 in. deck
Crew: 67–88
Service
Passaic: Commissioned November 1862
Montauk: Commissioned December 1862
Nahant: Commissioned December 1862
Patapsco: Commissioned January 1863; sunk by torpedo January 16, 1865
Weehawken: Commissioned January 1863; foundered December 6, 1863
Sangamon: Commissioned February 1863
Catskill: Commissioned February 1863
Nantucket: Commissioned February 1863
Lehigh: Commissioned April 1863
Camanche: Commissioned May 1865

CANONICUS CLASS

5 in class during war, plus 4 built after war ended
Built: Jersey City, NJ (3), Boston, MA (1), Wilmington, DE (1)
Displacement: 2,100 tons
Dimensions: 223 ft × 43 ft 4 in. × 13 ft 6 in. (*Saugus* and *Canonicus* were 235 ft × 43 ft 8 in. × 13 ft 6in)
Speed: 8 knots
Armament: 2 × 15 in. smoothbores in a single turret
Armor: 11 in. turret and pilothouse, 5 in. hull, 1.5 in. deck
Crew: 85
Service
Canonicus: Commissioned April 1864
Saugus: Commissioned April 1864
Tecumseh: Commissioned April 1864; sunk by torpedo August 5, 1864
Manhattan: Commissioned June 1864
Mahopac: Commissioned September 1864
Catawba, *Manaynuck*, *Oneota*, and *Tippecanoe* were completed after the war ended

DICTATOR

Built: New York, NY
Displacement: 4,438 tons
Dimensions: 312 ft × 50 ft × 20 ft 6 in.
Speed: 9 knots
Armament: 2 × 15 in. smoothbores in a single turret
Armor: 15 in. turret, 12 in. pilothouse, 6 in. hull,
                1.5 in. deck
Crew: 174
Service: Commissioned November 1864

ONONDAGA

Built: New York, NY
Displacement: 2,592 tons
Dimensions: 226 ft × 49 ft 3 in. × 12 ft 10 in.
Speed: 7 knots
Armament: 2 × 8 in. rifles in forward turret + 2 × 15
                in. smoothbores in after turret
Armor: 11.75 in. turrets and pilothouse, 5.5 in.
                hull, 1 in. deck
Crew: 130
Service: Commissioned March 1864

MONADNOCK CLASS

2 in class
Built: *Monadnock* Boston, MA; *Agamenticus*
                Portsmouth, ME
Displacement: 3,295 tons
Dimensions: 250 ft × 53 ft 8 in. × 12 ft 3 in.
Speed: 9 knots
Armament: 4 × 15 in. smoothbores in two turrets
                (two guns per turret)
Armor: 11 in. turrets, 8 in. pilothouse, 4.5 in.
                hull, 1.5 in. deck
Crew: 130
Service
Monadnock: Commissioned October 1864
Agamenticus: Commissioned May 1865

SPUYTEN DUYVIL

Built: Mystic, CT
Displacement: 207 tons
Dimensions: 84 ft 2 in. × 20 ft 8 in. × 7 ft 6 in.
Speed: 5 knots
Armament: One spar torpedo
Armor: 5 in. pilothouse, 5 in. hull, 3 in. deck
Crew: 23
Service: Commissioned October 1864

MILWAUKEE CLASS

4 built during war
Built: Carondelet, MO
Displacement: 1,300 tons
Dimensions: 229 ft × 56 ft 8 in. × 6 ft
Speed: 9 knots
Armament: 4 × 11 in. smoothbores in two turrets
                (two guns per turret)
Armor: 8 in. turrets and pilothouse, 4 in. hull,
                1.5 in. deck
Crew: 138
Service
Winnebago: Commissioned April 1864
Chickasaw: Commissioned May 1864
Kickapoo: Commissioned July 1864
Milwaukee: Commissioned August 1864; sunk by
                torpedo March 18, 1865

CASCO CLASS

4 in class during war, 16 built after war ended
Built: *Casco*, *Chimo* Boston, MA; *Tunxis*
                Chester, PA; *Naubuc* Williamsburg, NY
Displacement: 1,175 tons
Dimensions: 225 ft × 45 ft × 9 ft
Speed: 9 knots
Armament: *Casco*, *Naubuc* 1 × 11 in. smoothbore
                on an open pivot mount, spar torpedo;
                Tunxis 1 × 11 in. smoothbore and one
                150 pdr rifle in a single turret; *Chimo* 1 ×
                150 pdr rifle
Armor: 10 in. pilothouse, 3 in. hull and deck;
                Tunxis 8 in. turret
Crew: 69
Service
Casco: Commissioned April 1864
Tunxis: Commissioned July 1864
Chimo: Commissioned January 1865
Naubuc: Commissioned March 1865
*Cohoes, Etlah, Klamath, Koka, Modoc, Napa, Nausett,
Shawnee, Shiloh, Squando, Suncook, Umpqua, Wassuc,
Waxhaw, Yazoo*, and *Yuma* were completed after the
war ended, and most were never commissioned.

Ships not commissioned
The following ships were ordered during the war, but were never commissioned before the war ended.

Puritan
Monitor type; 2 x 20 in. smoothbores in a single turret. Built in Greenpoint, NY, she was launched in July 1864, but construction was suspended following the end of the war.

Dundenberg
Casemate ironclad; 4 x 15 in. smoothbores, 8 x 11 in. smoothbores, broadside mounted. Built in Greenpoint, NY, she was laid down in October 1862, but was not launched until after the end of the war. She was never completed or commissioned, but was sold to the French Navy in 1867.

Miantonomoh
Monitor type; 4 x 15 in. smoothbores in two turrets (two guns per turret). Built in Brooklyn, NY, she was launched in August 1863, but commissioned after the end of the war.

Tonawanda
Monitor type; 4 x 15 in. smoothbores in two turrets (two guns per turret). Built in Philadelphia, PA, she was launched in May 1864, but commissioned after the end of the war. She was renamed *Amphrite* in 1869.

Kalamazoo class
4 in class (*Kalamazoo, Passaconaway, Quinsigamond* and *Shakamaxon*); monitor type; 4 x 15 in. smoothbores in two turrets (two guns per turret). Built in various ports from Portsmouth to Philadelphia, they were laid down but never launched and scrapped while still on the stocks.

COLOR PLATE COMMENTARY

PLATE A
USS *Keokuk*

C. W. Whitney of New York designed this unusual ironclad, which proved to be one of the least successful vessels commissioned into the Union fleet. Whitney was a former partner of John Ericsson, the designer of the *Monitor*, but he lacked the Swedish engineer's flair for invention. *Keokuk* used an experimental armor scheme with a "sandwich" of 1 in. iron plates enclosing a 2 in. inner layer of wood, secured in vertical strips onto a thin wooden framework. These were then covered with a skin of boiler plate which was less than 0.5 in. thick. Her ordnance was carried in two casemates which resembled turrets, but were in fact immobile. Each carried an 11 in. Dahlgren smoothbore, capable of firing out of three fixed gunports (two broadside ports and one facing the bow or stern). She soon proved to be hopelessly under-protected.

The Passaic class monitor USS *Montauk* beached for repairs in March 1863, after she was damaged by a mine during the expedition up Georgia's Ogeechee River in late February. The damage was repaired in time for the *Montauk* to participate in the attack on Fort Sumter a month later. (HCA)

In February 1863 she joined the Union squadron off Charleston and under the command of Commander A. D. Rhind she participated in the attack on Fort Sumter in April. She was hit 90 times and, riddled with shot, she limped away from the action. She continued to take on water and sank the following day.

USS *Weehawken*

Following the success of the original *Monitor*, ten similar vessels were ordered, although the design would incorporate several improvements on the original vessel. In effect, the *Monitor* was a prototype for these vessels, which became known as the Passaic class. The greatest improvement was the mounting of the pilothouse over the turret, ensuring constant communication between the captain, the helmsman and the gun crews. The vessels were designed to carry two 15 in. Dahlgren

smoothbores, but a shortage of ordnance forced the fitting of one 11 in. gun in place of a larger piece. USS *Camanche* was armed with two 15 in. guns, but the remainder retained their original armament throughout the war. Under the command of Commander John Rodgers the USS *Weehawken* participated in the attack on Fort Sumter in April 1863 when she was hit 53 times without suffering serious damage. Together with the USS *Nahant* she captured the ironclad CSS *Atlanta* in June 1863, and bombarded Fort Sumter and Fort Fisher in late 1863. She foundered during a storm off Morris Island, near Charleston, on December 6, 1863.

PLATE B
USS *Tecumseh*

The USS *Tecumseh* was one of the nine vessels of the Canonicus class, five of which were commissioned before the war ended. The class was effectively an enlarged version of the Passaic class. Designed by John Ericsson, these vessels incorporated improvements over their predecessors, including the introduction of finer lines (giving an improved performance), thicker armor, a more efficient turret traversing mechanism and a low glacis protecting the vulnerable junction between the turret and the deck. Like the Passaic

The exterior of the turret of the USS *Monitor* photographed two months after the Battle of Hampton Roads. The improved sloping armor around the pilothouse can be seen behind the turret. (Naval Institute)

class monitors, vessels of the Canonicus class had the pilothouse mounted on top of the turret. The smokestack was retractable, which reduced the risk of damage. In addition, these monitors were fitted with a ventilation system, making living conditions relatively bearable compared to other ironclads of the period. The *Tecumseh* was commissioned in April, 1864, and first saw service on the James River near Richmond before being sent south to join the Gulf Blockading Squadron gathered off Mobile Bay. On August 5, 1864, she led the vanguard of Admiral Farragut's fleet as it forced its way into the bay, but the monitor struck a torpedo (mine), and sank within minutes. Most of her crew were lost, including her commander, Captain Craven.

The Passaic class monitor USS *Lehigh* photographed on the James River in July 1863. She later participated in the blockade of Charleston, and the attacks on Fort Sumter. Note the small field howitzer on her forecastle, designed for use against enemy sharpshooters on the riverbank. (National Archives)

USS *Chickasaw*

The USS *Chickasaw* was a shallow-drafted river monitor of the Milwaukee class, a double turret design developed by James Eads for use on the Mississippi River. Built in Cincinnatti, the monitor carried four 11 inch Dahlgren smoothbores, mounted two to each turret. The after turret was a standard Ericsson model, but the forward turret was designed by Eads, and was completely steam-operated, a novel design which proved highly effective. Both the USS *Chickasaw* and her sister the USS *Winnebago* saw service during the Battle of Mobile Bay (1864), and served in the Western Gulf Blockading Squadron. Thus, although designed for use on inland rivers, they proved seaworthy enough for use in coastal waters.

PLATE C
The bombardment of Fort Sumter, 1863

On April 7, 1863, Admiral Du Pont launched the Union ironclad fleet against the defenses of Charleston Harbor. The key to the Confederate defense was Fort Sumter, blocking the central channel into the harbor. Du Pont had nine ironclads at his disposal; his flagship the USS *New Ironsides*, seven monitors of the Passaic class (*Weehawken*, *Passaic*, *Montauk*, *Patapsco*, *Catskill*, *Nantucket*, and *Nahant*), and the unique USS *Keokuk*. The admiral formed his fleet into a single line, placing his flagship in its center. The lead ship was the USS *Weehawken*, commanded by Captain John Rodgers. Rodgers advanced north up the main ship channel,

approaching within 500 yards of Fort Sumter around 2.30 pm before the garrison opened fire. As he drew abreast of the fort he spotted a line of barrels ahead of him, which he surmised were torpedoes (mines). He stopped his ship, which plunged the line behind him into disarray. Communications had almost completely broken down, and after three hours, as the monitors began suffering heavy damage, Du Pont was forced to steam to the head of the line so he could order a withdrawal. The order was given at 5.30 pm, and the Union ironclads limped out of range. Some 439 shots from Fort Sumter and nearby Fort Moultrie had struck the fleet, and the USS Keokuk was almost sinking. The flagship alone was hit 93 times, but the total casualties belied the ferocity of the fighting. Only one Union sailor was killed and 22 injured, but there was no doubt that the action was an unmitigated disaster for the Union monitors.

The plate depicts the scene shortly after the Weehawken halted, then backed away from the line of suspected torpedoes. Rodgers' monitor is shown in the foreground, while the damaged *Keokuk* lies between her and the fort. The remainder of the Union fleet is shown in line astern, exchanging shots with the garrison.

PLATE D
USS *Monitor*

The USS *Monitor* was the forerunner of the US Navy's seagoing ironclad fleet. Designed by Swedish-born engineer John Ericsson, she was unlike any other warship that came before, and to many she was more a floating gun turret than a real combatant. She proved her worth during her one-day engagement with the CSS *Virginia*. Although later monitors were larger, better protected and carried a heavier armament, the USS *Monitor* was assured of her place in history as the most celebrated participant in the first battle between two ironclad warships. She was built specifically to counter the development of Confederate ironclads, and when she engaged Confederate batteries at Drewry's Bluff (May 15, 1862) her lack of deck protection left her vulnerable to enemy fire. During the summer of 1862 the *Monitor* was modified to incorporate improvements suggested by her officers. These included the addition of a sloped glacis to protect the pilothouse and a raised and linked smokestack. She foundered in a storm off Cape Hatteras on December 31, 1862, while she was being towed south to join the Union squadron off Charleston. The wreck now forms a protected Federal Marine Sanctuary.

PLATE E
USS *Monadnock*
The creation of a twin-turreted ironclad was the next logical step in the development of the monitor. USS *Monadnock* and her sister-ship *Agamenticus* were laid down in 1862, based on a design by John Lenthall, the Chief of the Bureau of Construction and Repair. Only the *Monadnock* saw service in the war, as her sister was only commissioned in May 1865.

The *Monadnock* was wooden hulled, which meant she could be built at the navy's Portsmouth Navy Yard in New Hampshire rather than in a specialist private yard. She was commissioned in October 1864, allowing her to participate in the bombardment of Fort Fisher in December 1864 and

The USS *New Ironsides* shown after her masts and rigging were removed, and her smokestack was cut down. Although she was sluggish, under-powered and difficult to handle by engines alone, her commander viewed the masts as an encumbrance in battle. (Private collection)

January 1865. Although criticized because her wooden hull was rotten, she confounded her critics after the war by sailing to San Francisco around Cape Horn in 1865. She remained in service for another two decades.

USS *Onondaga*
The USS *Onondaga* was ordered in 1862 and built by her designer, George W. Quintard, at the Continental Ironworks at Greenpoint, New York. The engine was produced under a separate contract in another New York foundry. She was designed to carry one 15 in. Dahlgren smoothbore in each of her Ericsson-designed turrets, alongside an 8 in. rifle, making her unique in the fleet for having mixed rifled and smoothbore guns in her turrets, an attempt to counter the Confederate reliance on rifled guns in their ironclads. Just before she entered service her 8 in. guns were replaced by more powerful 150 pdr rifles. Commissioned in the spring of 1864, she served on the James River, and participated in the Battle of Trent's Reach (January 24, 1865), although she also fought in several less spectacular engagements against Confederate batteries. Following the end of the war she was decommissioned and was subsequently sold to France. Her successful transatlantic passage proved her basic seaworthiness, despite her low freeboard.

PLATE F
The bombardment of Fort Fisher, 1865
By the end of 1864, Wilmington remained the only significant port on the Atlantic seaboard which remained in Confederate hands. The port lay on the Cape Fear River, whose mouth was protected by Fort Fisher. Built on a sand spit, the

A contemporary watercolor sketch by R. G. Skeret of the ironclad gunboat USS *Galena*. The sketch was made shortly after her abortive attack on the Confederate batteries on Drewry's Bluff on the James River, and the damage inflicted to her has not been fully repaired. (USN)

imposing fortification used sand earthworks to form the strongest defensive position in the Confederacy, with 44 heavy guns, guarded by minefields and trenches. It was garrisoned by 1,500 men, commanded by Colonel William Lamb. A Union fleet of 60 vessels was assembled to attack the fortress in late 1864, the largest naval concentration undertaken during the war. An initial assault was made on Christmas Day 1864, the land attack supported by a devastating naval bombardment. The attack was repulsed, giving the garrison a brief respite, but two weeks later the fleet returned. On January 13, 1865, the Union warships began a non-stop bombardment of Fort Fisher which lasted for 60 hours. The 40,000 shells and mortar bombs fired into the position destroyed many of the gun positions and caused over 300 casualties. The non-stop bombardment also demoralized the garrison, and prevented any return fire, as the defenders were forced to take shelter in their earthworks. On the afternoon of January 15 a force of 8,000 Union troops assaulted the fort, coming under heavy canister and rifle fire during their advance across the open neck of the sand spit. Despite heavy casualties the attackers entered the fort, and after a bitter hand-to-hand struggle lasting into the night the defenders were forced to surrender. A week later Wilmington fell to the Union, and the Confederacy was finally cut off from the sea.

The plate depicts the situation on January 14, when the fort had been subjected to constant bombardment for over a day. While the more vulnerable wooden warships remained at extreme range, the division of a dozen ironclads maintained a position 500–600 yards from the earthworks, while a squadron of four monitors positioned themselves between the line of ironclads and the shore. The USS *New Ironsides* is shown in the foreground, with the USS *Canonicus* astern of her. Between these ironclads and the

shore the USS *Mahopac* is shown leading the inshore squadron.

PLATE G
USS *New Ironsides*

The USS *New Ironsides* was commissioned as a prototype, and her armored casemate design was effectively a copy of that of the French ocean-going ironclad, the *Gloire*. Ordered at the same time as Ericsson's *Monitor*, the vessel presented a viable alternative to the monitor concept. She may have become the pattern for further Union ironclads, but after the Battle of Hampton Roads (1862) when "monitor fever" swept the North, only improved versions of the monitor design were ordered. The vessel had a protected casemate (or battery box) of 4.5 in. of forged metal plating backed by 15 in. of wood, making her one of the best protected warships in the fleet. She was also one of the best armed, carrying 16 heavy guns, including two rifles. Although her engines were under-powered, her sailing rig was removed soon after she was commissioned, as her commanders recognized that the masts were little more than a liability in action. This awkward vessel served as a flagship for the Atlantic Blockading Squadron, and spent most of her wartime career off Charleston, then participated in the bombardment of Fort Fisher.

USS *Galena*

A second alternative to the monitor design was the gunboat USS *Galena*, which carried a 3 in. protective layer of steel planking secured to her hull, with a pronounced tumblehome to encourage the deflection of enemy shot. Built at the Maxson Fish Yard in Mystic, Connecticut, according to a design devised by S. H. Pook, she was commissioned in April 1862, and saw action less than a month later at Drewry's Bluff, below Richmond, Virginia. Her armor proved woefully inadequate against plunging fire from the bluff, and she was withdrawn from active service. Her armor was removed, and the *Galena* returned to service in February 1864 as an unprotected wooden gunboat. She participated in the Battle of Mobile Bay in August 1864, and ended the war as part of the Western Gulf Blockading Squadron.

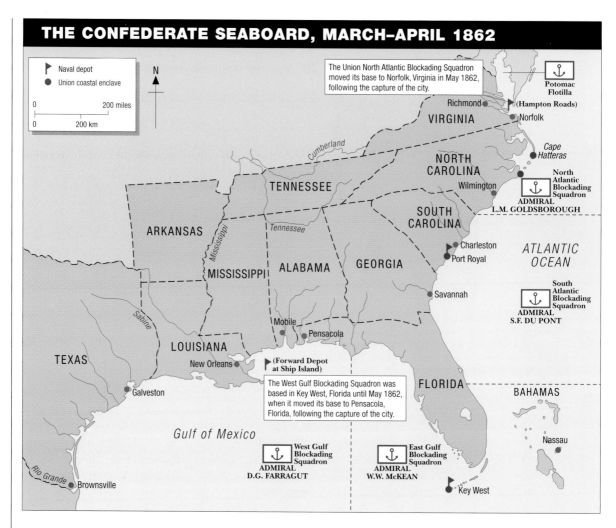

Naval depot

Union coastal enclave

0   200 miles

0   200 km

N

The Union North Atlantic Blockading Squadron moved its base to Norfolk, Virginia in May 1862, following the capture of the city.

Potomac Flotilla

Richmond

(Hampton Roads)

VIRGINIA

Norfolk

Cumberland

Cape Hatteras

NORTH CAROLINA

North Atlantic Blockading Squadron
ADMIRAL L.M. GOLDSBOROUGH

Wilmington

TENNESSEE

SOUTH CAROLINA

Tennessee

ARKANSAS

Mississippi

Charleston

Port Royal

ATLANTIC OCEAN

MISSISSIPPI

ALABAMA

GEORGIA

South Atlantic Blockading Squadron
ADMIRAL S.F. DU PONT

Savannah

Sabine

Mobile

Pensacola

LOUISIANA

New Orleans

(Forward Depot at Ship Island)

FLORIDA

BAHAMAS

TEXAS

The West Gulf Blockading Squadron was based in Key West, Florida until May 1862, when it moved its base to Pensacola, Florida, following the capture of the city.

Galveston

Gulf of Mexico

Nassau

Rio Grande

Brownsville

West Gulf Blockading Squadron
ADMIRAL D.G. FARRAGUT

East Gulf Blockading Squadron
ADMIRAL W.W. McKEAN

Key West

HAMPTON ROADS 1862

On 9 March 1862, the world's first battle between two ironclad warships took place in the confined waters of Hampton Roads, Virginia. Thousands of soldiers and civilians lined the shores to watch the Confederate casemate ironclad CSS *Virginia* and the Union turreted ironclad USS *Monitor*, which resembled no warships any of the onlookers had seen before. The previous day, the crew of the *Virginia* had demonstrated the vulnerability of wooden warships when faced by an armored opponent. She sank two Union warships, and left others stranded, vulnerable to attack the following day. During the night the tiny *Monitor* reinforced the battered Union fleet, so that when the *Virginia* sortied the following morning, the *Monitor* steamed out to meet her. Although the ensuing four-hour duel was a stalemate, with neither side causing any significant damage or even causing a fatality, the Confederate attempt to break the Union blockade of the Southern coastline had been thwarted. It can be argued that the stalemate at Hampton Roads ultimately led to the defeat of the Confederacy, as the Union naval blockade gradually bled the country of the means of defense. The battle was also a triumph for the naval designers who produced the two warships. In a single day, they had demonstrated that all unarmored wooden warships were obsolete, and the future of seapower lay in the creation of ironclad warships. As a result, the Battle of Hampton Roads has rightly been seen as a turning point in naval history.

When the Southern States seceded from the Union in 1861, neither the US Navy nor the nascent Confederate Navy was prepared for what was to follow. The Union had a handful of warships with which to institute a blockade of thousands of miles of enemy coastline, while the Confederates had no warships at all with which to defend themselves. Confederate Secretary of the Navy Stephen R. Mallory set into motion the train of events that culminated in the duel between the ironclads that morning in Hampton Roads. He decided that the best way to use the limited resources available to the Confederate Navy was the creation of a fleet of ironclad warships. Following the capture of the US Naval Yard in Portsmouth across the river from Norfolk, Virginia, the means to create a prototype ironclad were presented to him. Mallory and his advisors decided to raise the burned-out hulk of the steam frigate USS *Merrimac*, which lay in the Elizabeth River, and then convert her into an armored warship. When news of this work reached Washington, Union Secretary of the Navy Gideon Welles was allocated funds to create a Union ironclad to match the *Merrimac*. The result was the USS *Monitor*. From the moment work began on the *Monitor*, it was inevitable that the two warships would meet in battle. The result was the Battle of Hampton Roads. Participants and onlookers alike were well aware of the importance of the clash. At stake were the fate of the Union naval blockade and ultimately the survival of the Confederacy.

LEFT **The battle between the CSS *Virginia* and the USS *Monitor* on 9 March 1862 was the first naval engagement between two ironclad warships, and represented a turning point in naval history. *The Monitor and the Merrimac*, oil on canvas by Xanthus R. Smith. (Union League of Philadelphia, Philadelphia, PA)**

101

CHRONOLOGY

1861

17 April: Virginia secedes from the Union
19 April: Norfolk Navy Yard abandoned, and *Merrimac* destroyed
23 June: Plans proposed for conversion of the hulk of the *Merrimac* into an ironclad
4 October: John Ericsson signs contract to build the *Monitor*

1862

30 January: *Monitor* launched
17 February: CSS *Virginia* commissioned
25 February: USS *Monitor* commissioned
6 March: *Monitor* begins journey to Hampton Roads

8 March: Battle of Hampton Roads (First Day)
10.00hrs: The French sloop *Gassendi* prepares to move, raising the suspicions of General Wool
10.30: Flag Officer Buchanan orders the CSS *Virginia* be prepared for sea
11.00: The *Virginia* begins her journey down the Elizabeth River
11.15: Union signal station on Newport News Point sights smoke on the Elizabeth River
11.30: General Mansfield alerts General Wool to the possibility that the *Virginia* may be approaching
12.00: The *Virginia* approaches the mouth of the Elizabeth River
12.45: Union fleet sees the *Virginia* and her consorts off Sewell's Point
12.55: The tug *Zouave* is sent to investigate the Confederate naval activity
13.20: The tug *Zouave* opens fire on the *Virginia*
13.30: The *Minnesota*, *St. Lawrence* and *Roanoke* get under way, heading for Newport News Point
14.00: The tug *Beaufort* fires on the USS *Congress*
14.10: The Confederate batteries on Sewell's Point exchange fire with the Union flotilla
14.20: The *Virginia* and the *Congress* exchange fire
14.30: The *Virginia* closes to within 30 yards of the *Congress*
14.50: Leaving the battered *Congress*, the *Virginia* steers toward the *Cumberland*
15.05: The *Virginia* rams the *Cumberland*
15.10: The USS *Minnesota* and the *St. Lawrence* run aground
15.15: The *Virginia* withdraws, then rams the *Cumberland* a second time
15.20: The *Cumberland* sinks, and the *Virginia* commences her 180-degree turn
15.30: The James River Squadron begins its run past the Newport News batteries
15.45: The CSS *Patrick Henry* is hit by fire from shore batteries
16.10: The *Virginia* returns, and rakes the *Congress*
17.00: The *Congress* surrenders
17.10: Confederate vessels approaching the *Congress* come under fire from sharpshooters
17.35: Flag Officer Buchanan wounded
17.45: Heated shot fired at the *Congress*
18.00: Jones steams toward the *Minnesota*
18.30: The attack is abandoned, and the *Virginia* heads back toward Sewell's Point
19.45: The *Virginia* and her escorts anchor under the guns of Sewell's Point

9 March: Battle of Hampton Roads (Second Day)
00.30: The *Congress* explodes
05.00: Flag Officer Buchanan and other wounded sent ashore

06.00: The *Virginia* slips her moorings then waits off Sewell's Point for the fog to clear. The *Minnesota* prepares for action

08.00: The *Virginia* and her consorts steam into Hampton Roads

08.10: The *Monitor* heads south to intercept

08.25: The *Minnesota* and the *Virginia* exchange shots

08.35: The *Monitor* and the *Virginia* commence their duel, which continues for the next two hours

10.55: Lieutenant Worden in the *Monitor* attempts to ram the *Virginia*

11.05: The *Monitor* retires to shallow water to replenish her ammunition supplies

11.10: The *Virginia* steers toward the *Minnesota*

11.30: The *Monitor* returns to the battle, and attempts to ram the *Virginia* again

11.35: The *Virginia* runs aground, and the *Monitor* lies alongside the *Virginia* and fires at her

11.40: Jones signals his consorts to come to his aid, but the *Virginia* pulls herself off the shoal, and her consorts return to Sewell's Point

12.05: The *Virginia* attempts to ram and board the *Monitor*

12.10: Shot from *Virginia* hits the *Monitor's* pilot house, wounding Worden

12.15: Lieutenant Greene takes over command of the *Monitor*. He withdraws from the fight

12.30: The *Virginia* steams toward the *Minnesota* for a final attack

12.40: Attempt abandoned due to falling water levels

13.05: Jones holds a council of war then elects to return to his moorings off Sewell's Point, ending the engagement

13.30: The *Virginia* moors off Sewell's Point, while the *Monitor* anchors off Fort Monroe

21 March: Flag Officer Tattnal appointed to command *Virginia*

9 May: Fall of Norfolk

11 May: Destruction of the *Virginia*

15 May: Engagement at Drewry's Bluff

31 December: *Monitor* sinks during a gale off Cape Hatteras, North Carolina

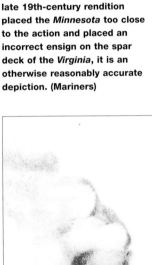

Few accurate depictions of the conflict exist, and although this late 19th-century rendition placed the *Minnesota* too close to the action and placed an incorrect ensign on the spar deck of the *Virginia*, it is an otherwise reasonably accurate depiction. (Mariners)

OPPOSING COMMANDERS

UNION

Gideon Welles, Secretary of the Navy (1802–79)

Born in Connecticut, Welles became the owner and editor of the *Hartford Times* newspaper in 1826. The same year he won a seat in the Connecticut Legislature that he held for nine years. In 1846 he began a four-year term in the Navy Department as the Chief of the Bureau of Provisions and Clothing, which provided him with a modicum of understanding of the Navy and its organization. In 1850 he failed to win a seat on the Senate as a Democrat, so he promptly switched to the Republican Party. In 1856 he founded the *Hartford Evening Press*, but failed in a bid to become Governor of Connecticut. When Abraham Lincoln became President in 1860, he appointed Welles to his cabinet, and in March 1861 he became the Secretary of the Navy, a post he held throughout the war. He quickly demonstrated the ability to select gifted subordinates, and under his tenure the Navy Department grew to meet its new wartime responsibilities. Welles worked hard to expand and modernize the navy, and pressed through the introduction of ironclads into naval service, while masterminding the blockade of the Confederate coastline. He was a staunch advocate of Ericsson and his monitor design, particularly after Hampton Roads. Welles was also a loyal supporter of the President throughout his term, but he still argued with Lincoln over several issues, such as press censorship and individual rights. In 1869 he retired from political life to write his memoirs.

Gideon Welles, the Union Secretary of the Navy was a former newspaper owner and an experienced politician. Although initially sceptical of Ericsson's design, he later became a whole-hearted supporter of the *Monitor* design. (Hensley)

John Ericsson, Designer of the USS *Monitor* (1803–89)

Born in Sweden, the young Ericsson was an engineer in the Swedish Army, but left for Britain in 1826 to promote his design for an engine. Although his machine evoked little interest, he stayed on, and in 1837 he built a twin-screwed steamboat, powered by his own propellers and engines. In 1839 he emigrated to the United States, where he began work on a steam warship for the US Navy. Ericsson fell from favor five years later when a fatal ordnance explosion occurred on his experimental warship. He concentrated on developing an ironclad turret warship, but as the Navy refused to deal with him, he tried unsuccessfully to sell his design to the French. Following the outbreak of the Civil War, Ericsson completed his design for his warship, and was encouraged by supporters to submit the plans to the Navy Department. After initial reluctance, the Navy decided to award Ericsson a contract to build his ironclad, which was completed in February 1862. Ericsson named her *Monitor*, and following her success at the Battle of Hampton Roads in March, the name was adopted by a succession of subsequent ironclads of similar type, many of which were designed by Ericsson. His patented turret

John Ericsson, the Swedish-born designer of the USS *Monitor* was plagued by criticism until the vessel's baptism of fire. Although his design had flaws, "Ericsson's Folly" proved her worth during the battle. (Mariners)

Lieutenant John Latimer Worden USN commanded the USS *Monitor* from her commissioning in Brooklyn until the final stages of the battle, when he was wounded. He demonstrated a remarkable coolness under fire, and good tactical ability. (Mariners)

design was used in most Union monitors throughout the war, and after the conflict his designs were copied or commissioned by several other navies. He continued to design new naval vessels and experiment with propulsion systems until his death.

Lieutenant John L. Worden, Commanding Officer of the USS *Monitor* (1818–97)

Born in New York, Worden entered the US Navy as a midshipman in 1835, and by 1846 he had reached the rank of lieutenant. He served both at sea and ashore until the outbreak of the war, when he was sent to Fort Pickens, Georgia. His orders were to encourage the garrison there to hold their fort until relieved, but during his return journey he was captured. Worden was exchanged as a prisoner of war in October, and on his return he was selected to command the experimental ironclad *Monitor*, then under construction in New York.

Following the battle, Worden recovered from his wounds in Washington, D.C., where he and his crew received the Thanks of Congress. He was promoted to the rank of Commander in July 1862, and he became a Captain in February 1863, when he was given command of the monitor USS *Montauk*. He destroyed the Confederate raider *Nashville* on Georgia's Ogeechee River and then his monitor participated in the bombardment of Fort Sumter in April. In May he returned to Washington, where he was attached to the Navy Department, tasked with advising on the development of new monitors. Following the end of the war he commanded the USS *Pensacola*, and became the Superintendent of the Naval Academy in 1870. He was promoted to the rank of Rear-Admiral, and commanded the European Squadron and served ashore until his retirement in 1886, after a half-century of service.

Lieutenant Samuel D. Greene, Executive Officer of the USS *Monitor* (1839–84)

Greene graduated from the US Naval Academy, Annapolis, in his native Maryland in 1859, and served as a midshipman aboard the USS *Hartford* in the Far East until the outbreak of the war, when the ship returned to the United States. He was promoted to lieutenant in 1861, and he duly volunteered for service on board the USS *Monitor*, then under construction. As the Executive Officer, his duty was to command the turret of the ironclad, and during the Battle of Hampton Roads he used his initiative and common sense to develop a way to use the turret and its guns to best effect. When Lieutenant Worden was wounded during the closing stages of the battle, Greene assumed command of the *Monitor*, and continued to hold the post until Commander John Bankhead was sent to relieve him. His decision not to pursue the *Virginia* and continue the battle preyed on him in later years.

Lieutenant Dana Greene USN was the Executive Officer of the USS *Monitor* during the battle. He supervised operations from the turret, and took over command of the vessel when his commanding officer was wounded. (Mariners)

Greene was a highly-strung officer, and although he served with distinction for the remainder of the war, and was eventually promoted to Commander in 1872, his guilt never left him. In December 1884, while serving as the Executive Officer in the Portsmouth Navy Yard in Maine, he put a pistol to his head, reputedly while "in a state of high nervous excitement," and killed himself. One historian argued that Greene's suicide was directly linked to the first duel between two ironclads, and the battle's only fatality.

CONFEDERATE

Stephen R. Mallory, Secretary of the Navy (1812–73)

Although he was born in Trinidad, Mallory was brought up in Key West, Florida, where he served as a customs inspector and port administrator. Trained as a lawyer, he became a local judge in 1840, and in 1851 he became a Florida senator. He served on the Naval Affairs Committee until the secession of Florida from the Union. He offered his services to the Confederate President Jefferson Davis, who appointed him Confederate Secretary of the Navy in May 1861. He held the position throughout the war, and was instrumental in developing new technologies to help offset Union naval superiority. These included the development of an ironclad fleet, torpedoes (mines), and rifled ordnance. In late 1861 he approved plans to raise the burned-out hulk of the USS *Merrimac* and to convert her into a casemate ironclad (the *Virginia*), and closely supervised the development of the project. The success of the design was an affirmation of Mallory's belief in ironclads.

A gifted politician and administrator, Mallory proved himself capable of dealing with the technical and logistical challenges of his job. Although his strategic vision of the *Virginia*'s ability to break the Union blockade was flawed, his reliance on developing a fleet of ironclads helped protect the major ports of the Confederacy for as long as practicable. Following the collapse of the Confederacy he was arrested and imprisoned for a year. After the war he moved to Pensacola where he practised law until his death.

Stephen Russell Mallory, the Confederate Secretary of the Navy. He was instrumental in developing an ironclad fleet to protect the Confederacy, and the *Virginia* was the prototype for this ambitious program. (Monroe County Public Library. Key West, FL)

John L. Porter, principal designer of the CSS *Virginia* (1821–84)

Porter was brought up in Portsmouth, Virginia, where his father owned a civilian shipyard close to the Norfolk Naval Yard. He was duly hired by the US Navy Department as a civilian naval designer, and worked on several projects in the Navy Department, including the development of steam warships. In 1859 he was appointed Naval Constructor, the leading warship design post in the Navy. When Virginia seceded in 1861, Porter resigned his post and returned to Virginia. For a few months he served on the staff of the Virginia State Navy, but following its amalgamation into the new Confederate Navy he joined the offices of the Navy Department in Richmond. Although he held no official position until 1864, he was de facto head of naval construction in the Department. Together with ordnance expert Lieutenant John M. Brooke and engineer William P. Williamson, Porter drew up plans for the conversion of the burned-out warship *Merrimac* into a Confederate ironclad. Although there was a degree of animosity between Porter and Brooke, the trio succeeded in converting the warship that was to become the casemate ironclad CSS *Virginia*.

Following the success of his design, Porter was authorized to develop plans for several new ironclads, including the highly successful *Richmond* Class. He continued to design the majority of new warships in the Confederacy, although his position as Chief Naval Constructor was only officially ratified in 1864. An extremely gifted designer, Porter became a businessman after the war.

Naval Constructor John L. Porter developed plans to convert the burnt-out remains of the *Merrimac* into the powerful casemate ironclad *Virginia*. He achieved miracles, given the limited resources available in the Confederacy. (Mariners)

Flag Officer Franklin Buchanan was a native of Maryland, who cast his lot with the Confederacy. A skilled naval tactician and administrator, he commanded his flagship the CSS *Virginia* during her attack on the *Cumberland* and *Congress*. (LoC)

Lieutenant Catesby ap Roger Jones, CSN was the Executive Officer of the CSS *Virginia*. He commanded the ironclad during her famous battle with the USS *Monitor*, as Flag Officer Buchanan was wounded during the previous day's fighting. (Mariners)

Flag Officer Franklin Buchanan, Commanding Officer of the CSS *Virginia* (1800–74)

Born in Maryland, Buchanan entered the US Navy in 1815, and gradually rose through the ranks, being promoted Commander in 1841. He assisted in the creation of the US Naval Academy at Annapolis, and in 1845 he became its first superintendent. He commanded the sloop USS *Germantown* during the Mexican-American War (1846–48), and in 1855 he was promoted to Captain and placed in command of the Washington Navy Yard. In 1861 he thought it certain that Maryland would secede from the Union, and he resigned from the Navy. When it transpired that Maryland remained loyal, Buchanan tried to withdraw his resignation, but the Navy Department refused his request. Consequently in August 1861 Buchanan headed south to offer his services to the Confederacy. He was appointed Captain in September, and served in the Navy Department, masterminding the drive to create a Confederate Navy from scratch. In February 1862 he was made Flag Officer, and given command of naval forces in Virginia. His decision to use his flagship the CSS *Virginia* to attack the Union blockading fleet in Hampton Roads initiated the Battle of Hampton Roads. He was wounded in the action, but was rewarded by promotion to full Admiral in August. He subsequently commanded the defenses of Mobile, Alabama, and during the Battle of Mobile Bay (August 1864) his flagship was the ironclad CSS *Tennessee*. After the war he worked as an insurance executive in Maryland until his death.

Lieutenant Catesby ap R. Jones, Executive Officer of the CSS *Virginia* (1821–77)

Born in Virginia, Jones entered the US Navy in 1836, and served in the Pacific before attending the Philadelphia Naval School, where he passed as midshipman in 1841. He then was posted to the Navy Department's Hydrographical Office, and he performed survey work off the Florida coast for several years. In 1853 Lieutenant Jones was assigned to the Washington Navy Yard, where he assisted John A. Dahlgren in developing a new system of smoothbore ordnance. He also served as gunnery officer on the USS *Merrimac*. When Virginia seceded in 1861 he resigned his commission and became a lieutenant in the Confederate Navy. He was appointed to the *Merrimac* during her conversion into the CSS *Virginia*, and Jones played a major role in preparing the ironclad for active service. During the first day of the Battle of Hampton Roads, Flag Officer Buchanan was wounded, and Jones assumed command of the Virginia in time for her duel with the USS *Monitor*, fighting her with skill. He continued as the *Virginia*'s Executive Officer until the vessel's destruction in May. By 1863 he had been promoted and was placed in charge of the Navy's Ordnance Works in Selma, Alabama. He settled there after the war, and became a businessman until his death in a quarrel. Jones remains the unsung hero of Hampton Roads, and historians have only recently acknowledged his true influence on the events of March 1862.

OPPOSING FORCES

CONFEDERATE

CSS *Virginia*

The decision to build an ironclad from the hulk of the burned-out steam frigate USS *Merrimac* was made by Stephen Mallory, the Confederate Secretary of the Navy. He realized that it was almost impossible for his Navy to break the Union blockade by conventional means, so he adopted a more radical approach, placing his faith in ironclads and rifled ordnance. The *Merrimac* had been burned and sunk when Union forces withdrew from Norfolk, but on inspection she was deemed to still be valuable. Although her upper works had been destroyed, her engines were salvageable, and her lower hull remained in good condition. The hulk was raised and brought into a dry dock in the Navy Yard for conversion. Mallory gathered a design team to work on the project. It consisted of leading naval constructor, John L. Porter, the ordnance expert John M. Brooke and naval engineer William P. Williamson – three of the best designers in the Confederacy. Given the lack of manufacturing capacity in the South, all three men realized that any attempt to produce a technically challenging design was beyond the abilities of Southern foundries. Following a series of meetings, Porter, Brooke and Williamson decided that the conversion of the burned-out hull of the *Merrimac* was far from ideal, as the vessel was cumbersome, and its engines were underpowered. Its principal advantage was that it allowed an ironclad to be built faster than if it were constructed from scratch. Mallory's directive to start work on the ironclad was issued on 11 June 1861, and she was commissioned into service just eight months later, on 17 February 1862. Given the limited industrial capacity of the Southern states, this represented an incredible accomplishment. The

The CSS *Virginia* was not completed when she fought the USS *Monitor*. She carried the wrong ammunition, and the gun port shutters designed to protect her gun crews were still not fitted. (Hensley)

The two 11in. Dahlgren smoothbore guns carried in the USS *Monitor* weighed 15,700lb, and fired a 165lb solid cast-iron roundshot or a 136lb conical shell. While Dahlgren limited their propellant to 15lb of powder, subsequent tests proved the barrels could withstand larger charges. (Author's Collection)

Confederacy lacked sufficient engineering plants, skilled workers and raw materials, and Porter and his team continually modified their design to suit the manufacturing capacity available to them. The main elements required were wood, rolled iron sheet for the armor plating, a propulsion system, and reliable ordnance. Wood was in plentiful supply, although the ramshackle rail infrastructure made the transport of shipbuilding lumber and metal plates a continual problem. Porter relied on the Tredegar Iron Works in Richmond, Virginia, to supply metal plates. Although the Richmond foundry was the largest ironworks in the Confederacy, it was small in comparison to its northern counterparts. The initial contract specified the use of 1in. iron plates, but tests conducted by John M. Brooke at Jamestown proved that a series of one-inch layers would be inadequate protection for the ironclad. Ironically, this was precisely the form of plating fitted to the USS *Monitor*, but she relied on eight layers of 1in. plate to protect her turret, twice the armor available to the *Virginia*'s designers. The vessel was finally protected with two layers of 2in. iron plate, and the Tredegar Works had to alter their machinery so it could roll the thicker plate, which delayed production, but the thicker metal greatly improved the defensive qualities of the vessel. It was bolted to the wooden backing by applying an inner horizontal belt and an outer vertical one. As for a propulsion system, Williamson oversaw the stripping and refurbishment of the *Merrimac*'s engines. Although underpowered, they were reliable, available, and could be fitted into the ironclad with minimal delay.

The basic design of the Confederate ironclad relied on a wooden casemate (shield) with rounded ends, erected on top of the existing hull. When coated with metal plate, this gave the warship the ungainly

appearance of an upturned bath. The wood was approximately 2ft thick and the casemate sloped inward at a 35-degree angle, which Brooke determined was the best to deflect enemy shot. The armor extended from the top of the casemate down to the lower hull and beyond, ending 6in. below the waterline. The decision to extend the armor below the point where the casemate joined the hull (known as the "knuckle") added weight to the vessel, and sacrificed maneuverability for protection, but it made the vessel virtually impervious to enemy shot. The upper spar deck (or "hurricane deck") on top of the casemate was unarmored, and fitted with ventilation grilles. The lower hull itself was all but submerged, offering virtually no target to the enemy, although on the second day of the battle more of it was exposed than had been the previous day. The ironclad had used up coal, and her bunkers were not replenished during the night of 8/9 March. Consequently, she rode higher in the water, exposing part of her lower hull below the protective "knuckle".

The ironclad's armament consisted of six 9in. Dahlgren smoothbore guns (part of the *Merrimac*'s original armament) plus two new 6.4in. Brooke rifled guns mounted as broadside weapons on conventional carriages. All these pieces were mounted on conventional carriages, and fired out of broadside ports, In addition, two 7in. Brooke rifles on pivot mounts were fitted at the bow and stern, so they could fire ahead, astern or at an angle out of the corner of the casemate. In theory, the ironclad had the capability of all-round fire, although her real strength lay in the power of her broadside armament. An even more potent offensive weapon was the 1,500lb cast-iron ram fitted to the bow, three feet below the waterline.

Christened the CSS *Virginia*, she was commissioned days before the battle, but she was still unfinished when Admiral Buchanan decided to use her to attack the Union blockading fleet. Much internal work remained to be done, her gunport shutters had not been fitted, and she lacked sufficient stores to allow her to remain at sea for more than a day

or two. There were still problems with her rudder, and it was estimated the cumbersome vessel would take almost 30 minutes to complete a 180-degree turn. Despite her lack of speed, poor maneuverability and a large draught (23ft), she was a powerful warship. She was also more than a match for all the Union vessels in Hampton Roads combined, until the arrival of her ironclad rival in time for the second day of the battle.

CSS *Virginia*'s Officers
Commanding Officer: Flag Officer Franklin Buchanan
Executive Officer: Lieutenant Catesby ap Roger Jones
Chief Engineering Officer: Lieutenant Ramsay
Lieutenants (6), Midshipmen (7)
Captain of Marines: Lieutenant Thom
Surgeon: Dinwiddie Phillips
Paymaster: James Semple

The James River Squadron

Waiting for the opportunity to pass through the Union fleet off Hampton Roads and slip into Norfolk was the James River Squadron; a collection of three wooden gunboats, under the command of Commander John R. Tucker. Tucker was the Commanding Officer of the sidewheel gunboat CSS *Patrick Henry*, a beautiful vessel that was formerly called *Yorktown*. She went on to become the Confederate Navy's training ship. She was accompanied by her sister ship the CSS *Jamestown* (commanded by Lieutenant Joseph M. Barney) and the small gunboat CSS *Teaser* (commanded by Lieutenant William A. Webb). At the start of

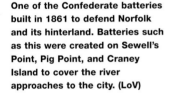

One of the Confederate batteries built in 1861 to defend Norfolk and its hinterland. Batteries such as this were created on Sewell's Point, Pig Point, and Craney Island to cover the river approaches to the city. (LoV)

the battle Tucker's squadron was moored off Jamestown, several miles up the James River from the Union fleet. They came under the overall command of Flag Officer Buchanan, who ordered Tucker to be ready to support the *Virginia* on the morning of 8 March 1862. All of the squadron's ships were converted merchant vessels, and lacked the strength to fight the more powerful Union warships on their own.

The *Virginia*'s escorts

The *Virginia* was supported by two small tugboats, which were based at Portsmouth or Norfolk. Their sole purpose was to tow the ironclad safely up the Elizabeth River into Hampton Roads, then to cut her loose. After that they were to stand by under the protection of the guns on Sewell's Point in case Buchanan required any further assistance. Both the CSS *Raleigh* and the CSS *Beaufort* were puny vessels, incapable of posing any threat to the Union fleet. Both vessels had escaped the Confederate defeat at Roanoke Island in February, and the subsequent destruction of the Confederate wooden gunboat squadron at Elizabeth City. They were both small enough to escape up the Dismal Swamp Canal to the safety of Norfolk, and were duly attached to Buchanan's "Chesapeake Bay Squadron", the grandly imposing name given to the motley collection of gunboats that sought refuge from the Union blockade behind the guns surrounding Norfolk. They were commanded by Lieutenant William L. Parker, who was also Captain of the *Beaufort*.

The Defenses of Norfolk

The Confederates, who had approximately 9,000 troops in the area, held the southern side of Hampton Roads. They came under the jurisdiction of Major General Benjamin Huger, commander of the Department of Norfolk, although in theory Flag Officer Buchanan was the senior officer there. Huger was also supposed to work in concert with the 12,000 troops screening the Union forces around

Fort Monroe and Newport News, who were commanded by Major General John B. Magruder. In reality, Huger was an independent commander, and the lack of communication between the Confederate Army and Navy in Norfolk would have severe repercussions. The Portsmouth–Norfolk–Gosport area was of major strategic importance to the Confederates, as the area housed the Confederacy's main naval base, and Norfolk was one of the largest cities in Virginia. It was, therefore, well defended, and Confederate batteries dominated the southern shore of Hampton Roads. These emplacements were sited on Sewell's Point, at the eastern mouth of the Elizabeth River, on Craney Island, blocking the river approaches to Norfolk, and further to the west, where the batteries protected both Norfolk and Suffolk. Further batteries lined the western shore of the Elizabeth River, between Sewell's Point and Norfolk. Magruder had his headquarters in the fortification immediately north of Norfolk. These troops manning the batteries and redoubts had an unobstructed view of the battle, and observers on Sewell's Point were ideally placed to watch both phases of the conflict, and to offer protection to the *Virginia* when required.

CONFEDERATE VESSELS

CSS *VIRGINIA* – Casemate Screw Ram (Armored)
Built: Boston 1855, converted Norfolk 1861–62. **Commissioned:** March 1862
Dimensions: 263ft (length) x 51ft 4in. (beam) x 22ft (draft)
Armament: 2 x 7in. rifles, 6 x 9in. smoothbores, 2 x 6.4in. rifles
Armor: 4in., with timber backing
Complement: 320
Speed: 8 knots

CSS *PATRICK HENRY*, CSS *JAMESTOWN* – Wooden Sidewheel Gunboats
(Unarmored)
Built: New York, 1853 [both]. **Commissioned:** April 1861
Dimensions: 250ft x 34ft x 13ft. **Displacement:** 1,300 tons
Armament: (*Patrick Henry*) 1 x 10in. smoothbore, 1 x 64-pdr. smoothbore, 6 x 8in. smoothbores, 2 x 32-pdr. rifles. Although details are unknown, the *Jamestown* was probably similarly armed, although she only carried 2 x 8in. smoothbores.
Complement: 150
Speed: 12 knots

CSS *TEASER* – Wooden Screw Tug (Unarmored)
Built: Philadelphia, c.1855. **Commissioned:** 1861
Dimensions: 80ft x 18ft x 7ft. **Displacement:** 65 tons
Armament: 1 x 32-pdr. rifle
Complement: 25
Speed: 10 knots

CSS *BEAUFORT* – Wooden Screw Tugboat (Unarmored)
Built: Wilmington, DE, c.1854. **Commissioned:** July 1861
Dimensions: 85ft x 17ft 6in. x 7ft. **Displacement:** 85 tons
Armament: 1 x 32-pdr. rifle
Complement: approx. 25
Speed: 9 knots

CSS *RALEIGH* – Iron Screw Tugboat (Unarmored)
Built: Not recorded. **Commissioned:** May 1861
Dimensions: 80ft x 18ft x 7ft. **Displacement:** 65 tons
Armament: 2 x 6-pdr. howitzers
Complement: approx. 20
Speed: Not recorded

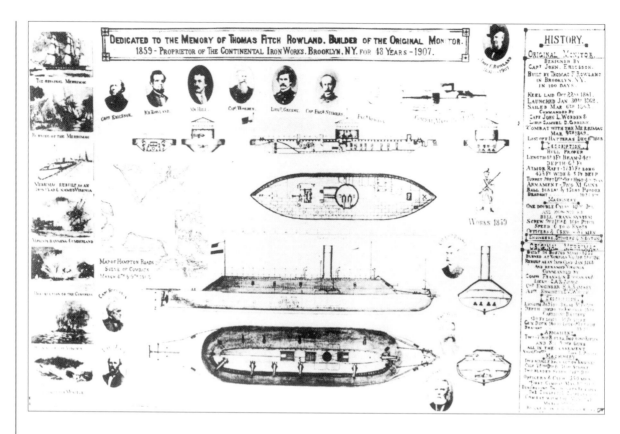

UNION

USS *Monitor*

When reports reached Washington that the Confederates were building an ironclad warship, the Navy Department became alarmed, and lobbied for funds to counter the threat with their own ironclad program. Gideon Welles, the Secretary of the Navy, was a highly experienced and competent administrator, but so far his efforts had been concentrated on expanding the navy by ordering new conventional warships and converting merchantmen for naval service. His primary aim was to create an effective blockade of the Confederacy, and the *Merrimac* threatened to break this maritime stranglehold. Congress was equally perturbed, and allocated funds for the creation of ironclads within days. Welles founded an "Ironclad Board", charged with examining proposals for ironclads, and following an appeal for designs the board retired to select the most promising. Three were chosen; a casemate ironclad similar to the French *Gloire* which became known as the USS *New Ironsides*, a small armored gunboat which became the USS *Galena*, and the revolutionary design proposed by Swedish-born designer John Ericsson for a turreted ironclad. This last vessel would become the USS *Monitor*. The Board was initially hesitant to approve Ericsson's design, as his vessel looked like no warship that had ever been seen before. One Board member even tried to force Ericsson to add masts and sails to the design, but the inventor refused. At a time when naval technology was being transformed, advocates of older, more traditional methods of ship construction were resistant to change.

A poster dedicated to Thomas F. Rowland of the Continental Iron Works gives a good impression of the difference in size between the two ironclads. Commissioned almost four decades after the battle, it emphasized the new spirit of unity in the nation by honoring the participants of both sides. (Hensley)

One of three sail-powered warships to participate in the battle, the USS *St. Lawrence* carried 44 guns. She ran aground during the afternoon of 8 March, but unlike her consort the *Minnesota*, the frigate could be refloated. (Mariners)

Ericsson's design was for a small armored hull to be fitted with a revolving gun turret containing two smoothbore guns. These guns were to be protected by eight layers of 1in. iron plate, bent into a curve to create the shape of the turret. The hull was constructed in two parts, the upper portion sitting on top of the lower hull like a raft. This upper part was protected by two ½in. deck plates laid over the deck beams, which provided little protection to fire from above, but as the design was meant to be a response to the threat of a Confederate ironclad, this was not considered a problem.

The sides of the hull were protected by 5in. of side armor in five 1in. strips, backed by just over 2ft of oak. When the guns were fitted and all the crew and stores embarked, the freeboard of the ironclad was less than 18in., which meant she was only capable of operating in calm coastal waters. It also meant that the hull presented an almost impossibly small target for enemy gunners. The hull was flat bottomed, and the upper portion of the hull extended over the lower part, protecting the rudder and screw. Unlike the *Virginia*, which had a draft of 22ft, Ericsson's ironclad could operate in less than 11ft of water.

She was powered by Ericsson's own "vibrating-lever" engines, which gave her a top speed of around 6 knots. A smaller engine powered the turret's rotation mechanism, which was controlled by an engineer inside the turret using a clutch mechanism. In theory, the 120-ton, 20ft diameter turret could rotate through 360 degrees in 24 seconds. It turned on a heavy central spindle, and to turn the whole device was elevated a few inches off the deck, so it effectively sat on the spindle's central column. Designed to house two powerful 15in. Dahlgren smoothbores, the turret was fitted with 11in. Dahlgrens instead, as the production of the larger guns was plagued by problems. The smaller 11in. pieces were available immediately, and were proven to be effective. Iron shutters known as "port stoppers" could be lowered over the gunports by means of pulleys inside the gun turret when the guns were not in use, or to protect the gunners from enemy fire.

When she was completed, the little ironclad was 179ft long, with a beam of 41½ft. Although newspapermen had dubbed her "Ericsson's folly", the ironclad was the only one of the three Union ironclads that were any way near completion in early 1862, and it became inevitable that as soon as she was completed, the ironclad would be sent south to Hampton Roads. The vessel was launched on 30 January 1862, when she was named the USS *Monitor*, a name chosen by her designer and approved by Gideon Welles. Her crew of 49 men was completely unused to any such vessel, and they had to discover the quirks of their vessel during the voyage south to Hampton Roads. Although far smaller than the *Virginia*, the *Monitor* was capable of virtually all-round fire, and was protected by thicker armor. She was also far more maneuverable than her opponent, but she lacked the sheer weight of armament of her rival. Although some naval officers who viewed her claimed she could "sink any vessel afloat," others expected her to sink as soon as she was launched. The all-volunteer crews were brave men to venture to sea in such an untested experimental vessel, let alone take her into action against the most powerful warship in the Confederacy.

USS *Monitor*'s Officers
Commanding Officer: Lieutenant John Worden
Executive Officer: Lieutenant Samuel Dana Greene
Chief Engineering Officer: Lieutenant Stimers
Lieutenants (3), Midshipmen (5)
Surgeon: Daniel C. Logue
Paymaster: William Keeler

The North Atlantic Blockading Squadron at Hampton Roads

The blockading squadron that lay in Hampton Roads during the first week of March 1862 was representative of the blockading forces that encircled the Confederacy. All were unarmored vessels, and almost all were wooden. The most powerful ships were the steam frigates USS *Minnesota* (Captain Gershon Van Brunt) and USS *Roanoke* (Captain John Marston), both well armed with the latest shell guns. Marston was also the acting commander of the squadron during the battle. The squadron also included several sailing warships, echoes of a bygone age. While they lacked the maneuverability of steam warships, they did possess a powerful enough armament, and were therefore useful, at least until more modern warships could be found to replace them. These sailing ships included the frigates USS *Congress* (Lieutenant Joseph Smith) and USS *St. Lawrence* (Captain H. Purvayance), plus the USS *Cumberland* (Captain William Radford), formerly a frigate that had been "razeed" or cut down to make a smaller but more useful warship. The squadron included myriad smaller ships, including transports, tugs to move the sailing vessels, supply ships, dispatch boats, small gunboats, a hospital ship, and a storeship. One oddity in the fleet was the *Vanderbilt*, a former iron paddlewheel steamer that had served as an ocean liner. She was due to be commissioned into the Navy, and was in Hampton Roads for the sole purpose of ramming the *Virginia* in the event of her appearance. As she had a top speed of 14 knots

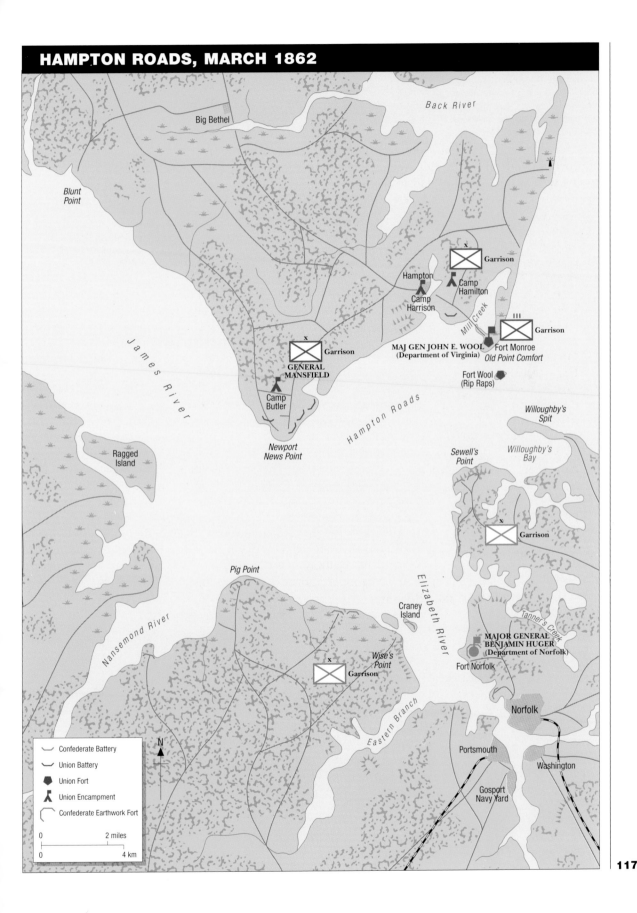

HAMPTON ROADS, MARCH 1862

Back River

Big Bethel

Blunt
Point

Hampton

Camp
Harrison

X **Garrison**

Camp
Hamilton

Mill Creek

X **GENERAL
MANSFIELD** **Garrison**

MAJ GEN JOHN E. WOOL
(Department of Virginia)

III **Garrison**

Fort Monroe
Old Point Comfort

Camp
Butler

James River

Newport
News Point

Hampton Roads

Fort Wool
(Rip Raps)

Willoughby's
Spit

Sewell's
Point

Willoughby's
Bay

Ragged
Island

X **Garrison**

Pig Point

Craney
Island

Elizabeth River

Wise's
Point

X **Garrison**

Tanner's Creek

MAJOR GENERAL
BENJAMIN HUGER
(Department of Norfolk)

Fort Norfolk

Nansemond River

Norfolk

Eastern Branch

Portsmouth

Washington

Gosport
Navy Yard

N

Confederate Battery

Union Battery

Union Fort

Union Encampment

Confederate Earthwork Fort

0   2 miles

0   4 km

The USS *Minnesota* was the most powerful wooden warship in Hampton Roads during the battle. During the second day of the battle she was also the most vulnerable, having run aground the previous afternoon midway between Old Point Comfort and Newport News Point. Unable to free herself, she lay at the mercy of the *Virginia*. (National Archives)

and displaced over 3,000 tons, she might well have been successful if she had been given the opportunity to try. Anchored amongst the Union fleet as an impartial observer, the small French warship *Gassendi* was present under a flag of neutrality. Her commander, Captain Gautier, was charged with determining the effectiveness of the Confederate ironclad. He would find plenty to write about.

The Union Defenses of Fort Monroe and Newport News

The northern shore of Hampton Roads was dominated by the imposing bulk of Fort Monroe, a brick-built fortification similar to other coastal fortifications that ringed the country from New England to the mouth of the Mississippi River. The fort was defended by 12,000 men, a total that included both its garrison and troops in outlying camps: Camp Butler at Newport News Point, Camp Hamilton two miles to the north, and Camp Harrison in the burned-out village of Hampton itself. The troops at Fort Butler were commanded by Brigadier General Joseph K. Mansfield, who also commanded the shore batteries lining Newport News Point. Halfway between Sewell's Point and Fort Monroe was a man-made island known as the "Rip Raps". A small round fortification

The sidewheel steamer *Vanderbilt* was a transatlantic liner that was donated to the US Navy as a free charter by the multimillionaire shipping tycoon Cornelius Vanderbilt. Plans were afoot to convert the liner into a giant ram to be used against the *Virginia*, but work had not yet started at the time of the battle. (US Navy)

had been built there, although work was far from complete. It was called Fort Wool, named after Major General John E. Wool, the commander of the Union Department of Virginia, whose headquarters was at Fort Monroe. Like their Confederate counterparts on the southern side of the Roads, these troops would have a grandstand view of the naval battle that would change the face of naval warfare.

UNION VESSELS

USS MONITOR – Single-turret screw monitor (Armored)
Built: New York. **Commissioned:** February 1862
Dimensions: 179ft (length) x 41ft 6in. (beam) x 10ft 6in. (draft).
Displacement: 987 tons
Armament: 2 x 11in. smoothbores
Armor: 8in. turret and pilothouse, 4½in. hull, 1in. deck, all with timber backing.
Complement: 49
Speed: 8 knots

USS CONGRESS – Wooden Sailing Frigate (Unarmored)
Built: Portsmouth. **Commissioned:** May 1842
Dimensions: 179ft x 47ft 6in. x 22ft 6in.
Displacement: 1,867 tons
Armament: 10 x 8in. smoothbores, 40 x 30-pdr. smoothbores
Complement: 480

USS CUMBERLAND – Wooden Sailing Sloop* (Unarmored)
Built: Boston. **Commissioned:** November 1843
Dimensions: 175ft x 45ft x 22ft 4in.
Displacement: 990 tons
Armament: 22 x 9in. smoothbores, 1 x 10in. smoothbore, 1 x 170-pdr. rifle
Complement: 190
* Converted from a frigate in 1855

USS MINNESOTA – Wooden Screw Frigate (Unarmored)
Built: Washington. **Commissioned:** May 1857
Dimensions: 265ft x 51ft 4in. x 23ft 10in.
Displacement: 4,833 tons
Armament: 28 x 10in. smoothbores, 1 x 10in. smoothbore, 14 x 8in. smoothbores
Complement: 646
Speed: 12 knots

USS ROANOKE – Wooden Screw Frigate (Unarmored)
Built: Norfolk. **Commissioned:** May 1857
Dimensions: 268ft 6in. x 52ft 6in. x 23ft 9in.
Armament: 2 x 10in. smoothbores, 28 x 9in. smoothbores, 14 x 8in. smoothbores
Complement: 674
Speed: 11 knots

USS VANDERBILT – Wooden Sidewheel Gunboat (Unarmored)
Built: New York, 1856 (former merchant vessel).
Acquired by Navy: March 1862
Dimensions: 340ft x 47ft 6in. x 21ft 6in.
Displacement: 3,360 tons
Armament: None fitted by 8–9 March 1862
Complement: skeleton crew
Speed: 14 knots

USS ST. LAWRENCE – Wooden Sailing Frigate (Unarmored)
Built: Norfolk. **Commissioned:** September 1848
Dimensions: 175ft x 45ft x 22ft 4in.
Displacement: 1,726 tons
Armament: 10 x 8in. smoothbores, 30 x 32-pdr. smoothbores, 2 x 12-pdr. smoothbores
Complement: 400

USS ZOUAVE – Wooden Screw Tug (Unarmored)
Built: Albany, 1861 (former merchant vessel).
Acquired by Navy: December 1861
Dimensions: 95ft x 20ft 10in. x 9ft
Armament: 2 x 30-pdr. rifles
Complement: 25
Speed: 10 knots

USS DRAGON – Wooden Screw Tug (Unarmored)
Built: Buffalo, 1861 (former merchant vessel).
Acquired by Navy: December 1861
Dimensions: 92ft x 17ft x 9ft 6in.
Armament: 1 x 30-pdr. rifle, 1 x 24-pdr. smoothbore
Complement: 42
Speed: 8 knots

BACKGROUND TO THE BATTLE

WAR AND BLOCKADE

I n 1860, the United States of America lay on the brink of Civil War as North and South were drawn apart on issues of slavery and state rights. To all but the most hot-headed secessionist, war between the predominantly agrarian South and the largely industrialized North would lead to the overwhelming of the rebelling Southern states by sheer weight of manpower and material. The only chance for the Confederacy was a rapid military victory, ending the conflict before Northern industrial might could be brought to bear. On 20 December 1860, South Carolina elected to secede from the Union, and within weeks six other states followed her lead. On 4 February 1861, representatives of these states met in Montgomery, Alabama, and agreed to form a Confederacy. Four days later a provisional constitution was ratified, and this group of secessionist states officially became the Confederate States of America. Conflict with the North seemed inevitable, but for the next eight weeks America's fate hung in the balance. Next, the Confederate Congress elected a new President, Jefferson F. Davis of Mississippi, who was inaugurated on 18 February. Two days later, President Davis created the Confederacy's own Navy Department, naming Florida senator Stephen R. Mallory as its first chief.

Mallory faced a daunting challenge. The Confederate coastline would eventually stretch from the Potomac River to the Rio Grande, and while many Southern ports were protected by relatively modern brick-

The CSS *Virginia*, shown during her passage down the Elizabeth River on the morning of 8 August 1862. In the background is the naval hospital at Portsmouth where Flag Officer Buchanan was taken after the battle. The two ensigns shown are incorrect, and post-date the engagement. (US Navy)

This view of Hampton Roads shows Fort Monroe in the foreground, and Fort Wool (5), Sewell's Point (7), Craney Island (8), and the mouth of the Elizabeth River (9) in the background. Newport News Point (17) is on the right of the illustration. (Casemate)

built fortifications, Mallory had no navy to help defend this long coastline. The situation improved during March and early April, as hundreds of Southern naval officers resigned their commissions and returned home. Ships were commandeered and converted to form the nucleus of State navies, and Mallory worked on plans to create a dedicated naval force capable of protecting the Confederate coastline, although throughout the war he was plagued by shortages of men and resources. On 12 April 1861, Confederate guns opened fire on Fort Sumter, the bastion that protected the entrance to Charleston, South Carolina. President Lincoln called for volunteers to defend the Union, and proclaimed the institution of a blockade of the Confederate coastline. The war had begun.

To Secretary of the Navy Gideon Welles, Union naval strategy was deceptively simple. General Winfield Scott developed the "Anaconda Plan", whereby a tight naval blockade would cut off the Confederacy from the outside world. A major thrust down the Mississippi River would cut the country in two, allowing Union forces to squeeze the remaining parts of the Confederacy by land and naval attacks. Deprived of supplies and faced with the industrial might of the North, defeat would be inevitable. When the war began the US Navy was desperately short of ships capable of blockading Southern ports. Although the fleet consisted of over 90 ships, in April 1861, most were either being refitted and repaired in port, or were on deployment overseas. While the Navy launched a major shipbuilding program, Welles ordered the purchase and conversion of dozens of merchant vessels to help maintain the blockade until purpose-built warships became available. During the remainder of 1861, token Union naval squadrons appeared at the mouth of major Southern ports, such as Charleston, New Orleans, Mobile, Pensacola, Savannah, and Wilmington.

Minor naval clashes on the Potomac River ended when a blockading squadron appeared in Hampton Roads, effectively sealing off tidewater Virginia, including links between Richmond and Norfolk. The squadron was based off Fort Monroe, whose formidable defenses remained in

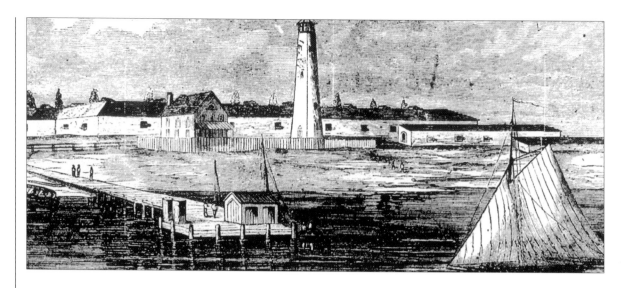

Union hands, and which served as a secure base in Virginia, across the bay from Norfolk. Combined naval and amphibious attacks secured the use of Hatteras Inlet in North Carolina's outer banks, and led to the capture of Port Royal, South Carolina. Both provided vital anchorages, as the only other secure Union anchorage south of Hampton Roads was Key West, off the southern tip of Florida. The Confederate capture of Norfolk ensured a sort of naval stalemate in Virginia's tidewater for another year. Although Union naval forces off Hampton Roads grew stronger during the winter and spring of 1862, and the strength of the Union garrison at Fort Monroe increased, neither side felt itself powerful enough to take offensive action. All that was to change with the conversion of the *Merrimac* into a powerful ironclad.

THE CAPTURE OF NORFOLK NAVY YARD

In 1861, the steam frigate USS *Merrimac* was one of the most powerful warships in the US Navy. She was one of a series of six 40-gun steam frigates ordered in 1854, and from her launch in Boston the following year she was regarded as the pride of the fleet. She served in the West Indies and the Pacific before being sent to Norfolk Navy Yard in February 1860 for a major refit. Norfolk Navy Yard was considered the "premier yard" in the country. It covered 108 acres in the Gosport suburb of Portsmouth, across the Elizabeth River from Norfolk itself, and combined being a major shipbuilding yard with service as the Navy's primary ordnance and munitions depot. It boasted a large granite dry dock, machine shops, a foundry, and three shipbuilding slips. Work continued in the yard in early 1861 even though war seemed imminent, as the base commandant was reluctant to begin any evacuation, which might provoke Virginia to secede.

When Virginia withdrew from the Union on 17 April 1861 (five days after the bombardment of Fort Sumter), the base commander finally made plans to evacuate Norfolk and to destroy the facilities. He achieved little, partly as he was hindered by Southern sympathizers amongst his staff and civilian workforce, most of whom refused to carry

The lighthouse on Old Point Comfort, with Fort Monroe behind it, viewed from the south. The jetty in the foreground was a hive of activity on 8 March, when the ironclad *Virginia* made her sortie into Hampton Roads, and the small vessels there fled behind the Point. (Casemate)

OPPOSITE TOP This emplacement to the northeast of Fort Monroe was sited to cover the passage between Fort Monroe and Fort Wool. Its primary function was to block the *Virginia*'s access to Chesapeake Bay. The 15in. Rodman smoothbore pictured here was nicknamed the "Lincoln Gun". (Casemate)

out his orders. On 20 April the commandant of the yard, Commodore Charles S. McCauley ordered the base destroyed and the *Merrimac* taken into the Elizabeth River, set on fire and scuttled, as he lacked the manpower to tow her to safety. Ironically a rescue party and a tug arrived from Fort Monroe to tow her away, but it was too late. If they had arrived earlier, the Battle of Hampton Roads would never have taken place. Of the 12 warships at the yard, only the sailing sloop USS *Cumberland* was towed to the safety of Fort Monroe, on the far side of Hampton Roads. Late the following evening the yard was abandoned, and the local Confederate militia marched in to claim their prize. Although an attempt had been made to destroy the dry dock, it was still serviceable, as were many of the shipyard facilities. Even more impressive was the haul of some 1,200 pieces of naval ordnance, including 300 modern Dahlgren smoothbores, 50 of them being his latest 11in. smoothbores. Within days, Confederate Secretary of the Navy Stephen Mallory visited the site, and work began hauling many of the guns away to arm coastal defenses in the Carolinas, Louisiana, and Georgia. Other pieces were hauled into place overlooking Hampton Roads to protect Norfolk itself. Two weeks later, scouting vessels dispatched from the north shore of Hampton Roads were turned back by fire from batteries on Sewell's Point and Pig Point. As trains brought up Confederate reinforcements from Richmond, General Wool at Fort Monroe deemed the Norfolk area too strong to be recaptured without a major and costly assault. Norfolk was safely in Confederate hands.

CONVERTING THE *MERRIMAC*

During his visit, Mallory examined the wreck of the *Merrimac*. Across Hampton Roads, Flag Officer Silas Stringham, commander of the newly formed North Atlantic Blockading Squadron, deemed the wreck "worthless" in a letter to the Secretary of the Navy Gideon Welles. Mallory thought otherwise, and weeks after the fall of the Norfolk Navy Yard, he formed a design team, consisting of naval constructor John L. Porter, Lieutenant John M. Brooke and naval engineer William

P. Williamson. Mallory asked the men to sketch out plans for the conversion of the hulk into an armored warship, able to "prevent all blockade and encounter … their entire navy." His trio of designers was perfectly chosen. They inspected the *Merrimac*, ordered her salvage, and designed her rebirth as a revolutionary new warship. On 11 July they presented their proposals to Mallory, who was delighted and immediately gave the design his approval. He immediately wrote to Flag Officer French Forrest, the new Confederate commandant of the yard: "You will proceed with all practical dispatch to make changes in the *Merrimack* and to build, equip and fit her in all respects … you will see that work progresses without delay to completion." As the Battle of Bull Run ensured the survival of the Confederacy for another year, work began on the creation of the Confederate answer to the Union's naval blockade.

As early as 24 May the *Merrimac* was raised and hauled into Norfolk's dry dock. Mallory estimated that the work to convert the *Merrimac* would cost $172,523, a sizeable portion of his Department's allocated budget. He went ahead with the work without arguing for additional funding from the Confederate Congress, now housed in Richmond, Virginia. He understood that time was vital. Mallory commissioned the building of other casemate ironclads to protect the Mississippi River, but he realized the importance of the *Merrimac* project. The Union was also becoming uneasy, particularly when, on 17 October, Stringham's replacement Flag Officer Louis M. Goldsborough reported to Gideon Welles that: "I am now quite satisfied that … she will, in all probability, prove to be exceedingly formidable." News of the project had already caused the Union Navy Department to launch their own ironclad program, but it was increasingly becoming clear that both navies were locked in a race. If the Confederates were first to commission their ironclad, they could decimate the Union blockading squadron lying off Hampton Roads. Goldsborough sent regular reports, reporting in mid-October that the *Merrimac* was, "still in the dry dock at Norfolk, and yet needs a goodly quantity of iron to complete her casing, all of which is furnished from Richmond. She has her old engines on board, and they have been made to work tolerably well." He expected her to be ready by the start of November. This was an estimate that failed to take the Confederacy's

ABOVE **When the decision was made to abandon Norfolk Navy Yard, the USS *Cumberland* protected the base with her guns as Union sailors and soldiers destroyed ships that couldn't be removed to safety and ferried stores to Fort Monroe. (LoV)**

RIGHT **The destruction of the wooden steam frigate USS *Merrimac* at Washington Navy Yard, early in the morning of 19 April 1861. The vessel was burned to the waterline, but her lower hull and engines escaped serious damage, and were reused by the Confederate Navy. (Hensley)**

industrial and transport problems into account. The Tredegar Iron Works was reportedly "pressed beyond endurance" to fulfill the demands of the Navy Department. When plate was ready, it was sent by train from Richmond to Portsmouth via Petersburg, although the Army had priority, and trains carrying iron plates were frequently shunted into sidings or re-routed to allow troop or munitions trains to pass. Another problem was the shortage of railroad flatcars that could carry the weight of the metal plates. According to their records, the Tredegar Iron Works supplied 725 tons of armored plates for use on the *Merrimac*, for a total cost of $123,615. The majority of these were 10ft long, 8in. wide

The Norfolk Navy Yard was actually located in the southern suburb of Portsmouth known as Gosport. This photograph was taken after the virtual destruction of the base on 18–19 April 1861. The US Navy's failure to destroy the dry dock would have major repercussions. (LoV)

and 2in. thick, pre-drilled to allow them to be bolted to the wooden framework of the *Merrimac*'s casemate.

The sheer scale of the casemate was a challenge to Porter and his team of engineers. The structure was 172ft long, 30ft wide, and 7ft high. The rounded corners were a problem, as plate had to be curved, and the Tredegar works lacked the powerful hydraulic presses found in other yards. Work on these corners was, therefore, slow and laborious. Another problem was the production of a huge 1,500lb iron ram, which Porter wanted attached to the ironclad's bow, some 2ft below the waterline. The piece was duly produced, but neither Porter or the ironworkers knew how this ram would perform in combat. Ramming was a tactic used by galleys in the Mediterranean as late as the Renaissance, but the advent of reliable firepower at sea made the device redundant. Porter's "re-invention" of the ram demonstrated the extent to which he, Mallory, and other Confederate designers were leading a revolution in naval warfare.

The armament was supplied from two sources: the six 9in. Dahlgren's, which formed the bulk of the vessel's broadside armament, came from the stockpile of weapons captured when the Norfolk Navy Yard was captured. Some accounts claim they were the guns that were originally carried on the *Merrimac*, but there is no hard evidence to support this. Mallory was a strong advocate for the adoption of rifled ordnance. Under the guidance of Lieutenant Brooke, four rifled guns were cast at the Tredegar ironworks; two 6.4in. pieces, which would be fired as part of the main broadside, and two 7in. rifles, mounted at the bow and stern. The rifled guns were Brooke's own design, although they were for the most part improved versions of the Parrott guns used by the Union. The Confederates recognized the advantages of rifled guns, but although highly accurate, in practice their effectiveness was limited by problems with the supply of reliable projectiles and powder.

By the New Year of 1862, deserters reported to the Union that "the last of the iron plates for the *Merrimac* were put on". In fact, the ironclad was far from ready, as shortages of iron, guns, fittings, and almost all types of supplies delayed her construction. The ironclad was still weeks from completion, and although Flag Officer Buchanan arrived to oversee her completion, the ironclad was still short of a crew to man her.

ERICSSON'S FOLLY

On 3 August 1861, the Union Navy Department secured Federal funding to build ironclads in response to the threat posed by the *Merrimac*. The "Ironclad Board" reviewed the 16 tenders that had been submitted, and encouraged by the financier Cornelius Bushnell, and prompted by Welles, the Board reluctantly approved the design proposed by John Ericsson. None of the board members were engineers, or even advocates of ironclad warships, but all three members understood the danger facing the blockading squadron in Hampton Roads. Of the two other tenders approved, the ironclad gunboat USS *Galena* would be commissioned in April 1862, and the powerful casemate ironclad USS *New Ironsides* would enter service four months later. As reports suggested the *Merrimac* would be ready for service by February at the latest, Ericsson's design for a turreted

When the Confederates captured Norfolk Navy Yard on the morning of 19 April 1861, they found 1,085 pieces of ordnance that had survived the destruction. These included modern Dahlgren smoothbores, which were subsequently mounted in the *Virginia*. (Hensley)

ironclad was the only vessel of the three that stood any chance of being commissioned in time to counter the *Merrimac*.

Ericsson was a designer of moderate means, and he lacked the capital needed to start work on the project. His alliance with the Connecticut financier Cornelius Bushnell ensured he had the support of Bushnell's friend Gideon Welles. It also brought Ericsson into contact with Bushnell's two partners, John Griswold and John Winslow, both of whom owned foundries on the Hudson River. It also ensured funds were available to undertake the project. On 27 September the four men signed a contract with the Navy and work began immediately.

The agreement signed by Ericsson and his three backers specified the vessel would be completed in just over four months. Sub-contracting much of the work helped speed the process, and the constituent parts would then be brought to the Continental Iron Works in Brooklyn for final assembly, under the supervision of Ericsson. The turret plates were to be manufactured in the Abbot foundry in Baltimore, while the hull plates came from John Winslow's own works in New York. Ericsson made all the design decisions; many of which involved compromises, such as the decision to use 1in. rather than 2in. plate for the turret, as the thicker metal would take too long to produce. The Novelty Iron Works of New York constructed the turret, as they had the most suitable hydraulic presses to bend the plate supplied by Abbot. Ericsson's friend Cornelius Delamater built the engines in his foundry in New York, while auxiliary engines were produced under contract in another foundry. As Ericsson boasted afterwards, production began even before the Navy Department clerks had drawn up the contract.

To many serving naval officers, the idea of a semi-submerged floating ironclad warship was preposterous, and they ridiculed the project in the press. Newspaper reporters dubbed the vessel "Ericsson's folly", and some contemporaries even doubted she would float. The initial contract specified the inclusion of "masts, spars, sails and rigging", a freeboard of 18in., and demanded that the vessel carry sufficient stores and water to

Camp Butler was sited close to Newport News Point, and served as a holding camp for troops garrisoning the tip of the Virginia Peninsula. Detachments of sharpshooters from the camp were used to provide supporting fire for the *Cumberland* and *Congress*. (LoV)

feed 100 men for three months. Clearly these were all devices added by the Navy to compromise the project, as was the clause whereby Ericsson and his backers remained liable for the vessel until the Navy approved its design. Twenty-five percent of the cost of the vessel was withheld by the Navy Department until the vessel's captain pronounced her a seaworthy and effective warship. This meant that when the *Monitor* steamed toward the *Virginia*, she was still partly owned by her builders!

The keel was laid on 25 October, and during the following month the project took shape. The lower hull was completed within three weeks, and work began on the raft-like upper hull. The turret was shipped to the Brooklyn yard in pieces, then assembled *in situ*. The engines were tested, then disassembled and installed before the vessel's deck beams were fitted. Ignoring the contract stipulations, the *Monitor*'s coal bunkers were sufficient for just over a week of steaming, which Ericsson considered sufficient for the needs of the vessel. By the first days of January, the vessel was nearing completion, and Ericsson informed the Navy Department that he wanted to call her the *Monitor*, so that "the ironclad … will thus prove a severe monitor" to the Confederacy. He added that "this last Yankee notion, this monitor" would also amaze the British. The name was approved, and on 30 January 1862 the *Monitor* was launched into the East River. Thousands had come to watch the launch, and many considered her the epitome of the "iron coffin" the vessel had been dubbed in the press. Confounding many of her critics, she floated. Ericsson's folly was almost ready for service, just four months after the Navy ordered her to be built. Ericsson ignored the contractual obligations to supply stores, masts, and other non-essentials, and instead he supplied the Navy with a revolutionary warship, custom built to fight Confederate ironclads.

Two weeks before the launch, the Navy Department named Lieutenant John Worden her first Commanding Officer, and Worden duly arrived at the Brooklyn Yard on 16 January. Worden was an experienced naval officer, and although a quiet, retiring man, one of his officers reckoned, "he will not hesitate to submit our iron sides to as severe a test as the most warlike could desire." As soon as the *Monitor* was launched he led his volunteer crew on board and together with Ericsson he examined his new command. He also supervised the installation of the two 11in. Dahlgren smoothbore guns into the *Monitor's* turret. Despite pleas for larger 12in. Dahlgren pieces, the commandant at Brooklyn Navy Yard reported that none were available. It was the Navy's last attempt to prevent the ironclad's completion. Like many other features about the *Monitor*, her armament was a compromise, as Worden and Ericsson settled for 11in. guns instead. Worden formally took command of the ironclad at 2.00pm on 19 February 1862, and although an initial trial demonstrated problems with her engines, the vessel was duly commissioned into the Navy six days later. The USS *Monitor* was ready for active service.

THE LONG VOYAGE SOUTH

John Ericsson never claimed that the USS *Monitor* was an ocean-going vessel. Instead, it was designed for use in shallow coastal waters such as Hampton Roads. Lieutenant Worden completed his provisioning of the *Monitor* in Brooklyn Navy Yard, and on 4 March he received his orders to take her to Hampton Roads. The Atlantic seaboard was in the grip of a severe storm, so Worden delayed his departure for two days, waiting for the storm to subside. At 11.00am on 6 March he secured a towline from the screw tug *Seth Low*, and was led out of New York harbor. The tug was there to augment the small engines of the *Monitor*, and to be ready to help in the event of any mishap. The wooden screw gunboats USS *Sachem* and USS *Currituck* provided an armed escort.

By the end of the afternoon watch (4.00pm), the flotilla rounded Sandy Hook and turned south to follow the New Jersey coast. The

The incomplete walls of Fort Wool were built on the Rip Raps shoal, halfway between Old Point Comfort and Willoughby's Spit. It, therefore, helped seal off the entrance into Hampton Roads from Chesapeake Bay. (Casemate)

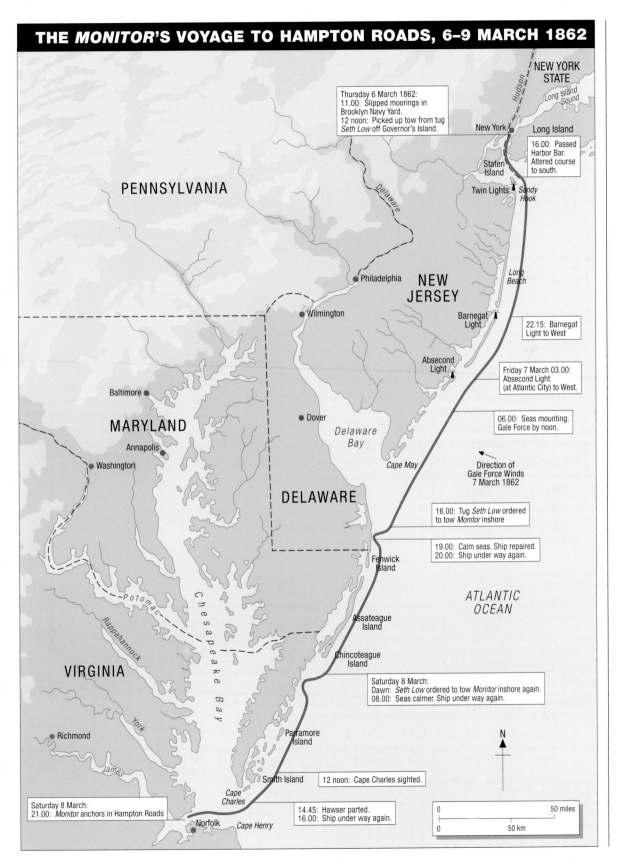

THE *MONITOR*'S VOYAGE TO HAMPTON ROADS, 6–9 MARCH 1862

NEW YORK STATE

Long Island Sound

Hudson

New York

Long Island

Staten Island

16.00: Passed Harbor Bar. Altered course to south.

Twin Lights

Sandy Hook

Thursday 6 March 1862:
11.00: Slipped moorings in Brooklyn Navy Yard.
12 noon: Picked up tow from tug *Seth Low* off Governor's Island.

PENNSYLVANIA

Delaware

Philadelphia

NEW JERSEY

Long Beach

Wilmington

Barnegat Light

22.15: Barnegat Light to West

Absecond Light

Friday 7 March 03.00: Absecond Light (at Atlantic City) to West.

Baltimore

Dover

Delaware Bay

06.00: Seas mounting. Gale Force by noon.

MARYLAND

Annapolis

Washington

Cape May

Direction of Gale Force Winds 7 March 1862

DELAWARE

16.00: Tug *Seth Low* ordered to tow *Monitor* inshore

19.00: Calm seas. Ship repaired.
20.00: Ship under way again.

Fenwick Island

Potomac

C h e s a p e a k e   B a y

ATLANTIC OCEAN

Rappahannock

Assateague Island

Chincoteague Island

VIRGINIA

Saturday 8 March:
Dawn: *Seth Low* ordered to tow *Monitor* inshore again.
08.00: Seas calmer. Ship under way again.

York

Richmond

Parramore Island

James

N

Smith Island

12 noon: Cape Charles sighted.

0 ——— 50 miles

0 ——— 50 km

Saturday 8 March:
21.00: *Monitor* anchors in Hampton Roads

Cape Charles

14.45: Hawser parted.
16.00: Ship under way again.

Norfolk

Cape Henry

Brigadier General Joseph K. F. Mansfield (center figure) **commanded the Union forces at Camp Butler and Newport News Point during the battle. His attempts to prevent the Confederates reaching the** *Congress* **after she had surrendered led to the destruction of the vessel. (Hensley)**

Monitor continued on throughout the night, and sea conditions were relatively calm. The Navy Department's Chief Engineer, Alban Stimers, was attached to the ship to see how she performed. He recorded that despite the lack of swell, "as soon as we were outside of Sandy Hook the sea washed over the deck so deeply that it was not considered safe to permit the men to go on deck." Whatever the conditions, they seem to have deteriorated during the night. By 10.15pm Barnegat Light on Long Beach was due west, and the log recorded "fine weather." Seven hours later it reported it was "cold and clear," and the flotilla was six miles to seaward of the Absecond Light at Atlantic City. This meant the *Monitor* made an average speed of 5 knots throughout the night. By dawn conditions had worsened. A light gale had reappeared from the west, and at 6.00am the log recorded "very heavy sea. Ship making heavy weather." Worden was suffering from severe sea sickness, and moved to the top of the turret to revive himself. By mid-morning it was clear the *Monitor* had been caught in a full gale, and water broke over the turret. It even slammed through the vision slit in the pilothouse with such force that the helmsman was knocked over. The ship started leaking from the base of the turret. It had been designed to rest on a brass ring when not in use, and Ericsson argued that the weight of the turret provided an adequate seal. Worden had ignored Ericsson's advice, and had raised the turret, caulked the ring with oakum and lowered it again. The oakum had washed away, and water poured through "like a waterfall". Seawater also poured down into the engine room through ventilation ducts, soaking the leather belts that turned the engine fans. They were designed to remove poisonous fumes, and the water stopped them working. Within an hour the engine room was filled with carbon dioxide and carbonic gas. During the afternoon the engineers struggled to restart the blowers, but the fumes forced them to abandon the attempt. Chief Engineer Isaac Newton ordered the engine room abandoned, but the fumes quickly spread throughout the ship. Half-sinking and filled with poisonous gases, the *Monitor* was in danger of foundering, and Worden signaled for help. The *Seth Low* towed her into the shore, and in calmer waters, the engineers managed to vent the engine room and restart their machinery, including the pumps. Disaster had been averted.

The launch of the USS *Monitor* on 30 January 1862 was witnessed by thousands of spectators, many of whom were convinced the ironclad would never float. This contemporary lithograph is incorrect, as her turret was fitted after she was launched. (US Navy)

By 8.00pm on Friday 7 March, the *Monitor* was ready to resume her journey. The gale had passed on to the north and sea conditions were moderate as she steamed southwards past Fenwick Island. Lieutenant Greene reported a "smooth sea, clear sky, the moon out, and the old tank going along five and six knots very nicely." Around midnight they passed Chincoteague Island on the Maryland coast, but soon afterwards the swell increased. Water passed through the hawsepipe, making a "dismal, awful sound", and Worden ordered the hawsepipe stopped up to prevent any leaks. The seas started breaking over the smokestacks and ventilation ducts again. For the next few hours it remained doubtful whether the engines could continue, but somehow they kept turning. At one point the tiller ropes came loose, and the vessel turned "broadside to the seas and rolling over and over in all kinds of ways." It seemed likely the *Monitor* would be capsized if struck by a rogue wave, but within half an hour the wheel was working again. By dawn the seas had abated slightly, allowing Worden to signal the *Seth Low* to tow her inshore again. By 8.00am the *Monitor* and her escorts were in sheltered coastal waters again, and the crew ate breakfast. They had come close to disaster twice, but the ironclad remained afloat and her engines still worked. She was pumped dry and the voyage south continued.

At noon the quartermaster recorded "fine weather and clear sky." The worst was behind them, and Worden sighted Cape Charles, marking the northern entrance to Chesapeake Bay. The *Monitor* was on the last leg of her epic maiden voyage. At 2.45pm the *Seth Low's* towing hawser parted, but this was quickly replaced and the flotilla resumed its progress. A few minutes later Cape Henry Light became visible, and further to the right smoke lingered over Hampton Roads. Lieutenant Keeler recorded "as we approached still nearer little black spots could occasionally be seen." These were shells bursting in the air. Worden assumed the worst. Unable to steam any faster, he prepared his ship for action. When a pilot boat came out to meet the *Monitor*, the Pilot confirmed their fears. The *Merrimac* was destroying the blockading squadron. It was 9.00pm when Worden finally dropped anchor in Hampton Roads alongside the flagship USS *Roanoke*. He immediately sent a message to Washington announcing his safe arrival. Captain and crew then prepared themselves for the battle that would almost certainly take place the following morning.

BUCHANAN TAKES COMMAND

On or around 14 February the *Merrimac* was relaunched, and on 16 February 1862 the Navy officially acquired the *Merrimac*, which was duly, renamed the CSS *Virginia*. There was no ceremony, and one sailor recorded "only four marines and a corporal were on board at her launching." A week later Flag Officer Franklin Buchanan arrived in Norfolk to oversee the completion of the ironclad. "Old Buck" and his staff found her far from ready for action, particularly as the vessel was still short of crewmen. While the Executive Officer, Lieutenant Smith, supervised the last-minute preparations of the *Virginia*, Buchanan sent Lieutenant John Wood, the grandson of President Zachary Taylor, to ask the Army for help. Wood met General Magruder near Yorktown, and of the 200 men who volunteered, the naval officer selected 80 artillerymen or former seamen to serve on board the *Virginia*. Jones was a hard taskmaster, and he hounded the construction crew and dockyard staff, while complaining to Buchanan about "the want of skilled labor and

The USS *Monitor* as she looked when she was commissioned. Following the battle, improvements were made to her pilot house and to her smokestacks (funnels), which were too low to prevent seawater from pouring into the boilers. (Hensley)

lack of proper tools and appliances." Everything in the wartime Confederacy was in short supply, and constant delays in the delivery of iron, coal, ammunition, powder, caulking, ropes, and lubricating oil kept Jones fully occupied. At one stage he even sent a naval party up the railroad track toward Petersburg to locate a missing shipment of iron.

While these preparations continued, Buchanan considered how best to use the ironclad. She drew 22ft of water, and the waters of the Elizabeth River and Hampton Roads were a maze of shallows and narrow channels. She was going to be difficult to turn, and given the constricted waters between Norfolk and Newport News Point, Buchanan was severely limited as to where he could steam. Even with a good local pilot, he would be unable to get close to either Fort Monroe or Newport News, and a large patch of shallows between Sewell's Point and Pig Point limited her area of operations even further. It was unlikely that the *Virginia* could sail far up the James River toward Richmond, but at least she could attack the larger vessels of the blockading squadron, forcing them to flee or run aground to avoid destruction.

On 4 March, Buchanan wrote to Mallory from "aboard the C.S. Steam Frigate *Virginia*." He acknowledged receipt of his appointment as Flag Officer commanding "the Naval Defenses of the James River," and he reported that "today I hoisted my flag aboard this ship." He went on to outline his plan of operation. "On Thursday night the 6th instant, I contemplate leaving here to appear before the Enemy's Ships at Newport News. Should no accident occur to this ship, when I feel confident that the acts of the *Virginia* will give proof of the desire of her officers and crew to meet the views of the Department as far as practicable." Buchanan was referring to Mallory's stated aim to use the ironclad to break the Union blockade of the Chesapeake. He added: "From the best and most reliable information I can obtain from experienced pilots it will be impossible to ascend the Potomac in the *Virginia* with the present draft of water, nearly 22 feet." He was gently letting Mallory know that his pipe dream of using the *Virginia* to bombard Washington was exactly that.

Buchanan wrote to Commander Tucker of the "James River Squadron," asking him to stand by to assist his attack. Jones counseled a delay. None of the gunport shutters had been fitted, and powder and shot had only just arrived. The attack was delayed for a day, allowing Jones to grease the casemate sides to "increase the tendency of projectiles to glance," and to rig temporary gunport shutters at the bow and stern. All the crew went on board on Thursday 6 March, and in Jones' words, "all preparations were made." Pilots were consulted, and a further postponement was recommended, as navigation of the Elizabeth River would be easier. The *Virginia*'s sortie against the enemy fleet would take place at dawn on Saturday 8 March 1862.

THE BATTLE OF HAMPTON ROADS

"BLACK SMOKE IN THE ELIZABETH RIVER"
The Sortie of the CSS *Virginia*, Saturday 8 March 1862

Flag Officer Buchanan's plan to attack the Union blockading fleet in Hampton Roads on Thursday 6 March was cancelled. The CSS *Virginia* was still not ready for action, and Lieutenant Jones begged for a few more days to finish preparing the ironclad. Buchanan had planned a night attack, but local pilots refused to take responsibility for guiding the ship up the Elizabeth River in the dark. The attack was postponed until Saturday morning. Even then, the gunport shields would still not be fitted, and finishing work on the warship such as the construction of internal compartments had to wait until after her maiden voyage. Lieutenant Wood recorded that prior to her sailing into action, "not a gun had been fired, hardly a revolution of her engines had been made." The ugly, ungainly *Virginia* would have to go into battle without the luxury of being fully completed, or even having run sea trials to test her performance. Neither her officers nor men knew what to expect. As the ironclad prepared for action, Buchanan claimed that she was only going to

The tug *Seth Low* towed the USS *Monitor* out of the Brooklyn Navy Yard, and then escorted her during the ironclad's eventful voyage south to Hampton Roads. On two occasions the tug had to tow the *Monitor* inshore to prevent her from being swamped. (US Army Military History Institute)

Sailors manning the hand-operated pumps inside the USS *Monitor*. During her voyage from New York to Hampton Roads the ironclad was almost swamped in heavy seas. Nine months later she foundered off Cape Hatteras in similar conditions. (Author's Collection)

perform trials on the Elizabeth River. Nobody seemed fooled by this, and the local press and public were well aware that the ironclad would sail into action against the enemy on Saturday morning. Buchanan briefed the commander of the James River Squadron, and requested that the three gunboats be ready to cooperate with him on Saturday morning. Apart from the ironclad itself, everything else was ready for the coming battle.

Lieutenant Jones later wrote of her condition before she went into action. "The lower part of her shield forward was only immersed a few inches instead of two feet as intended, and there was but one inch of iron on the (lower) hull. The port-shutters, etc. were unfinished. The *Virginia* was unseaworthy; her engines were unreliable, and her draft, over 22 feet, prevented her from going to Washington ..." The surgeon Dinwiddie Phillips wrote that "many of those who watched us predicted failure." A naval friend of H. Ashton Ramsay, the *Virginia's* Chief Engineer took the opportunity to tease his colleague, exclaiming "Goodbye Ramsay. I shall never see you again. She will prove your coffin." Many others probably shared these sentiments. Ramsay claimed there was an air of desperation in Flag Officer Buchanan as he ordered the workmen to leave the ship, and prepared the ironclad for her

The USS *Monitor* in heavy seas. Given her low freeboard, even a gentle swell could be enough to cause the ironclad to founder. Watercolor by Clary Roy, c.1900. (US Navy)

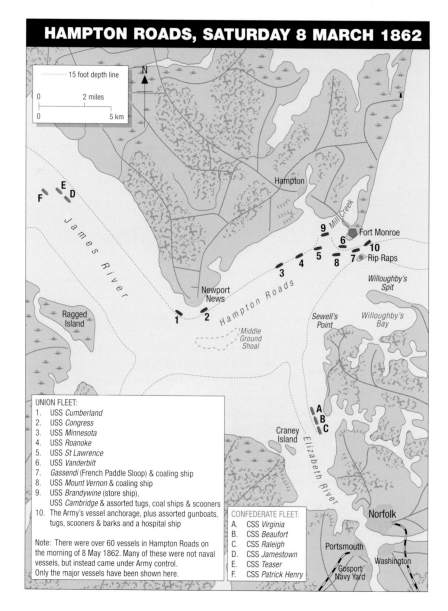

---- 15 foot depth line

0   2 miles
0   5 km

N

Hampton

James River

Mill Creek

Fort Monroe

Newport News

Hampton Roads

Ragged Island

Middle Ground Shoal

Willoughby's Spit

Willoughby's Bay

Sewell's Point

Rip Raps

Craney Island

Elizabeth River

Norfolk

Portsmouth

Washington

Gosport/ Navy Yard

UNION FLEET:
1. USS *Cumberland*
2. USS *Congress*
3. USS *Minnesota*
4. USS *Roanoke*
5. USS *St Lawrence*
6. USS *Vanderbilt*
7. *Gassendi* (French Paddle Sloop) & coaling ship
8. USS *Mount Vernon* & coaling ship
9. USS *Brandywine* (store ship),
    USS *Cambridge* & assorted tugs, coal ships & scooners
10. The Army's vessel anchorage, plus assorted gunboats,
    tugs, scooners & barks and a hospital ship

Note: There were over 60 vessels in Hampton Roads on
the morning of 8 May 1862. Many of these were not naval
vessels, but instead came under Army control.
Only the major vessels have been shown here.

CONFEDERATE FLEET:
A. CSS *Virginia*
B. CSS *Beaufort*
C. CSS *Raleigh*
D. CSS *Jamestown*
E. CSS *Teaser*
F. CSS *Patrick Henry*

journey down the river. The tug CSS *Beaufort* (commanded by Lieutenant William H. Parker, CSN) nudged the ironclad away from the dock, and the *Virginia* slowly moved into the river channel, the Beaufort following like a protective hen. It was 11.00am.

It was ten miles from the wharf in Gosport to Hampton Roads. The ironclad had a top speed of about five or six knots, but made seven with the river current. It would be at least 1½ hours before she would engage the enemy, giving ample time for the entire garrison and population of Norfolk and its hinterland to watch her journey down the Elizabeth River. While Flag Officer Buchanan paced the upper spar deck of the *Virginia*, thousands of onlookers crowded the banks and waved at him. One crewman also noted that some "seemed too deeply moved by the gravity of the moment to break into cheers." Small boats jostled for position as the *Beaufort* and *Virginia* steamed past them, but "no voice broke the silence of the scene; all hearts were too full for utterance. All

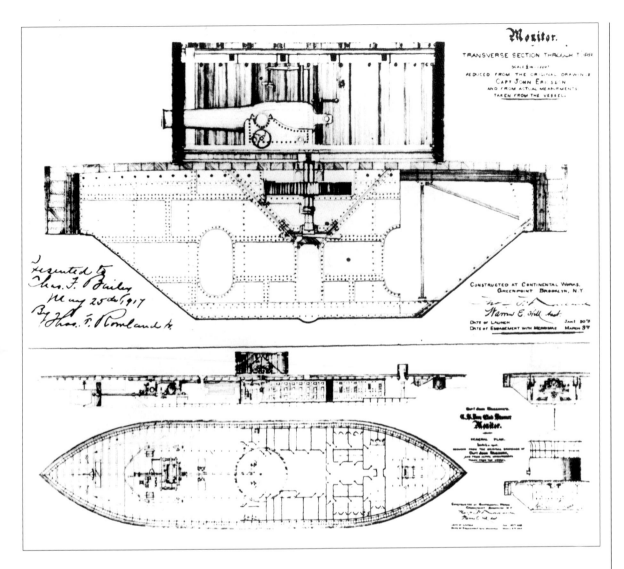

A cross-section through the turret of the USS *Monitor*, showing her guns run forward into their firing position. Thomas Rowland of the Continental Iron Works presented the plan to the Mariners Museum. (Mariners)

present knew that this was a decisive moment for the Confederacy. If the *Virginia* broke the enemy blockade, then there was a significant chance that the nation would gain the recognition and support of foreign powers such as Britain and France. With their support, the survival of the Confederacy was far more likely. William F. Drake, an artilleryman who had volunteered to crew one of the guns knew "ten thousand waving handkerchiefs told us that in their hearts they were bidding us Godspeed!" A local journalist was more eloquent. "It was a gallant sight to see the ironclad leviathan gliding noiselessly through the water flying the red pennant of her commander at the fore flag staff and the gay Confederate ensign aft…" To the inexperienced eye, all was going smoothly. In fact, the *Virginia's* steering mechanism was proving to be highly erratic, and two miles below Norfolk, Jones hailed the *Beaufort* and requested a tow. The ironclad would continue down the river under tow from the tugboat. A second armed tugboat, the CSS *Raleigh* was also called to help keep the *Virginia's* bows pointed down river.

It was at this stage that Buchanan stopped pacing and questioned Ramsay, his engineer. He asked him: "what would happen to your

engines and boilers if there should be a collision?" Ramsay replied that they would take the shock of impact. Buchanan then turned and addressed his senior officers. "I am going to ram the *Cumberland*. I am told she has the new rifled guns, the only ones in their whole fleet we have cause to fear. The moment we are in the roads, I'm going to make right for her and ram her." The decision had been made. The hands were piped to dinner, and the crew prepared themselves for battle. Ramsay went to join the other officers behind the curtained-off wardroom, but he passed the assistant surgeon laying out his instruments. "The sight took away my appetite," he recalled.

By noon, the *Virginia* and her consorts had drawn level with Sewell's Point, guarding the mouth of the Elizabeth River. For the first time, the crew could make out the enemy ships on the northern shore of Hampton Roads. Ramsay remembered seeing: "*Congress* and *Cumberland*, tall and stately, with every line and spar clearly defined against the blue March sky." The journalist from the *Norfolk Day Book* described his first view of the two Union ships "rising like prodigious castles over the placid water." The rigging of the USS *Cumberland* was covered with sailors' clothing hung out to dry, giving the ship a somewhat festive appearance. It looked as if the *Virginia*'s sortie had taken the Union fleet by surprise.

There were over 60 Union vessels in Hampton Roads that morning; warships, transports, supply ships, tugs, dispatch vessels, and tenders. Most of the vessels were powered by sail, and all lacked any form of armored protection. While many were naval vessels (or at least operated by the Navy), others came under the control of the Army Quartermaster Corps. Even the warships included a strange assortment of vessels, from powerful wooden steam frigates to former New York ferry boats that had been hastily converted into gunboats. The flagship of the Hampton Roads squadron was the USS *Minnesota*, an unarmored wooden steam-powered frigate mounting 43 large smoothbore guns. Rear-Admiral Louis M. Goldsborough was away at Hatteras Inlet, so Captain John Marston, the commander of the USS *Roanoke* was the senior Union naval officer in Hampton Roads that morning. The *Roanoke* was another

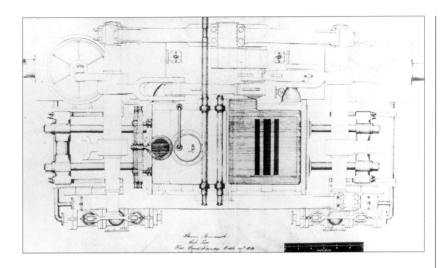

When Confederate engineers inspected them, they discovered that given work, the engines of the sunken wooden frigate *Merrimac* could be made to function again. Built at the West Point Foundry in New York State, the engines could produce 869 horsepower. (US Navy)

unarmored steam-powered frigate, but her engines were in the process of being overhauled, and her screw (propeller) shaft had been sent to Brooklyn Navy Yard. In order to join in any fight, she would have to use her sails, or else be towed into action. She carried 44 smoothbore guns. Captain Van Brunt commanded the *Minnesota*. She was anchored next to the *Vanderbilt*, one of the oddest ships in the squadron.

As a countermeasure against the *Virginia* the 5,000-ton transatlantic steamship had been recently chartered by the Navy. It was intended to plate her sides with iron, and to reinforce her bow with timber. If the *Virginia* appeared, the *Vanderbilt* would be used to ram her. The unarmed paddlewheel liner was still waiting for the work parties to begin her conversion when the *Virginia* sortied from the Elizabeth River. Anchored close to her was the USS *St. Lawrence*, a wooden sailing frigate that carried 42 guns of various sizes. All three of these warships lay off Fort Monroe, to the northeast of the mouth of the Elizabeth River.

Two more sailing warships lay to the northwest, off Newport News Point. The USS *Congress* was a wooden sailing frigate that carried 50 smoothbore guns. She was short of crew to man her, and although her full complement was 480 men, she was short of 80 men that morning, and even then her crew included a detachment of 89 soldiers from the 99th New York Infantry. She also had two captains. Commander W.B. Smith had just handed his ship over to Lieutenant Joseph B. Smith, but the Commander remained on board, waiting for a passage to take him to his new appointment. The Paymaster of the *Congress* was McKean Buchanan, the brother of the Confederate commander. Neither sibling knew that the other was on board either the *Virginia* or the *Congress*. Further to the west lay the wooden sailing sloop USS *Cumberland*, commanded by Captain William Radford. That morning he was away from his ship, as he was taking part in a court-martial on board the USS *Roanoke*. This meant his Executive Officer, Lieutenant George U. Morris was left in command. The *Cumberland* started her career as a sailing frigate, a sister ship of the *St. Lawrence*. Commissioned in 1845, she was "razeed" ten years later. This involved having her upper deck removed, making her a lower, lighter vessel. She was reclassified as a sloop. In March 1861 she carried 24 guns, including one rifled gun, mounted in her stern.

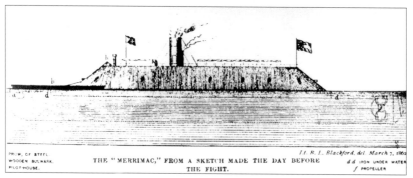

PROW, OF STEEL
WOODEN BULWARK,
PILOT-HOUSE.

THE "MERRIMAC," FROM A SKETCH MADE THE DAY BEFORE
THE FIGHT.

lt. R. L. Blackford, del. March 7, 1862

d d IRON UNDER WATER
f PROPELLER

The tugboat *Zouave* (commanded by Acting Master Henry Reaney) began her career towing grain barges on the upper Hudson River. Now she was berthed at the dock at Newport News, where she acted as the tug and guard vessel for the two sailing warships off the Point. Sources contradict each other, but two army transport vessels were probably moored to the same wharf. Of the remainder of the shipping in Hampton Roads, most were clustered around Fort Monroe, either on the eastern, Chesapeake Bay side of Point Comfort, or off her southwest side. Other vessels lay further inshore, closer to the burned remains of the village of Hampton. These ships included the store ship *Brandywine*, a sister ship of the *St. Lawrence* and the *Cumberland*.

Anchored between Fort Monroe and Fort Wool was the small French paddlewheel gunboat *Gassendi*, commanded by Captain Ange Simon Gautier. She was there to observe any clash between the blockading squadron and the *Virginia*, and report the outcome to the French government. A group of her officers had just returned from a visit to Norfolk under a flag of truce. As neutral observers, the French naval officers were allowed to see the *Virginia*, but kept their observations to themselves. They were there as impartial observers, and over the next two days they were presented with a spectacle that her Captain would find "très intéressante."

The *Gassendi* provided the Union Navy with the first indication that something was about to happen. Around 10.00am she began taking on coal, an indication that she planned to shift her anchorage. Protocol demanded that she inform the Union flagship of any plan to depart, so that both nations could exchange the correct salutes. No such notification had been made. As the staff in Fort Monroe were well aware

The powerful wooden steam frigate USS *Merrimac* pictured entering Southampton Harbour during a courtesy visit to Britain in September 1856. In her day she was the most powerful and up-to-date vessel in the US Navy. (Mariners)

that the French had visited Norfolk the previous day, they suspected the French knew something, and planned to get out of the line of fire of the Fort. The Fort's commander, Major General John E. Wool, sent a telegram to Brigadier General Joseph K. Mansfield, commanding the Union troops encamped near Newport News Point. It asked him to keep a sharp lookout. Mansfield duly ordered the gun batteries lining the point to be manned and ready. Despite the warning, there was little other activity among the Union ships and men in the area. Many believed that the *Virginia* was far from ready, and there was little chance of action that morning. Soon after 11.00am, the signalers manning Mansfield's lookout station on Newport News Point reported seeing smoke rising far up the Elizabeth River. There was some form of Confederate naval activity going on, and Mansfield sent a telegram to Wool, claiming that "the *Merrimack* is close at hand." Apparently, neither General saw fit to share their suspicions with their naval colleagues. When the *Virginia* appeared off Sewell's Point, the Union blockading squadron was caught completely unprepared. The washing hanging from the rigging of the *Cumberland* was ample evidence of the fleet's lack of readiness.

To Lieutenant Tom Selfridge of the *Cumberland*, the early spring morning was "mild, bright and clear." With hardly any wind to ruffle the glassy surface of Hampton Roads, it promised to be a beautiful day. This all changed at about 12.45pm, when Henry Reaney on the *Zouave* noticed "black smoke in the Elizabeth River." He cast off and steamed alongside the *Cumberland*, where Selfridge was the officer of the deck. He had also spotted the smoke, and ordered Reaney to investigate. Within minutes the *Zouave* was heading south toward Pig Point, on the southern shore of the Roads. Reaney later reported: "It did not take us long to find out, for we had not gone over two miles when we saw what to all appearances looked like the roof of a very large barn belching forth smoke as from a chimney fire." The *Zouave* fired her 30-pdr. Parrot

Representation of the gun crews in action on board the CSS *Virginia*. Although the gun ports are too large and the wrong shape, the details of the guns, carriages and crew are accurate. The guns shown are her 9in. Dahlgren smoothbores, part of her broadside armament. (Hensley)

rifle six times, then spun around and headed back towards the relative safety of Newport News. The time was 1.20pm. Reaney had fired the opening shots in the Battle of Hampton Roads. At the same time as Selfridge and Reaney spotted the *Virginia*, lookouts elsewhere in the squadron spotted the enemy warships. The logbook of the *Minnesota* that morning recorded that: "at 12.45pm saw three steamers off Sewell's Point standing towards Newport News; one of these was supposed to be the *Merrimack* from the size of her smokestack. We immediately slipped chain with buoy and rope attached at the 15-fathom shackle and steamed towards Newport News." Signals alerted the rest of the fleet, and the alarm drum call alerted the garrisons of Fort Monroe and Camp Butler. The French Captain Gautier shared Reaney's views concerning the appearance of the *Virginia*, which he described as "a barracks room surmounted by a large funnel." On board the Confederate ironclad, Chief Engineer Ramsay recorded the effect the *Virginia* had on the shipping in Hampton Roads. "The white-winged sailing craft that sprinkled the bay and long lines of tugs and boats scurried to the far shore like chickens on the approach of a hovering hawk." The *Minnesota* was seen to raise steam, and the clotheslines on the *Cumberland* were ripped down. Sails were raised on the *Congress*. The combatants on both sides prepared for battle.

"All was lost except honor." The destruction of the *Cumberland*

Before he led the *Virginia* into action, Flag Officer Buchanan addressed his crew. "Sailors, in a few minutes you will have the long-looked-for opportunity of showing your devotion to our cause. Remember that you are about to strike for your country and your homes. The Confederacy expects every man to do his duty. Beat to Quarters!" The crew went to their stations, and one would note that: "the strictest discipline was in force on our gun deck, no one at the guns was allowed to talk, not even in a whisper. Everything was ready, guns loaded, and run out for action...." On the *Congress*, Captain Smith made a less Nelsonian speech.

"My hearties, you see before you the great southern bugaboo, got up to frighten us out of our wits. Stand to your guns, and let me assure you that one good broadside from our gallant frigate and she is ours!" A similar silence then descended on the *Congress* as her crew watched the *Virginia* approach. Further to the east, the *Minnesota* was steaming toward Newport News, while the tugs *Dragon* and *Young America* were preparing to tow the *Roanoke* into action. The gunboat USS *Cambridge* already had the *St. Lawrence* under tow. An observer on the gunboat USS *Mystic* described it as "a sorry fleet to attack a vessel like the *Merrimack*...." The *Virginia* veered a little to starboard, then to port, as she tested her steering. She then headed straight for the *Congress*.

At around 2.00pm, the *Beaufort* fired the first Confederate shot of the day at the *Congress*. She was steaming on the port beam of the *Virginia*, and the shot was in response to Buchanan's signal, ordering "Close Action." The shot fell short. The fragile little armed tug stayed in the middle of Hampton Roads, as closing any further with the *Congress* would be suicidal. The *Virginia* steamed on alone. A few miles to the east, the wooden Union warships making their way toward Newport News came under fire from Sewell's Point soon after 2.00pm. One shot hit the *Minnesota's* mainmast, and she returned the fire while repairs were made. The other Union warships altered course to stay out of range.

The *Congress* held her fire until her gunners could make out the ports and armored plates on the casemate of the *Virginia* (around 500 yards). She then "tried her with a solid shot from one of our stern guns, the projectile glancing off her forward casemate like a drop of water from a duck's back...." At approximately 2.20pm the *Virginia* replied by firing a round of grapeshot from her forward gun, which killed or wounded about a dozen sailors on board the frigate. Next, with "a tremendous roar," the *Congress* fired her full broadside of 25 guns, including five 8in. Dahlgren smoothbores. Watching from the shore, Private Josh Lewis of the 20th Indiana Regiment recalled that the broadside "rattled on the armored *Merrimack* without the least injury."

The CSS *Virginia* managed to rake the stern of the stranded wooden frigate USS *Congress* from a range of less than 200 yards. Her fire turned the frigate into a "charnel house". (VWM)

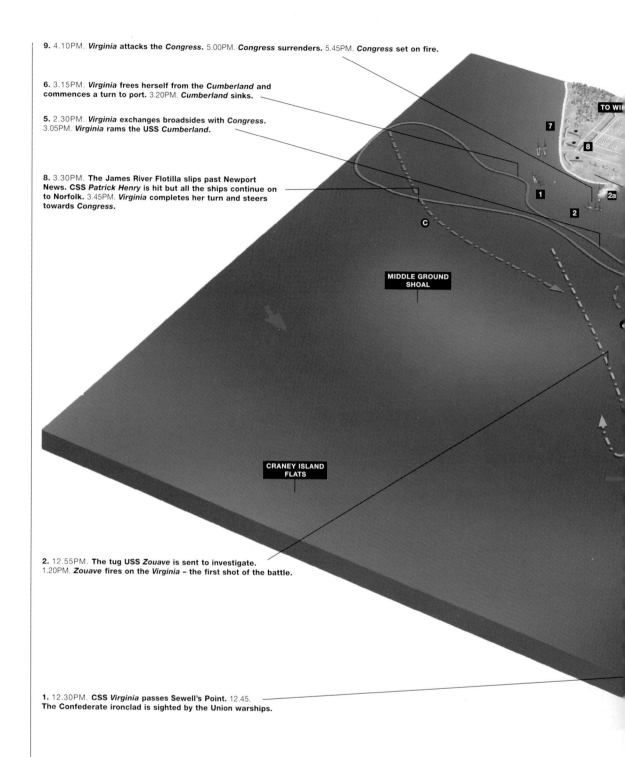

9. 4.10PM. *Virginia* attacks the *Congress*. 5.00PM. *Congress* surrenders. 5.45PM. *Congress* set on fire.

6. 3.15PM. *Virginia* frees herself from the *Cumberland* and commences a turn to port. 3.20PM. *Cumberland* sinks.

5. 2.30PM. *Virginia* exchanges broadsides with *Congress*. 3.05PM. *Virginia* rams the USS *Cumberland*.

8. 3.30PM. **The James River Flotilla slips past Newport News. CSS** *Patrick Henry* **is hit but all the ships continue on to Norfolk.** 3.45PM. *Virginia* completes her turn and steers towards *Congress*.

TO WI

7

8

1

2a

2

C

MIDDLE GROUND
SHOAL

CRANEY ISLAND
FLATS

2. 12.55PM. **The tug USS** *Zouave* **is sent to investigate.** 1.20PM. *Zouave* fires on the *Virginia* – the first shot of the battle.

1. 12.30PM. **CSS** *Virginia* **passes Sewell's Point.** 12.45. **The Confederate ironclad is sighted by the Union warships.**

THE ATTACK ON USS *CUMBERLAND* AND USS *CONGRESS*

8 March 1862, 12.30pm–5.45pm, viewed from the southeast, showing the CSS *Virginia*'s first attack on the Union blockading squadron, including the ramming of the USS *Cumberland* and the destruction of the USS *Congress*. The wind was 10mph from west-southwest throughout the action.

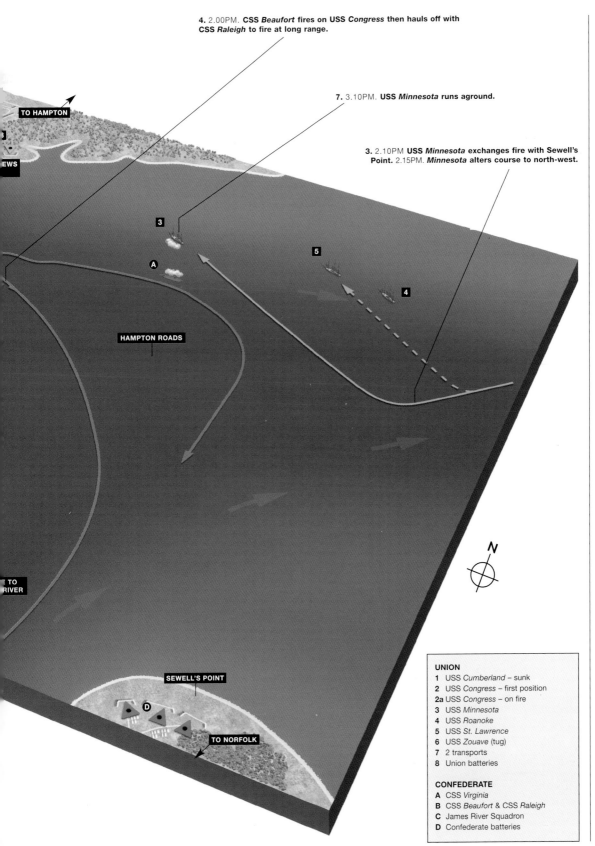

4. 2.00PM. **CSS** *Beaufort* fires on **USS** *Congress* then hauls off with **CSS** *Raleigh* to fire at long range.

7. 3.10PM. **USS** *Minnesota* runs aground.

3. 2.10PM **USS** *Minnesota* exchanges fire with Sewell's Point. 2.15PM. *Minnesota* alters course to north-west.

TO HAMPTON

3

A

5

4

HAMPTON ROADS

TO
RIVER

N

SEWELL'S POINT

D

TO NORFOLK

UNION
1 USS *Cumberland* – sunk
2 USS *Congress* – first position
2a USS *Congress* – on fire
3 USS *Minnesota*
4 USS *Roanoke*
5 USS *St. Lawrence*
6 USS *Zouave* (tug)
7 2 transports
8 Union batteries

CONFEDERATE
A CSS *Virginia*
B CSS *Beaufort* & CSS *Raleigh*
C James River Squadron
D Confederate batteries

The ramming of the USS
Cumberland by the CSS *Virginia*.
While the two ships were locked
together they continued to fire at
each other at point-blank range.
From "Battles and Leaders",
1894. (Hensley)

Captain Smith of the *Cumberland* recalled they bounced off the casemate "like India-rubber balls". By this stage the *Virginia* had closed to within 300 yards. She turned and presented her full starboard broadside to the frigate, then fired. The effect was devastating, particularly as her smoothbore guns had been loaded with heated shot. As Dr. Edward Shippen on the *Congress* recalled: "One of her shells dismounted an eight-inch gun and either killed or wounded every one of her gun's crew, while the slaughter at the other guns was fearful. There were comparatively few wounded, the fragments of the huge shells she threw killed outright as a general thing. Our clean and handsome gun-deck was in an instant changed into a slaughter-pen, with lopped-off legs and arms and bleeding, blackened bodies scattered about by the shells". She then fired a second broadside, overturning guns and sweeping men over the side. By this stage the two ships were so close that Frederick Curtis, the gun captain on one of the *Congress*'s 32-pdrs. thought that the *Virginia* was about to send over a boarding party. Paymaster Buchanan survived the broadside delivered at the orders of his brother. The crew of the *Congress* expected the *Virginia* to turn around and fire her port broadside, but she continued on her course, heading towards the *Cumberland*. The *Congress* was left burning from the heated shot, and her decks covered in blood and gore. Lieutenant Smith knew his ship was likely to sink under him, so he ordered her anchor cables to be cut and set his jib. He called on the tug *Zouave* to come to his aid, as he planned to beach his ship to prevent her from sinking. She ran aground in 17ft of water, effectively becoming a battered wooden fort, immobile but ready to fight. Pumps began to fight the fires, and the wounded were taken below for Dr. Shippen to tend. Her remaining crew watched the *Virginia* approach the *Cumberland*.

On the sloop the crew had rigged "springs", a system of anchors and cables that allowed the warship to be pulled around so she presented her broadside to the enemy. This also meant the *Virginia* was heading straight toward her beam amidships, in the ideal angle for a ramming attempt. The *Cumberland* opened fire with "a few forward 9-inch guns" and her 150-pdr. rifle. Both the heavy smoothbore shot and the 6in. rifled shot failed to penetrate the *Virginia*'s casemate, although they damaged her davits and rails. The *Virginia* opened fire on the *Cumberland* with her bow guns, while her starboard battery engaged the shore batteries on Newport News Point. The shore batteries replied, creating a hail of fire. On the *Gassendi*, Captain Gautier was "able to estimate the force of the fire, which during a quarter of an hour particularly, was of the hottest." This was the period around 3.00pm, when the *Virginia* was lining herself up to ram the *Cumberland*. Gautier continued, reporting that "we could see the entrance of the river constantly swept in all directions by the shot that ricocheted…." At first, the *Virginia* was able to rake the *Cumberland* as she approached, before the sloop was winched round on her "springs". Lieutenant Selfridge on the *Cumberland* described these raking shots as "a situation to shake the highest courage and the best discipline." He described the carnage:

Another depiction of the CSS *Virginia* ramming the USS *Cumberland*. Although the blow was a mortal wound for the Union warship, the ram jammed in the side of the *Cumberland*, and for a moment it appeared that the *Virginia* might be pulled under with her victim. (Author's Collection)

VIRGINIA SINKING THE CUMBERLAND, MARCH 8th 1862

"The dead were thrown to the disengaged side of the deck; the wounded carried below. No one flinched, but everyone went on rapidly loading and firing; the places of the killed and wounded taken promptly by others.... The carnage was frightful. Great splinters torn from the ship's side and decks caused more casualties than the enemy's shell." By this time Buchanan had worked the *Virginia* into a position where she could ram her opponent. William Drake, the artillery volunteer, recalled hearing the order "Stand Fast! We are going to run into her!" As the *Virginia* surged forward, the engine room was given the signal to disengage her engines, then to go astern. Ramsay recalls: "There was an ominous pause, then a crash, shaking us all off our feet." To Lieutenant Jones, the *Virginia's* Executive Officer, "crashing timbers was distinctly heard above the din of battle." The 1,500lb iron ram bolted to the bow of the *Virginia* plowed into the side of the *Cumberland*, crushing her hull. The iron ram was buried deep inside the hull of the wooden sloop, which started to settle in the water. For a moment it seemed as if the *Cumberland* would take the *Virginia* down with her. The two ships were almost touching, and the *Cumberland* fired three broadsides in quick succession, the shot scraping down the ironclad's casemate. The shot shattered the muzzles of two of the *Virginia's* broadside smoothbores. Another shell hit the smokestack, causing "a terrible crash in the fire room," caused by the concussion. On the *Cumberland*, Lieutenant Selfridge described the view from the sloop. "Cheer after cheer went up from the *Cumberland*, only to be followed by exclamations of rage and despair as the enemy slowly moved away...." The *Virginia* had managed to free herself, leaving her ram embedded inside the *Cumberland*. Water rushed into the huge hole in her hull, which one witness described as being "wide enough to let in a horse and cart. The forward magazine was flooded ... As the water gained the berth deck, which by this time was filled with the badly wounded, heart-rending cries above the din of combat could be heard from the poor fellows as they realized their helplessness to escape slow death from drowning." Both ships continued

The ramming of the USS *Cumberland* was a popular subject for maritime artists and contemporary engravers. A naval tactic from antiquity had been resurrected in an age of modern shell and armor. The *Virginia's* ram proved as deadly as her guns. (Mariners, courtesy of the Chrysler Museum of Art)

Commander John Randolph Tucker, CSN was the commander of the James River Squadron. Although his small flotilla ran past the batteries of Newport News Point on 8 March, his flagship, the CSS *Patrick Henry,* was damaged during the action (Museum of the Confederacy, Richmond, VA.)

to pour shot into each other, and as the *Virginia* backed away, the shore batteries added their weight to the barrage. A Confederate officer hailed the *Cumberland,* calling on her to surrender. Lieutenant Morris yelled the response: "Never! We will sink alongside with our colors flying." His ship was already doomed, as her decks were awash in blood and she was settling in the water. For some reason the *Virginia* rammed her again. The *Cumberland* was still firing, but she began to sway wildly as the *Virginia* pulled away again. A lucky shot from the sloop hit the bow gunport of the ironclad, killing two of the crew and wounding several more. These were the first Confederate casualties of the day. Morris gave the order to abandon ship, adding "Every man look out for himself!"

The crew began throwing themselves overboard, while a few of the wounded were lowered into boats. Lieutenant Selfridge was one of the last to abandon ship, but found his way to the upper deck blocked by an overweight drummer and his drum who was stuck in the hatch. He squirmed through a gunport instead, only to break the surface next to the musician, who was using his drum as a raft. As they struggled ashore, the survivors were offered whiskey and blankets. Observers on the *Congress* saw the confusion, and watched the *Cumberland* lurch, "then she went down like a bar of iron, but her flag still flew at her mast head; all was lost except honor." A Confederate observer declared her crew was "game to the last."

"A terrible scene of carnage." The second attack on the *Congress*

It was now around 3.20pm. The *Virginia* had destroyed or damaged two powerful enemy warships, and was relatively unscathed. She was also facing in the opposite direction from the rest of the Union fleet. She continued bombarding the shore, destroying both the wharf and General Mansfield's headquarters. The *Virginia* had to turn to port, but it would take about 30 minutes to turn the ungainly ironclad through 180 degrees. In the meantime she provided enough of a distraction to allow the James River flotilla to steam past the Union batteries at Newport News. Following Buchanan's orders, Captain John R. Tucker's flagship, the CSS *Patrick Henry,* was "standing down James River under

Although inaccurate, as it combines both days of the battle into one scene, this lithograph gives a fair impression of the scene near Newport News Point on the first day, as the survivors from the *Cumberland* struggled ashore. In the foreground Brigadier General Mansfield is shown surveying the carnage. (Mariners)

full steam, accompanied by the *Jamestown* and *Teaser*. They were all nobly into action, and were soon exposed to heavy fire of the shore batteries." The *Patrick Henry* was hit several times, but managed to continue on with only minor damage, screening her consorts which were on her starboard side. The trio of gunboats continued on to the mouth of the Elizabeth River and the protection afforded by the batteries on Sewell's Point.

While the *Virginia* was busy attacking the two warships off Newport News, the other major warships in the blockading squadron tried to come to their aid. The *Minnesota* ran aground about 1½ miles east of Newport News Point. As the tide was ebbing, there was no chance of moving her for six hours. The *Roanoke* was duly towed back under the guns of Fort Monroe, while the *St. Lawrence* ran aground, but at least she was in a position where she could support the *Minnesota*. Buchanan recalled the problems he encountered turning his flagship. "I was obliged to run the ship a short distance above the batteries … Thus we were subjected twice to the heavy guns of all the batteries in passing up and down the river, but it could not be avoided."

By 4.00pm she was back in position, her broadside facing the stern of the stranded *Congress*. The frigate was still on fire, and her decks were still filled with dead and wounded sailors. At a range of 150 yards the ironclad raked the frigate, overturning her remaining stern-firing guns and according to the ship's doctor, "Men were being killed and maimed every minute." He recalled how a line of cooks and stewards who were passing ammunition up from the hold were "raked by a shell, and the whole of them killed or wounded…." Captain Smith was amongst the casualties; killed by a splinter that sliced into his head. Lieutenant Austin Pendergast and Commander William Smith were now in command, and after almost 30 minutes of this carnage, the officers decided to surrender. Two white flags were raised and the *Virginia* ceased firing. It was just after 5.00pm. On the ironclad, Lieutenant Jones ordered his men to remain at their posts while Flag Officer Buchanan and several officers climbed onto the spar deck. Ramsey noted, "a pall of black smoke hung about the ships and obscured the clean-cut outlines of the shore. Down the river were the three frigates *St. Lawrence*,

A shell from the CSS *Virginia* penetrates the hull of the wooden sloop USS *Cumberland* and explodes inside her sick bay. Most of the wounded were unable to escape from below decks when the sloop sank. (Hensley)

Roanoke and *Minnesota*.... The masts of the *Cumberland* were protruding above the water. The *Congress* presented a terrible scene of carnage." A small boat was sent from the *Virginia* to the *Congress*, in itself a miracle given the damage to the deck fittings of the ironclad. Next, the *Beaufort* arrived to take the frigate's surviving officers off as prisoners, then burn the enemy ship. She was followed by the Confederate tug *Raleigh*. The two tugs had scarcely come alongside the *Congress* when they came under heavy fire from the shore. General Mansfield refused to support the frigate's peaceable surrender, and fired his batteries, supported by the rifle fire of two infantry companies. He ordered a subordinate to "send down marksmen and do not permit them to board the *Congress*." His actions were effectively a death warrant for the wounded sailors on board the frigate. Lieutenant Parker on the *Beaufort* recalled that bullets were hitting his tug "like hail." He withdrew to join two other Confederate tugs (*Harmony* and *Teaser*) that had just reached the scene,

Around 12.20am during the night of 8/9 March, the *Congress* finally exploded, after having burned all evening. It provided a dramatic finale to the events of the previous day, which demonstrated the vulnerability of wooden warships to modern shells. (VWM)

JACK: "Mr. Secretary! Mr. Secretary! Wake up! Here's the *Merrimac* got out and sunk the *Cumberland* and taken the *Congress!*"

MR. SECRETARY [Welles]: "Ah! (*yawns*) you don't say so? I must get Morgan to buy some more boats then!"

intent on capturing prisoners. The *Patrick Henry* made an attempt to divert the shore batteries, but her engines were hit by a shot from the *Minnesota*, releasing scalding steam into her engine room. The *Jamestown* towed her into Norfolk. By this time Flag Officer Buchanan had seen enough. He was still standing on the *Virginia*'s spar deck, watching the drama unfold. He ordered Jones to "plug hot shot into her and don't leave her until she's afire!" Just then he was hit in the groin by a rifle bullet. As he was carried below, he cried out: "That ship must be burned! They must look after their own wounded, since they won't let us!" Several heated shot were fired into the *Congress*, which was blazing from stem to stern. The crew abandoned ship while many of the wounded succumbed to the flames. Others escaped overboard, to be rescued by soldiers from the 20th Indiana. Paymaster Buchanan emerged unhurt but dazed, as did the surgeon, Dr. Shippen. An English observer described the burning *Congress* as a "helpless, hopeless charnel house."

Lieutenant Jones was now in command of the *Virginia*, and as the *Congress* was clearly burning, he turned his attention to the stranded *Minnesota*, 1½ miles away to the east. He quickly realized that the ironclad's draft was too deep to allow her to approach within close range of the Union frigate. He opened fire on the *Minnesota*, but it was getting harder to see the target as dusk approached. His pilots advised him to abandon the attack, as the water levels were dropping, and it was getting dark. Reluctantly Jones ordered his helmsman to steer toward the mouth of the Elizabeth River. It was 6.30pm, by 8.00pm the ironclad was riding at anchor, protected by the Confederate guns on Sewell's Point. Buchanan and the other wounded were taken ashore, along with the bodies of the two crewmen who had been killed. Union prisoners were sent under guard to the Norfolk hospital, and Jones and his officers inspected their vessel for damage. The crew ate their evening meal around midnight, while Jones finished his report on the action. The Confederates had just inflicted a humiliating defeat on the US Navy, the worst day in its history since the capture of the USS *Chesapeake* in 1812. Over 2,650 sailors had been killed, and almost as many were wounded. The Navy had also lost two powerful warships, and the rest of their fleet lay exposed and vulnerable. Captain Gautier reported that; "Panic appeared to take possession of everyone. Several vessels changed their anchorage, and all held themselves in readiness to stand out to sea at the first movement of the enemy." Although the *St. Lawrence* was refloated, the *Minnesota* remained hard aground. She would be the obvious target when the *Virginia* resumed her attack in the morning.

The *Congress* had continued to burn all evening, and just after 12.30am she exploded "like a tremendous bombshell, and with a roar that could be heard for miles around." A Confederate witness described the end of the Union warship in "an enormous column of fire." A Union observer recalled that the sight "went straight to the marrow of our bones." Jones recounted that by the light of the flames, a Confederate pilot on the *Virginia* noticed "a strange-looking craft, brought out in bold relief by the light of the burning ship, which he at once proclaimed to be the Ericsson". His sighting was dismissed, and Jones continued to plan a second sortie to finish the piecemeal destruction of the entire blockading flotilla. In fact the pilot was correct. As the *Congress* burned, the *Monitor* steamed into Hampton Roads. After reporting to the squadron commander on board the *Roanoke*, Lieutenant Worden's ironclad was ordered to guard the *Minnesota*. When the battle was

Captain Gersholm Jaques Van Brunt, USN, the Commanding Officer of the USS *Minnesota*, had the unenviable task of facing the CSS *Virginia* in an immobile wooden frigate. His vessel was saved by the actions of the USS *Monitor* on 9 March. (US Army Military History Institute)

THE NAVAL ENGAGEMENT BETWEEN THE MERRIMAC AND THE MONITOR AT HAMPTON ROADS
ON THE 9TH OF MARCH 1862.

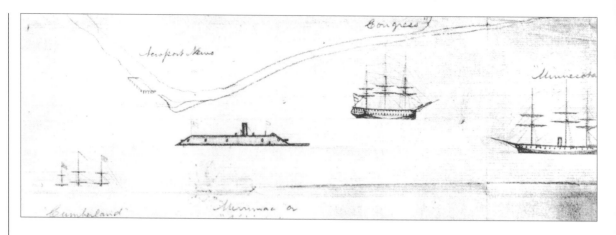

resumed the following morning, the Confederate ironclad would meet Ericsson's *Monitor*. Instead of fighting against unprotected wooden warships, the *Virginia* would be fighting another ironclad.

"I WILL STAND BY YOU TO THE LAST"
The first clash between the ironclads, Sunday 9 March 1862

In the predawn darkness, the *Virginia*'s officers examined their ship. Surgeon Philipps wrote: "I found all her stanchions, iron railings, boat davits and light work of every description swept away, her smokestack cut to pieces, two guns without muzzles, and 98 indentations on her plating, showing where heavy iron shot had struck, but glanced off without doing any injury." Water was also seeping in through a crack in the bow, caused when the iron ram had been wrenched off. Only Lieutenant Jones and the pilot knew of the possible presence of the *Monitor*, and everyone seemed to believe that the *Minnesota* would be the only real opponent that morning. The crew ate breakfast, which included "two jiggers of whiskey," then prepared for action. On the other side of Hampton Roads the *Monitor* had spent the night anchored alongside the *Minnesota*, "like some undersized sheepdog in the shadow of a very large but partially incapacitated ram." As the skies lightened, the crews of both vessels scanned the opposite sides of the Roads. Lieutenant Rochelle on the *Patrick Henry* observed that: "The *Minnesota* was discovered in her old position, but the *Minnesota* was not the only thing to attract attention. Close alongside of her lay such a craft as the eyes of a seaman never looked upon before – an immense shingle floating on the water, with a gigantic cheesebox rising from its center; no sails, no wheels, no smokestacks, no guns. What could it be"? Some thought it was a water raft, or a floating magazine. Others though she might be the *Monitor*. Lieutenant Jones seemed in little doubt. He told Lieutenant Hunter Davidson of "his determination to attack and ram her, and to keep vigorously at her until the contest was decided." On the *Monitor*, Lieutenant Worden spotted the "*Merrimack*" with several consorts at anchor off Sewell's Point. He also ordered his men to breakfast, then prepared his ship for action. Captain Jaques Van Brunt of the *Minnesota* was also getting his ship ready to face the *Virginia*. A cluster of tugs and small boats was busy removing her stores, baggage, even her paychest, in

This contemporary sketch gives a good impression of the location of the *Cumberland* (left) and the *Congress* (right) in relation to Newport News Point, although the *Minnesota* is depicted too close to the *Congress*. She grounded 1½ miles east of the frigate. (Museum of the Confederacy, Richmond, VA.)

A highly inaccurate view of the interior of the gundeck of the CSS *Virginia* appeared in the contemporary French publication *Le Monde Illustré*. The breech-loading gun, its carriage and even the uniforms are incorrect, but it retains something of the flavor of conditions inside a casemate battery. (Author's Collection)

The interior of the turret of the USS *Monitor*. Although somewhat inaccurate it was evidently based on experience, as the depiction of the gunport stoppers and their attendant pulley system is accurately shown. (VWM)

order to try to lighten the ship. There was a general assumption that she would be destroyed just like the *Cumberland* and *Congress*. Around 6.00am, Van Brunt saw the enemy "coming down from Craney Island." His men raced to their guns.

The *Virginia* had indeed slipped her mooring off Sewell's Point just before 6.00am, but a heavy bank of fog lay over Hampton Roads, and Lieutenant Jones wanted to wait until the tide had risen and the fog dispersed. He remained in station off the Point, while the sidewheel gunboats *Patrick Henry* and *Jamestown,* and the tug *Teaser* joined him. By 8.00am conditions had improved, and Jones conned his ship in the direction of Fort Wool preceded by the two gunboats before curving back toward the stranded *Minnesota*. The Union frigate lay two miles to the northwest, across the Roads. On the French sloop *Gassendi*, Captain Gautier reported that: "at eight-o-clock the fog completely disappeared." Van Brunt and Lieutenant Worden saw the move, and exchanged a last

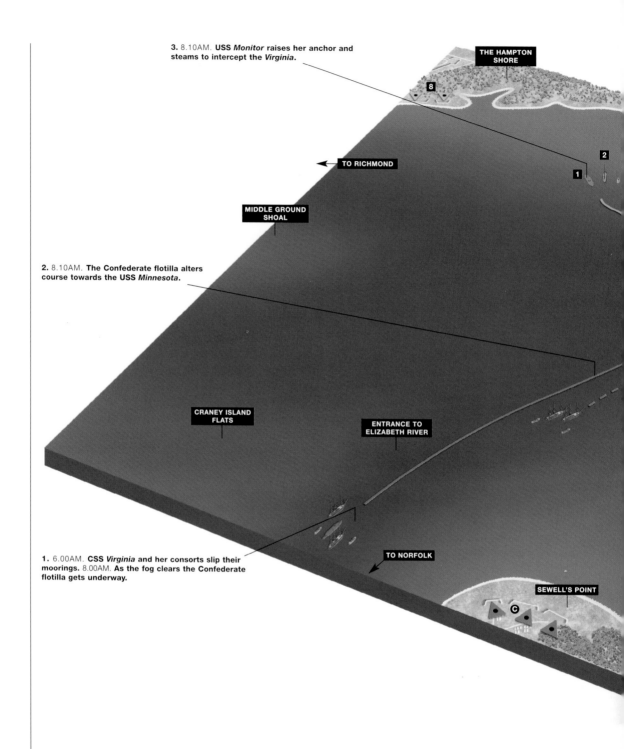

3. 8.10AM. **USS *Monitor* raises her anchor and steams to intercept the *Virginia*.**

THE HAMPTON SHORE

8

TO RICHMOND

2

1

MIDDLE GROUND SHOAL

2. 8.10AM. **The Confederate flotilla alters course towards the USS *Minnesota*.**

CRANEY ISLAND FLATS

ENTRANCE TO ELIZABETH RIVER

1. 6.00AM. **CSS *Virginia* and her consorts slip their moorings.** 8.00AM. **As the fog clears the Confederate flotilla gets underway.**

TO NORFOLK

SEWELL'S POINT

C

THE BATTLE OF HAMPTON ROADS

9 March 1862, 6.00am–10.00am, viewed from the southeast. CSS *Virginia* returns to finish off the Union blockading squadron, in particular the USS *Minnesota*. The *Virginia* is intercepted by the Union ironclad USS *Monitor*, however, and their epic confrontation begins. Wind is 5mph from the west throughout the morning.

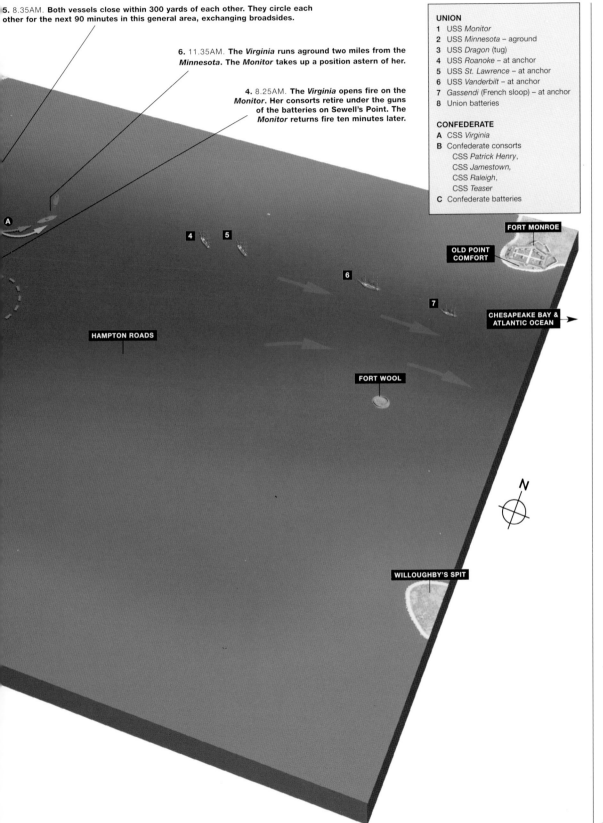

5. 8.35AM. **Both vessels close within 300 yards of each other. They circle each other for the next 90 minutes in this general area, exchanging broadsides.**

6. 11.35AM. **The *Virginia* runs aground two miles from the *Minnesota*. The *Monitor* takes up a position astern of her.**

4. 8.25AM. **The *Virginia* opens fire on the *Monitor*. Her consorts retire under the guns of the batteries on Sewell's Point. The *Monitor* returns fire ten minutes later.**

UNION
1 USS *Monitor*
2 USS *Minnesota* – aground
3 USS *Dragon* (tug)
4 USS *Roanoke* – at anchor
5 USS *St. Lawrence* – at anchor
6 USS *Vanderbilt* – at anchor
7 *Gassendi* (French sloop) – at anchor
8 Union batteries

CONFEDERATE
A CSS *Virginia*
B Confederate consorts
  CSS *Patrick Henry*,
  CSS *Jamestown*,
  CSS *Raleigh*,
  CSS *Teaser*
C Confederate batteries

A

4   5

6

7

FORT MONROE

OLD POINT
COMFORT

CHESAPEAKE BAY &
ATLANTIC OCEAN →

HAMPTON ROADS

FORT WOOL

N

WILLOUGHBY'S SPIT

This atmospheric engraving is probably the most accurate depiction of conditions inside the turret of the USS *Monitor* that was produced by contemporary artists. Eighteen men and two 15,700lb guns and their slide carriages were crammed into the 20ft diameter space. The conditions during action could only be described as "hellish". (VWM)

OPPOSITE TOP

In this contemporary depiction of the scene inside the USS *Monitor*'s turret, the gun crew is shown peering out through the gun port, waiting for the CSS *Virginia* to appear in their line of sight. (Hensley)

OPPOSITE BOTTOM

Although inaccurate, this detailed engraving shows the final moments of the battle, just before a shot from the stern gun of the CSS *Virginia* hit the USS *Monitor*'s pilot house. Although several other ships are included in the scene, the closest wooden vessel to the action was the USS *Minnesota*, stranded over a mile to the north. (VWM)

few words before they went into action. The captain of the *Minnesota* told Worden: "If I cannot lighten my ship off, I will destroy her." Worden replied: "I will stand by you to the last if I can help you." Van Brunt's thoughts on the *Monitor* probably mirrored those of Dr. Shippen, watching from Fort Monroe: "she seemed so small and trifling that we feared she would only constitute additional prey for the leviathan."

When the *Virginia* was a mile away from the *Minnesota*, the Union vessel opened fire with her stern guns. Others claim that the *Virginia* fired first, while Captain Tucker commanding the *Virginia*'s consorts recorded that his gunboats opened the engagement. William Keeler, the paymaster of the *Monitor*, was watching from the ironclad's deck, and wrote that the *Virginia* fired, and "a shell howled over our heads and crashed into the side of the *Minnesota*." Worden ordered everyone to go below. It was shortly before 8.30am. After the *Virginia* fired, Worden reported that: "I got underway as soon as possible and stood directly for her, with the crew at quarters, in order to meet and engage her as far away from the *Minnesota* as possible." Van Brunt wrote that the *Monitor* "laid herself right alongside of the *Merrimack*, and the contrast was that of a pigmy to a giant." As Ashton Ramsay, the *Virginia*'s Chief Engineer recalled, "suddenly to our astonishment a black object that looked like… a barrelhead afloat with a cheesebox on top of it moved slowly out from under the *Minnesota* and boldly confronted us."

In the *Monitor*'s turret, Lieutenant Greene supervised the loading of the twin 11in. Dahlgrens with solid shot. Each gun was crewed by eight men, while Greene and Acting Master Louis N. Stodder supervised their operation. These two men had some idea of what was going on, as they could see out of the gunports. The only other viewpoint on the *Monitor* was the pilot house, where the Pilot, Samuel Howard, and the Quartermaster, Peter Williams, accompanied Lieutenant Worden. Williams manned the ship's wheel. As the speaking tube linking turret to pilot house had broken down, Worden in the pilot house and Greene in the turret could only communicate by message carriers in the berth deck. Paymaster Keeler volunteered to maintain the link between the two parts of the ship. He was assisted by Captain's Clerk Daniel Toffey. Greene called down: "Paymaster, ask the captain if I shall fire!"

The reply came back: "Tell Mr. Greene not to fire till I give the word, to be cool and deliberate, to take sure aim and not waste a shot". The gunboats peeled away from the *Virginia* as the two ironclads approached each other, returning to lie underneath the guns on Sewell's Point. As the Frenchman Gautier put it: "they were seen to abandon the attack and retire under the batteries of Sewell's, leaving the *Merrimack* to defend alone the honor of their young flag." When the two were within

100 yards of each other, Worden turned the *Monitor* so her bows faced upstream, taking the way off the ship. He then gave the order to open fire. Greene decided to fire the first shot himself. "I triced up the port, ran out the gun, and taking deliberate aim, pulled the lockstring." The *Monitor* shuddered under the impact. Observers thought the first shot hit the *Virginia* "plumb on the waterline." Jones was in the process of turning his ship to starboard, which presented his full broadside to the enemy. Both ships were now parallel to each other, but headed in opposite directions; the *Monitor* facing west and the *Virginia* east. He gave the order to fire. According to Greene, it was "a rattling broadside … the turret and other parts of the ship were heavily struck, but the shots did not penetrate; the tower was intact, and it continued to revolve."

Greene later wrote that "a look of confidence passed over the men's faces, and we believed the *Merrimack* would not repeat the work she had accomplished the day before." One gunner even thought the Confederates were firing canister at them, as the shots "rattled on our iron decks like hailstones."

Worden recalled that "at this period I felt some anxiety about the turret machinery, it having been predicted by many persons that a heavy shot with great initial velocity striking the turret would so derange it as to stop its working; but finding that it had been twice struck and still revolved as freely as ever, I turned back with renewed confidence and hope, and continued the engagement at close quarters; every shot from our guns taking effect on the high sides of our adversary, stripping off the iron freely." This was the ultimate test of Ericsson's invention. Both the *Monitor*'s hull and turret armor were proof to the rifled shot fired by her opponent.

Worden "passed slowly by her, within a few yards, delivering fire as rapidly as possible and receiving from her a rapid fire in return, both from her great guns and musketry – the latter aimed at the pilot house, hoping undoubtedly to penetrate through the lookout holes and to disable the commanding officer and the helmsman."

Although the *Virginia* maintained a heavy fire, its shot seemed to be incapable of damaging the *Monitor*. Officers in the attendant flotilla of Confederate vessels near Sewell's Point were heard to say "the unknown craft was a wicked thing, and that we better not get too near her." It was becoming increasingly apparent that the *Virginia* had met her match. This ineffectiveness frustrated Jones, who recalled, "she and her turret appeared to be in perfect control. Her light draft enabled her to move about us at pleasure. She once took position for a short while where we could not bring a gun to bear on her." Jones would have been relieved to know that the heavy smoothbore guns on the *Monitor* were firing using reduced charges, a safety precaution that reduced velocity at short range. The *Monitor* was firing 168lb solid roundshot using 15lb of gunpowder to propel the shot, two thirds of the normal charge. This reduction in powder was made in accordance with the instructions of Captain John A. Dahlgren, the inventor of the *Monitor*'s guns, and the Chief of Naval Ordnance. He was concerned that the guns could burst if fired using a larger charge, but subsequent tests proved the reliability of his guns.

If the *Monitor* had used full charges of gunpowder, her shots might have had more chance of penetrating the *Virginia*'s lighter armor. Ramsay recalled that; "we hovered about each other in spirals, gradually contracting the circuits until we were within point-blank range, but our shell glanced from the *Monitor*'s turret just as hers did from our sloping sides". These sloping sides were angled inward at 35 degrees from the vertical. The *Virginia*'s designer, John L. Porter, and ordnance expert, John M. Brooke, worked out that this was the optimal angle of deflection to confound incoming roundshot, while retaining enough space inside the casemate to house the battery. The same angle was used in almost all subsequent Confederate casemate ironclads, as the theory was proved in battle. The 11in. roundshot fired by the *Monitor*'s two guns tended to strike the casemate, and were then deflected upwards by the slope. This significantly reduced the effect of the impact, and rendered the *Virginia* relatively impervious to enemy fire. The weakness with the casemate design was also becoming apparent. Two layers of two-inch-thick metal plate protected her casemate. These were bolted into place on top of a wooden frame, and although the armor was thick enough to

Another stylized 20th-century depiction of the Battle of Hampton Roads, this painting manages to include the sinking of the CSS *Cumberland* into an otherwise correct representation of the second day's battle. (Casemate)

withstand the enemy shot, each hit caused damage to the retaining bolts. Both Worden and Greene noticed this, and thought it possible that by concentrating their fire at a particular spot, sections of the armor plating could be shot away. Another problem with the *Virginia* was her armament. Two of her 9in. smoothbores had been damaged in the previous day's battle, and although they could still be fired even though their muzzles had been shot away, they were wildly inaccurate. The minor damage to her forward-facing 7in. Brooke rifle had been repaired by the time the battle began, and the piece appeared to function normally during the engagement with the *Monitor*.

More serious was her shortage of appropriate ammunition. The previous day, when she sailed out to fight the wooden ships of the blockading squadron, her solid cast-iron roundshot had been left behind, as it was less effective against unarmored opponents. Her ammunition had not been replenished, and when she steamed into battle against the *Monitor* she only had explosive shells in her magazines, apart from canister, which was an anti-personnel projectile. She also had the facilities to fire heated shot, which proved useful the day before, but was of no value in her fight against another ironclad. As her Chief Engineer related: "If we had known we were to meet her, we would have been supplied with solid shot for our rifled cannons." Another officer wrote: "our only hope to penetrate the *Monitor's* shield was in the rifled cannon, but as the only projectiles we had for those were percussion shells, there was barely a chance that we might penetrate our adversary's defense by a lucky shot." Jones was well aware of the problem, and although he had every faith in the superb rifled guns that had been designed by John M. Brooke, he knew that only a very lucky shot would have any effect on his opponent. Later in the day a shot from one of his Brooke rifles would prove his faith was well placed. If his guns were relatively ineffective against the *Monitor*, Jones still retained the perfect means of destroying the wooden frigate *Minnesota*, so this remained his priority throughout the morning. Similarly, Worden's objective was to keep the *Virginia* as far away from the frigate as possible. To the observers lining both shores of Hampton Roads, the duel between the two ironclads appeared ferocious. William E. Rogers of the 10th New York Regiment felt that "truly this odd little craft was no match for this great monster. They closed in, however, and a curtain of smoke settled down over the scene with the Confederate batteries on Sewell's Point, Pig Point and Craney Island in the fray. With breathless suspense we listened to this firing, but could see nothing for the clouds of smoke. We heard the whistle of the shells and the shot, and we could recognize the shots of the *Monitor*. One takes no note of time under such circumstances. How long that first round lasted before the firing ceased I have no idea. When the thunder ceased, oh! We thought the 'cheesebox' had gone to the bottom. Gradually the smoke lifted and there lay the two antagonists, backing, filling and jockeying for position, then at it again, and again the cloud of smoke which settled over their struggle hid them from view."

The conflict was also a confusing one for those taking part. In the *Virginia*, Ramsay recalled that "on our gun deck all was bustle, smoke, grimy figures and stern commands, while down in the engine and boiler rooms the sixteen furnaces were belching out fire and smoke, and the firemen standing in front of them like so many gladiators, tugging away with devil's claw and slice-bar, inducing by their exertions more and more intense combustion and heat. The noise of the crackling, roaring fires, escaping steam, and the loud and labored pulsations of the engines, together with the roar of battle above, and the thud and vibration of the huge masses of iron which were hurled against us produced a scene and sound to be compared only with the poet's picture of the lower regions."

Conditions were as bad, if not worse, on board the *Monitor*, and at one stage Lieutenant Worden had to clamber out onto the open deck to look around, assess the damage inflicted on his ship, and to get his bearings. This display of calm bravery under fire was typical of the man who Acting Master John Webber described as being "as cool as a man playing a game of chess." While he was standing there he was subjected to volleys of musket fire from the *Virginia*, the bullets flying "as thick as hailstones in a storm". He noted the turret bore the dents from the conical shells fired by the *Virginia*'s Brooke rifles. The 68lb projectiles created 4in. dents in the sides of the turret, but failed to cause any real damage. Even these non-penetrating shots could be dangerous, although the armor was sufficient to protect the turret crew. Acting Master Stodder was busy operating the machinery that rotated the turret. As he leaned against the turret side the structure was hit by one of these non-penetrating rounds. He was stunned by the vibration, and had to be carried below, suffering from concussion. He was replaced by Chief Engineer Alban C. Stimers, the man who had supervised the ironclad's construction on behalf of the Navy Department. Although her armored protection proved more than adequate, other features of Ericsson's design proved less reliable. The lack of communication between turret and pilot house was a significant problem, and however quickly messages could be relayed from one position to the other, it was still too slow to be able to react to events with any degree of alacrity. Another problem was that both the Paymaster and the Captain's Clerk

Lieutenant John Taylor Wood, CSN fired the last shot of the battle. The conical shell fired from the CSS *Virginia*'s stern 7in. Brooke's Rifle hit the USS *Monitor*'s pilot house and wounded Lieutenant Worden. (VWM)

were not real sailors or gunners, so lacked the technical vocabulary to perform their job properly. As Lieutenant Greene later described it: "The situation was novel: a vessel of war was engaged in desperate combat with a powerful foe, the captain, commanding and guiding, was enclosed in one place, and the Executive Officer, working and fighting the guns, was shut up in another."

Lieutenant Greene described the situation inside the *Monitor*'s turret. "My only view of the world outside the tower was over the muzzles of the guns, which cleared the ports by only a few inches. When the guns were run in, the portholes were covered by heavy iron pendulums, pierced with small holes to allow the iron rammer and sponge handles to protrude while they were in use. To hoist these pendulums required the entire gun's crew and vastly increased the work inside the turret." Eighteen men were trapped inside a smoke-filled metal box 20ft in diameter, and filled with two massive guns. They were also under near-constant fire, as marksmen tried to fire in through the gun ports, and the *Virginia*'s shells tried to penetrate the turret, the rounds clanging into its sides and shaking the whole structure. Green recalled that: "the effect upon one shut up in a revolving drum is perplexing, and it is not a simple matter to keep the bearings. White marks had been placed upon the stationary deck immediately below the turret to indicate the direction of the starboard and port sides, and the bow and the stern; but these marks were obliterated early in the action. I would continually ask the captain, 'How does the *Merrimac* bear?' He replied 'On the starboard beam', or 'on the port quarter", as the case might be. Then, the difficulty was to determine the direction of the starboard beam or port quarter, or any other bearing."

The gun crews had no idea where the enemy was most of the time, let alone which direction their own ship was pointing. After a few rounds, Greene developed a solution that solved both the problem of the cumbersome gun port covers and the confusion over direction. "It finally resulted, that when a gun was ready for firing, the turret would be

started on its revolving journey in search of the target, and when found it was taken 'on the fly', because the turret could not be accurately controlled." In other words, Greene's solution was to keep the gun port covers open all the time. When a gun had fired, he ordered the turret to be turned, so the open ports faced away from the enemy. Protected by the bulk of the turret itself, the gun was then reloaded and run out again. Greene would then give the order to turn the turret, and he peered through the small gap around the muzzle until the *Virginia* filled his view. He then pulled the lanyard and fired the gun. During the action he elected to fire each gun himself, moving constantly from gun to gun throughout the action.

Below the *Monitor*'s turret, Paymaster Keeler was unable to see the action develop, but he heard everything, and both Worden and Greene kept him abreast of developments as they relayed information from one part of the ship to the other. Keeler wrote: "The sounds of the conflict were terrible. The rapid fire of our guns amid the clouds of smoke, the howling of the *Minnesota's* shells, which were firing broadsides just over our heads (two of her shots struck us), mingled with the terrible crash of solid shot against our sides (not from the *Virginia*) and the bursting of shells all around us. Two men had been sent down from the turret, knocked senseless by balls striking outside the turret while they happened to be in contact with the inside wall of the turret". In a letter to his wife Anna, he recalled some of the orders passed back and forth. "Tell Mr. Greene that I am going to bring him on our Starboard beam, close alongside," or, "They're going to board us, put in a round of canister." He also passed on Worden's comments about the shooting; "That was a good shot, went through her waterline," or, "That last shot brought iron from her sides".

"A moment of terrible suspense." The battle of maneuver

After two hours of dueling, both captains were beginning to realize that they had little chance of damaging their opponent through gunfire alone. While Jones had the option of trying to maneuver closer to the *Minnesota* to attack her, both captains could also try to ram their opponent. The duel

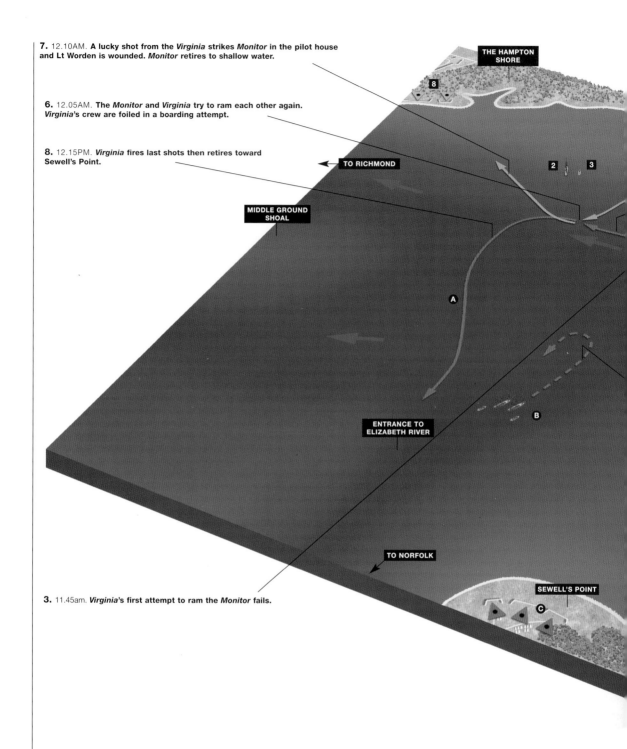

7. 12.10AM. **A lucky shot from the *Virginia* strikes *Monitor* in the pilot house and Lt Worden is wounded. *Monitor* retires to shallow water.**

THE HAMPTON SHORE

8

6. 12.05AM. **The *Monitor* and *Virginia* try to ram each other again. *Virginia*'s crew are foiled in a boarding attempt.**

8. 12.15PM. ***Virginia* fires last shots then retires toward Sewell's Point.**

← **TO RICHMOND**

2   3

MIDDLE GROUND SHOAL

A

B

ENTRANCE TO ELIZABETH RIVER

TO NORFOLK

SEWELL'S POINT

C

3. 11.45am. ***Virginia*'s first attempt to ram the *Monitor* fails.**

THE BATTLE OF HAMPTON ROADS

9 March 1862, 11.40am–12.15pm, viewed from the southeast. With *Virginia* having freed herself, the two vessels make various attempts to ram and board each other. A lucky shot strikes the pilot house of the USS *Monitor*, wounding Lt Worden. The *Monitor* retires to shallow water and, with the water levels falling, *Virginia* retires towards Sewell's Point. Wind is 5mph from west-northwest; it shifted at around 10.15am.

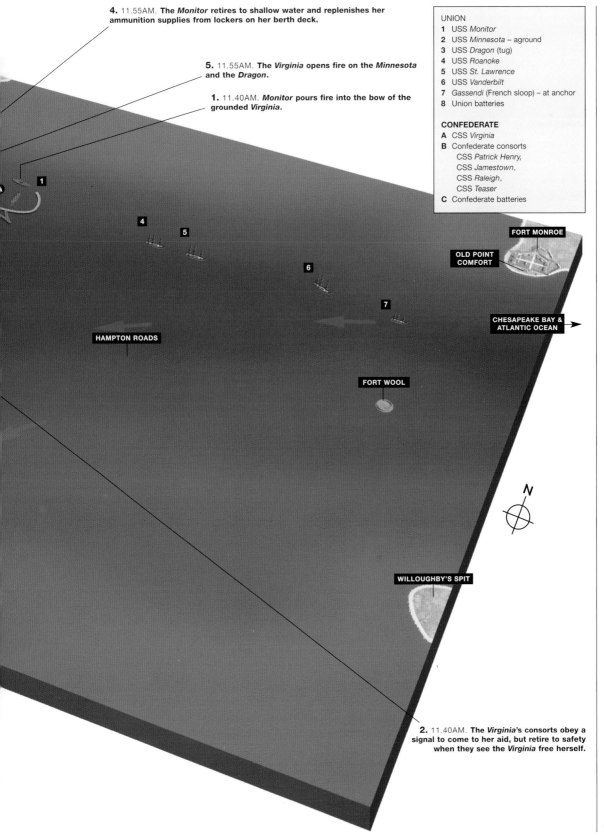

4. 11.55AM. The *Monitor* retires to shallow water and replenishes her ammunition supplies from lockers on her berth deck.

5. 11.55AM. The *Virginia* opens fire on the *Minnesota* and the *Dragon*.

1. 11.40AM. *Monitor* pours fire into the bow of the grounded *Virginia*.

UNION
1 USS *Monitor*
2 USS *Minnesota* – aground
3 USS *Dragon* (tug)
4 USS *Roanoke*
5 USS *St. Lawrence*
6 USS *Vanderbilt*
7 *Gassendi* (French sloop) – at anchor
8 Union batteries

CONFEDERATE
A CSS *Virginia*
B Confederate consorts
    CSS *Patrick Henry*,
    CSS *Jamestown*,
    CSS *Raleigh*,
    CSS *Teaser*
C Confederate batteries

1

4

5

6

7

FORT MONROE

OLD POINT COMFORT

CHESAPEAKE BAY & ATLANTIC OCEAN

HAMPTON ROADS

FORT WOOL

N

WILLOUGHBY'S SPIT

2. 11.40AM. The *Virginia*'s consorts obey a signal to come to her aid, but retire to safety when they see the *Virginia* free herself.

continued, but instead of a contest between two ships steaming in circles around each other, around 11.00am Jones and Worden began to try other stratagems. Of the two ships, the *Monitor* was by far the more maneuverable, and Worden decided to try to ram the stern of her opponent, hoping to damage her screw (propeller) or rudder. If the *Virginia* could be disabled, then the *Monitor* could find a blind spot and pour fire into her without danger. First, Worden had to deal with a logistical problem. His guns had run out of ammunition, and in order to replenish the supplies within the turret, he had to disengage, and steam away from his opponent. Shot was brought up out of the hold, and while this was going on, Jones edged his ship closer to the *Minnesota.* Both he and his pilot were unsure of how deep the water was beneath their keel, and by the time they had charted a course to get as close to the wooden frigate as they could, the *Monitor* was steaming back into the fray. Worden made a dash for the *Virginia*'s stern, but missed by just two feet. Jones also decided to break the circling pattern adopted by the two ships in an attempt to attack the *Minnesota.* He steered northwest, forcing the *Monitor* to chase after him, and try to cut in between the *Virginia* and the stranded frigate. Just at that moment, in Lieutenant Jones's words, "In spite of all the cares of our pilots, we ran ashore". The surgeon, Dr. Phillips, was less reluctant to place blame: "the pilot purposely ran us aground nearly two miles off from the *Minnesota,* fearing that frigate's terrible broadside." This was a potential disaster for the Confederates, and Worden was quick to take advantage of their plight. He laid his ship alongside the *Virginia* so that the smaller ironclad lay beneath the muzzles of the Confederate

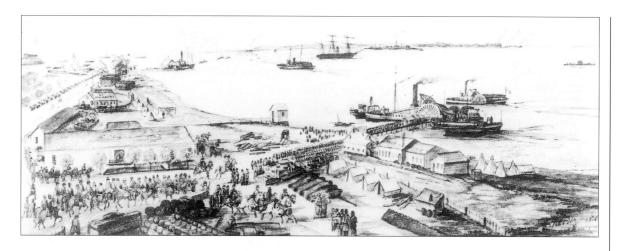

OVERLEAF
THE CSS *VIRGINIA* ATTEMPTS TO RAM THE USS *MONITOR*, 9 MARCH 1862
After the first hour or so of duelling between the two ironclads, both commanders were running out of options. It had become clear that the under-charged propellant used on the USS *Monitor* was insufficient to allow its 11in. roundshot to penetrate the *Virginia*'s armor. Similarly, the hollow shells used on the CSS *Virginia* were unable to do more than dent the turret of her opponent. Lieutenant Catesby ap Jones had just pulled his ship off a mudbank, and found that the *Monitor* was lying off his bow. He ordered for full steam in an attempt to ram his adversary, but without his iron ram, he was reluctant to damage his own ship. Consequently he reversed his engines immediately before the collision, and the glancing blow to the *Monitor* did little damage. Although accounts vary (one claims the blow struck the *Monitor*'s starboard beam), the scene depicts the *Virginia* striking a glancing blow to the *Monitor*'s stern, on her port quarter. (Adam Hook)

guns. As Van Brunt described it; "the contrast was that of a pygmy to a giant." Phillips recalled that "she directed a succession of shots at the same section of our vessel, and some of them striking close together, started the timbers and drove them perceptibly in ... she began to sound every chink in our armor – every one but that which was actually vulnerable, had she known it." He was referring to the waterline. As the *Virginia* burned coal, she became lighter, and consequently her protective knuckle at the bottom of the casemate rose closer to the surface. It was designed to extend almost three feet below the waterline. After two days of fighting, it was only six inches below the surface. As Ramsay reported: "Lightened as we were, these exposed portions rendered us no longer an ironclad, and the *Monitor* might have pierced us between wind and water had she depressed her gun." Worden was oblivious to the opportunity this presented.

With the *Virginia* aground, Jones tried everything he could to move her off the mud bank. Ramsay was the man of the moment. "We lashed down the safety valves, heaped quick-burning combustibles into the already raging fires, and brought the boilers to a pressure that would be unsafe under ordinary circumstances. The propeller churned the mud and water furiously, but the ship did not stir. We piled on oiled cotton waste, splits of wood, anything that would burn faster than coal. It seemed impossible that the boilers could stand the pressure we were crowding upon them. Just as we were beginning to despair, there was a perceptible movement, and the *Merrimack* slowly dragged herself off the shoal by main strength. We were saved." To the crew, this seemed a miracle. By placing everyone at risk by straining the engines and boilers almost beyond endurance, Ramsay managed to develop enough reverse thrust to drag the vessel back into open water.

Minutes before, Jones had ordered his yeoman to signal the wooden consorts lying off Sewell's Point. When Captain Tucker saw the signal "my screw is disabled", he realized that by going to the rescue of the ironclad, he would be sacrificing his ship. As his Executive Officer, Lieutenant Rochelle, put it, "No wooden vessel could have floated twenty minutes under the fire the *Virginia* was undergoing, but if her propeller was disabled it was necessary to tow her back to the cover of our batteries, so the *Patrick Henry* and *Jamestown* started to make the attempt." The crews of the two gunboats must have been immensely

relieved to see the ironclad pull herself off without help. While all this was going on, Lieutenant Jones passed through the ship, visiting every gun crew. He noticed that the division of two smoothbore guns commanded by Lieutenant J.R. Eggleston had ceased firing. When asked why his guns were not returning the fire of the *Monitor*, Eggleston replied with the perfect summation of the gunnery duel: "Why, our powder is very precious, and after two hours incessant firing I find that I can do her about as much damage by snapping my thumb every two minutes and a half." Jones decided not to press the matter. What Eggleston had said was perfectly true.

If it was too difficult to approach the *Minnesota* without running aground, and if his gunnery was ineffective, Jones had one other tactical option. He could ram the *Monitor*. Using the ship herself as a weapon had worked well the day before, but the *Cumberland* was a stationary target, and as one critic on board put it, the *Virginia* "was as unwieldy as Noah's Ark." It took the better part of an hour to maneuver into a position where the *Virginia* could ram her opponent. After a run of half a mile, Jones was on target. Worden called out to Keeler: "Look out now, they're going to run us down! Give them both guns!" He also turned the ship, which almost escaped the collision completely. What followed was described by the Paymaster as "a moment of terrible suspense." The *Virginia* caught the *Monitor* a glancing blow, "nearly throwing us from our feet," as Keeler recalled. Jones had reversed the engines immediately before impact, which reduced the effect of the collision on both ships. The *Monitor* "spun around like a top." All he managed to do was to dent the hull of the *Monitor*, but the blow produced a leak in the bow of the Confederate vessel. As the *Virginia* plowed past the *Monitor*, Greene fired both his guns, driving in the armor protecting the stern of the casemate. A second hit in the same spot would probably have penetrated the hull. Jones was more concerned with the leak, and rigged pumps to deal with the flooding. He was also running out of options. For a moment he considered boarding. A group of volunteers was organized, led by Captain Reuben T. Thom, commander of the *Virginia*'s marines. Thom planned to jump onto the *Monitor* when the opportunity presented itself.

Robert E. Lee's son Colonel Custis W. Lee fortified Drewry's Bluff, overlooking the James River. When Norfolk fell, the fortification was all that lay between the Union fleet and Richmond. The gun shown in the photograph is a 10in. Columbiad smoothbore. (US Army Military History Institute)

Once on board his men would throw a coat over the slits in the pilot house, and jam the turret using metal spikes. Worden obviously took the threat seriously, as at one stage he ordered Greene to load his guns with canister. He had seen the boarding party gathering on the *Virginia's* spar deck. The *Monitor* dropped astern, and the opportunity passed. Thom ordered his men back to their guns. About this time the Confederate ensign was shot away, raising a cheer from the Union soldiers watching the fight from the shore. A replacement ensign was rigged and the fight continued, with Jones edging as close as he dared to the *Minnesota*. One shot struck the boiler of the tug USS *Dragon*, which was lying alongside the frigate. Other shots burst inside the *Minnesota*, and fires were started, although these were soon extinguished. It was now around noon. The two main protagonists had been fighting for 3¾ hours. The basic tactical situation remained the same: Jones wanted to attack the *Minnesota*, and Worden wanted to protect her. At that stage the *Monitor* passed close to the stern of the *Virginia*, almost catching her screw for a second time. As the smaller ship passed by, Lieutenant John Taylor Wood fired a 7in. Brooke rifle at the *Monitor's* pilot house. The shell scored a direct hit, blowing off one of the plates that protected the position. When the shell struck, Worden was peering out through the vision slit. The explosion blinded the *Monitor's* captain. Worden fell back, but could still sense the bright light and cool air coming from the hole in the armor. Miraculously, the helmsman was unhurt. Keeler saw "a flash of light and a cloud of smoke." Racing through the ship, he heard the captain call out: "My eyes. I am blind." He called for medical aid, and while Worden lay there, he ordered the helmsman to alter course to starboard, and head for shallow water, where the *Virginia* couldn't follow. He thought the damage to the pilot house was serious enough to break off the fight. Lieutenant Greene arrived, and assumed command. As he was carried below, Worden begged his replacement to "save the *Minnesota* if you can." It was 12.15pm.

The Battle of Drewry's Bluff, 15 May 1862. After nearly four hours, the battered ironclads *Monitor* and *Galena* were forced to retreat, abandoning their attempt to force a route to Richmond by way of the James River. *Harper's Weekly*, 31 May 1862. (Hensley)

Jones guessed something was amiss, and the *Monitor* was running from the fight. On board the *Minnesota*, Van Brunt realized his protector was out of the battle, and he prepared for the worst. The attack never came. The tide was ebbing, and as the water levels went down, the *Minnesota* gained a new protector. The *Virginia* had a draft of 22ft, and the area she could safely operate in was getting smaller by the minute. The pilots argued that the wooden frigate was too far away, and Jones complained that the "pilots will not place us nearer the *Minnesota*, and we cannot run the risk of getting aground again." He could only get within a mile of the enemy frigate, and the tide was still falling. He called his officers together and presented them with the situation. His ship was leaking, the crew was exhausted, and they were unable to fight either the *Monitor* or the *Minnesota*. He proposed a return to Norfolk. Almost all of his officers agreed, although Jones noted: "had there been any sign of the *Monitor*'s willingness to renew the contest we would have remained to fight her". Ramsay said the news was a "wet blanket," and claimed that Jones "ignored the moral effect of leaving the Roads without forcing the *Minnesota* to surrender." Jones ignored his protests, and ordered the helmsman to set a course for Sewell's Point and the mouth of the Elizabeth River. Lieutenant Wood had fired the last shot in the Battle of Hampton Roads.

Both ironclads returned to their respective berths, and were met with a hero's welcome. The *Monitor* had limped from the battleground, but remained undefeated. After four hours of battle, neither ship could claim a victory.

AFTERMATH

Neither side could claim a victory in the Battle of Hampton Roads. The four-hour battle between the ironclads had been a stalemate. The *Monitor* had been hit 23 times, and the *Virginia* 20 times. Neither ship was badly damaged in the engagement. Although Lieutenant Worden was badly scarred, he survived, and eventually regained his eyesight. There were no other casualties. The day before, the *Virginia* had destroyed two powerful warships and killed or wounded hundreds of Union sailors. Why did the Union regard the battle as a victory? The threat posed by the *Virginia* had been countered. There was no longer any chance of her being able to break the Union blockade, and the industrial capacity of the North ensured the Union would win any ironclad arms race. The first day of the battle demonstrated the vulnerability of wooden ships, and made them obsolete as warships. It also highlighted the danger facing the Union blockading fleets. The second day ushered in the era of the armored warship, and demonstrated that any hopes the Confederates had entertained of breaking the maritime stranglehold around the Confederacy had been dashed. In a single, four-hour battle, the nature of naval warfare had been changed forever.

In a tactical sense, the *Virginia* still dominated Hampton Roads, and therefore controlled access to the James River. As General McClellan was planning an offensive against Richmond, and planned to use Fort Monroe as his base, the Confederate ironclad was a serious threat. She had won a strategic victory by her very existence. McClellan sought assurances from the Navy Department that the *Monitor* could hold the *Virginia* in check. McClellan moved his planned base of operations to the York River, out of reach of the ironclad. For its part, the Navy Department was reluctant to risk the *Monitor* in battle. Under her new captain, Lieutenant Thomas O. Selfridge, she was modified to incorporate improvements to the pilot house and smokestacks, and she was ordered to keep out of the way of her adversary. For its part, the *Virginia* was repaired, and she was issued with new, specially designed armor-piercing bolts. A new and improved ram was also fitted to her bow, and the missing gun port lids were finally fitted. As Buchanan was in hospital, Flag Officer Josiah Tattnal arrived to hoist his flag in the ironclad on 21 March. He was more than willing to renew the fight. Work also began on another casemate ironclad in the Norfolk Yard. Buchanan and Jones were both aware that the *Monitor* had proven to be the equal of the *Virginia*, but neither Tattnal, the Confederate Navy Department, the press, nor the Southern public would hear of it. For them, the *Virginia* was still the victor of the battle, and would eventually prevail over her opponents. Tattnal's orders were to "Strike when, how and where your judgment may dictate." On 4 April 1862, the *Virginia* was ready to reenter the fray, and Secretary of the Navy Stephen Mallory

ordered Tattnal to launch an attack on the transports of the Army of the Potomac, which were lying at anchor in Hampton Roads. A week later, on 11 April, the *Virginia* sailed down the Elizabeth River, but the Union transports scattered and ran for the protection of Fort Monroe. Obeying orders to avoid battle, the *Monitor* also fled from Hampton Roads, and headed into Chesapeake Bay. The Union fleet hoped to lure the Confederate ironclad out into deep water, where they could surround her and overwhelm her by sheer numbers. The fleet included the *Vanderbilt*, whose sole purpose was to ram the *Virginia*. Tattnal refused to fall into the trap, and was content with holding Hampton Roads, and the capture of three Union transports. The *Monitor*'s crew was indignant. As one crewman put it, "I believe the Department is going to build us a big glass case to put us in for fear of harm coming to us." The *Virginia*'s reign of terror would not last much longer.

On 3 May, the Confederate Army in the Virginia Peninsula abandoned its defensive lines around Yorktown, and slipped away. Faced with overwhelming numbers of Union troops, General Joe Johnston had no option but to retreat. Three days later President Lincoln arrived at Fort Monroe, and on 8 May he discussed the *Virginia* with General Wool. While the President watched, a Union flotilla moved up to Sewell's Point and began shelling the Confederate batteries there. Suddenly the *Virginia* appeared, and the entire Union fleet turned tail and fled. Once again, the *Monitor* chose to flee rather than to fight. According to the *Virginia*'s Lieutenant Wood, "it was the most cowardly exhibition I have ever seen." Lincoln was less than impressed, but General Wool had already planned a second attack. While the *Virginia* was distracted he slipped the new armored gunboat USS *Galena* and a few wooden warships past Newport News and into the James River. The plan was to seal Norfolk off from Richmond. The following afternoon (9 May), under cover of a second naval demonstration, Wool ferried 6,000 men across Chesapeake Bay and landed them at Ocean View, to the east of Willoughby's Spit. A second wave of troops landed the following morning. The Union army now had a divisional-sized force of 10,000 troops in a position to outflank Sewell's Point, and poised to capture Norfolk itself. Although Confederate Major General Benjamin Huger commanded a similar number of troops, they were scattered between several defensive positions on both sides of the Elizabeth River. He had also been recalled to help in the defense of Richmond, and was in the process of abandoning Norfolk. By nightfall General Wool's troops had entered the city. The first the crew of the *Virginia* knew of the retreat came the following morning (10 May), when they noticed the emplacements on nearby Sewell's Point had been abandoned. Huger's retreating army destroyed the Norfolk Navy Yard, and the *Virginia* was left without a base. The ironclad had too deep a draft to escape up the James River to Richmond, although the rest of the flotilla managed to escape. Lieutenant Jones tried to lighten the ironclad, but by 1.00am on 11 May, it became clear the task was impossible. By lightening the ship, Jones had stripped her of most of her armor, which meant she was unable to attack the enemy fleet. Tattnal had no choice but to scuttle his ship. The *Virginia* was run aground off Craney Island, and her crew prepared the ship for destruction. Jones and Wood lit the fuse and rowed away. The once-proud ironclad caught light then exploded. Her

The USS *Monitor* foundered during a gale off Cape Hatteras, North Carolina, early in the morning of 31 December 1862. The sidewheel gunboat USS *Rhode Island* is shown coming to her aid. Note the temporary modification to the ironclad's smokestack, to prevent waves dousing her engines. (Mariners)

crew marched inland in the wake of Huger's army, and their officers cursed the folly of both the army and their administration. The pride of the Confederate Navy had been destroyed.

Richmond seemed to be wide open, and the Union Navy immediately launched an expedition up the James River. The plan was to force their way as far as Richmond. The *Monitor* and the armored gunship *Galena* led the flotilla, and it seemed that nothing could stop them. The Union squadron was halted at Drewry's Bluff, some 15 miles below the Confederate capital. A fort had been built on top of the bluff overlooking the river, and Tattnal's sailors arrived just in time to help crew the heavy guns that had been placed there. The *Jamestown* was scuttled to block the river, and the defenders ranged their guns in just beyond the obstacle. On 15 May, the *Monitor* and *Galena* appeared and came under heavy fire. They soon found the bluff was too high for their guns to shell, while the plunging fire from Drewry's Bluff threatened to pierce the virtually unprotected decks of the Union ironclads. After four hours, the *Monitor* and its consorts limped away. Richmond had been saved.

The *Monitor* remained on the James River throughout McClellan's peninsular campaign, and covered the retreat of the Army of the Potomac. The new threat was the CSS *Richmond*, the ironclad that had been partially built in Norfolk, and then towed to Richmond to be completed. Captain Jeffers was replaced by Commander Bankhead, and on Christmas Day he received orders to steam south to join the blockade off Wilmington. Towed by the sidewheel steamer USS *Rhode Island*, the *Monitor* reached Cape Hatteras before she was overtaken by a storm. By the late evening of 30 December it became clear that the *Monitor* was sinking. The *Rhode Island* was called on to send boats, and Bankhead gave the order to abandon ship. The steamer was still trying to rescue the crew when the *Monitor* sank, taking four officers and 12 men down with her. At 12.30am on 31 December 1862, the second of the two ironclads was no more. Her remains still lie in 220ft of water.

183

THE END OF THE *VIRGINIA*, MAY 1862

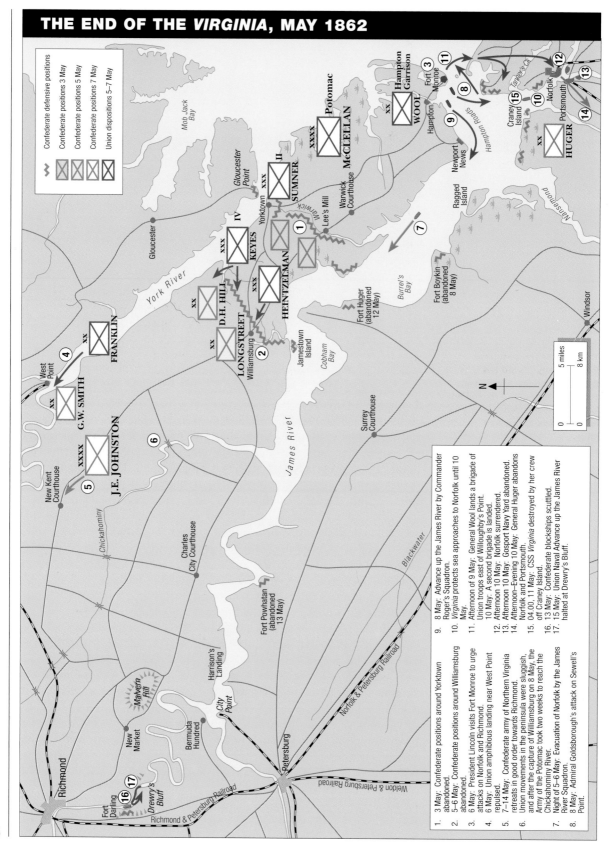

Confederate defensive positions

- Confederate positions 3 May
- Confederate positions 5 May
- Confederate positions 7 May
- Union dispositions 5–7 May

1. 3 May: Confederate positions around Yorktown abandoned.
2. 5–6 May: Confederate positions around Williamsburg abandoned.
3. 6 May: President Lincoln visits Fort Monroe to urge attacks on Norfolk and Richmond.
4. 6 May: Union amphibious landing near West Point repulsed.
5. 7–14 May: Confederate army of Northern Virginia retreats in good order towards Richmond.
6. Union movements in the peninsula were sluggish, and after the capture of Williamsburg on 8 May, the Army of the Potomac took two weeks to reach the Chickahominy River.
7. Night of 5–6 May: Evacuation of Norfolk by the James River Squadron.
8. 8 May: Admiral Goldsborough's attack on Sewell's Point.
9. 8 May: Advance up the James River by Commander Roger's Squadron.
10. 5–6 May: *Virginia* protects sea approaches to Norfolk until 10 May.
11. Afternoon of 9 May: General Wool lands a brigade of Union troops east of Willoughby's Point. 10 May: A second brigade is landed.
12. Afternoon 10 May: Norfolk surrendered.
13. Afternoon 10 May: Gosport Navy Yard abandoned.
14. Afternoon–Evening 10 May: General Huger abandons Norfolk and Portsmouth.
15. 04.00, 11 May: CSS *Virginia* destroyed by her crew off Craney Island.
16. 13 May: Confederate blockships scuttled.
17. 15 May: Union Naval Advance up the James River halted at Drewry's Bluff.

184

THE BATTLEFIELD TODAY

Hampton Roads has changed almost beyond recognition over the past 160 years. The only constant is the water itself, dark, deep, and cold. Once a sleepy Tidewater port, Norfolk is now a major American city, and home to what is probably the largest naval base in the world. Much of the shoreline around Sewell's Point and the eastern bank of the Elizabeth River where Confederate soldiers watched the drama unfold is now part of Norfolk Navy complex. In the waters off the point where the *Virginia* spent the night before her battle against the *Monitor*, lines of US Navy supercarriers and amphibious assault ships continue the naval legacy. Further down the river are the berths for smaller vessels: destroyers, frigates, and support vessels. The base is not entirely off limits to the public, although access is still restricted, particularly in the vicinity of Sewell's Point. The US Navy run tours for interested civilians, and the "Norfolk Navy Base Tour Office" is close to the site of the encampment of the Confederate garrison during the spring of 1862. The office can be reached by following Interstate 64 as far as Junction 276C, then following State Road 564 (Admiral Taussig Boulevard) past Base Gate 2. The office is on the right.

The shore of Newport News Point, looking toward Sewell's Point (now Norfolk Navy Base). The USS *Cumberland* foundered in the shallow waters in the foreground of the picture. (Author's Photograph)

The Norfolk Navy Yard in Portsmouth, Virginia, still exists as a naval establishment, and is located on the western bank of the Elizabeth River, immediately over the Jordan Bridge, off Route 337 (Elm Avenue). Parts of the shipyard are open to the public, and the Portsmouth Naval Shipyard Museum interprets the history of the base, and the story of the building of the *Merrimac/Virginia*. Of particular interest is a model of the dry dock where the *Merrimac* was converted into the *Virginia*. A pedestrian ferry that runs seven days a week links the site with downtown Norfolk. Visitors to the area should also visit the nearby Lighthouse Museum, which provides a useful insight into maritime activity on the Elizabeth River. The Old Naval Hospital Building is located close to the riverfront at the northern end of Portsmouth, and stands on the site where Flag Officer Buchanan and other Confederate and Union wounded were taken for treatment after the first day's battle. Across the river lies downtown Norfolk, which can be reached by three main Interstates (164, 264, and 464). Interstate 64 serves as a bypass road, linking all three roads with the Hampton Bridge Road Tunnel, one of three major road crossings in the Hampton Roads and Chesapeake Bay area. The museum and maritime science exhibit Nauticus is located on the bank of the Elizabeth River in the southwest corner of downtown Norfolk. On its upper floor it contains a maritime museum dedicated to the naval history of Norfolk and Hampton Roads (The Hampton Roads Naval Museum). A major portion of the museum is devoted to the interpretation of the battle between the ironclads, and contains a full-sized reconstruction of the *Monitor*'s turret, and a cross-section of the *Virginia*'s casemate. Interpretation is augmented by a fascinating collection of artifacts, and an extremely well-presented audio-visual display. While in the area, visitors might consider strolling down through Town Point Park to the river itself, and imagine the scene on that Saturday morning, when thousands lined the shore and silently watched the *Virginia* on her way down the river.

While the Chesapeake Bay Bridge Tunnel links Norfolk with Delaware across the Bay, two other crossings connect Norfolk and Portsmouth with Newport News and Hampton. To the west Route 664 doglegs its way across Hampton Roads, from Pig Point to Newport News Point. To the east of its southern approach is Craney Island, where the *Virginia* was scuttled. The area is now a disposal area run by the US Army Corps of Engineers. The wreck site was located, and artifacts from the *Virginia* are now housed in several collections, including the Museum of the Confederacy in Richmond, Virginia, probably one of the best Civil War museums in the country. The northern end of the crossing is the site where Union batteries fired on the *Virginia* while it attacked the two Union sailing frigates. Once again, the wrecks of both the *Congress* and the *Cumberland* have been located, and artifacts recovered from them are now housed in the Mariners Museum in Newport News, one of the premier maritime collections in the world. Further to the east, Route 64 links Willoughby Spit (now called Willoughby Beach) to Hampton via the Hampton Roads Bridge Tunnel. The bridge itself links the Rip Raps (the site of Fort Wool) with the southern shore, while at the northern end the tunnel emerges immediately to the west of Fort Monroe, located on Old Point Comfort.
The fort is open to the public, and contains the Casemate Museum.

One of a series of interpretative markers located on the shore of Newport News, explaining the events which took place beyond the shoreline to the left a century and a half ago. (Author's Photograph)

Visitors can reach it by turning east onto Mallory Street (named after the Confederate Secretary of the Navy), then following directions. The museum contains a *Monitor–Merrimac* display (which includes scale models), an interpretation of the history of the fort, and displays dealing with coastal fortifications and artillery. As its name suggests, the museum is located in the inner casemates of the Fort. By driving west from Hampton to Newport News along Chesapeake Avenue, travelers are presented with an excellent view over Hampton Roads, looking out over the piece of water where the two ironclads fought their duel. A series of interpretative signs provides a brief outline of the battle, and shows where certain events took place. Near the western end of the avenue is a small car park, and close by, several signs tell how the *Virginia* destroyed the *Congress* immediately in front of the car park. By standing on the shoreline, you can imagine the scene as the survivors swam ashore, or were rescued in the shallows by Union soldiers. The wreck lies in the mud some 80 yards from the shore. Unfortunately the waterfront in front of the area where the *Cumberland* went down is more commercial, and railroad tracks and the slip-roads onto the Route 664 tunnel and bridge make it difficult to imagine the shore as it looked in 1862. Two museums in the Newport News area are well worth visiting and contain information or artifacts that are relevant to the battle. The Virginia War Museum is situated close to the junction of Route 60 and Mercury Boulevard (leading to the James River Bridge). Incidentally, the bridge crosses the part of the river where the *Virginia* turned around before returning to finish off the *Congress*. The museum covers military activity in Virginia from 1775 to the present day, and provides a venue for the interpretation of the Union batteries and garrisons on the northern bank of Hampton Roads in 1862. Further up Route 60 is the Mariners Museum. Apart from the artifacts from various shipwrecks that have already been mentioned, the museum contains extensive displays of ship models, historical artifacts, and documents relating to the naval side of the American Civil War in general and the Battle of Hampton Roads in particular. It also boasts a world-class book store and gift shop. For researchers, it offers an excellent library and an extensive photo archive.

As for the two ships themselves, the *Virginia* has gone, destroyed by a mixture of treasure hunting, salvage, and dredging operations. Only a handful of artifacts remain in the care of museums in Richmond and Newport News. The Washington Navy Yard in Washington D.C. houses a collection of artillery, including all the guns carried by both of the ironclads during the battle, but the *Virginia's* original guns have been lost. The *Monitor* sank off Hatteras Inlet, North Carolina, in 220ft of water. The site now forms part of an underwater marine sanctuary administered by NOAA (The National Oceanic and Atmospheric Administration). Several artifacts have been raised, and the wreck has been extensively surveyed and the results published. The vessel sank upside down, so the hull rests on her turret. Scientists have recently become concerned for the stability of the wreck, and are considering plans to ease the turret out from beneath the hull in order to preserve it. If the turret and any other part of the ship were raised and conserved, it would provide a direct link with the dramatic events that took place in the waters of Hampton Roads in 1862.

BIBLIOGRAPHY

Bauer, Jack K., & Roberts, Stephen, S., *Register of Ships of the US Navy, 1775–1990*, Greenwood Press (Westport, CT, 1991)

Bennett, Frank, M., *The Steam Navy of the United States*, Warren and Company (Pittsburgh, PA, 1896)

Brophy, Ann, *John Ericsson and the Inventions of War*, Silver Burdett Press (Eaglewood Cliffs, NJ, 1991)

Canney, Donald, L., *Lincoln's Navy: The Ships, Men and Organization, 1861–65*, Conway Maritime Press, (London, 1998)

Canney, Donald, L., *The Old Steam Navy* [2 volumes], Naval Institute Press, (1990 & 1993)

Chapelle, Howard, I., *The History of the American Sailing Navy*, W.W., Norton (New York, NY, 1949)

Church, William Conant, *The Life of John Ericsson* [2 volumes], Scribner's Press (New York, 1891)

Daly, R.W., *How the Merrimac won: The strategic story of the CSS Virginia*, Crowell Press, (New York, NY, 1957)

DeKay, James Tertius, *Monitor: The story of the legendary civil war ironclad and the man whose invention changed the course of history*, Ballantine Books, (New York, 1997)

Gardiner, Robert (ed.), *Steam, Steel and Shellfire: The Steam Warship, 1815–1905*, Conway Maritime Press and Naval Institute Press (London, UK and Annapolis, MD, 1992)

Gentile, Gary, *Ironclad Legacy*, Gentile Productions (Philadelphia, PA, 1993)

Hoehling, A.A., *Thunder at Hampton Roads: The U.S.S Monitor –It's battle with the Merrimack and its recent rediscovery*, Da Capo Press (New York, NY, 1993)

Holcombe, Robert, *Notes on the Classification of Confederate Ironclads*, US Army Corps of Engineers (Savannah, GA, 1980)

Jones, Virgil Carrington, *The Civil War at Sea* [2 volumes], Rinehart and Winston (New York, NY, 1960, reprinted in three volumes by Broadfoot Press, Wilmington, NC, 1990)

Luraghi, Raimondo, *A History of the Confederate Navy*, Naval Institute Press (Annapolis, MD, 1996)

Rush, Richard (ed.), *Official Records of the Union and Confederate Navies in the War of the Rebellion* [30 volumes], Government Printing Office (1895–1921)

Silverstone, Paul H., *Warships of the Civil War Navies*, Naval Institute Press, (1989)

Smith, Gene, A., *Iron and Heavy Guns: Duel between the Monitor and Merrimac*, McWhiney, Foundation Press [Civil War Campaigns and Commanders Series], (Abilene, TX, 1998)

Stern, Philip van Doren, *The Confederate Navy: A Pictorial History*, Da Capo Press (New York, NY, 1992)

Still Jr., William, N., *Iron Afloat: The Story of the Confederate Ironclads*, University of South Carolina Press (Columbia, SC, 1985)

Still Jr., William, N., (ed.), *The Confederate Navy: The Ships, Men and Organization 1861–65*, Conway Maritime Press (London, 1997)

Underwood, Robert, & Buel, Clarence Clough, (eds.), *Battles and Leaders of the Civil War* [volume 1], Century Company (New York, NY, 1887), reprinted by Castle, Edison, (NJ, 1987). **Note.** This source contains articles originally published in *Century Magazine*, including accounts by John Ericsson, Dana Greene, Henry Reany, and others.

Ward, James, H., *A manuel of Naval Tactics*, Appleton and Company (New York, NY, 1859)

West Jr., Richard, S., *Gideon Welles: Lincoln's Navy Department*, Bobbs-Merril Company (New York, NY, 1943)

Ehite, William Chapman, & White, Ruth, *Tin Can on a Shingle*, Dutton Press (New York, NY, 1957)

Worden, John Lorimer, *The Monitor and the Merrimac: Both sides of the story*, Harper & Brothers (New York, NY and London, 1912)

INDEX

Figures in **bold** refer to illustrations, plates are shown as
plate/page number (caption page number)